THE JAZZ AGE

Recent Titles in Historical Explorations of Literature

The Harlem Renaissance: A Historical Exploration of Literature
Lynn Domina

American Slavery: A Historical Exploration of Literature
Robert Felgar

THE JAZZ AGE

A Historical Exploration of Literature

Linda De Roche

HISTORICAL EXPLORATIONS OF LITERATURE

BLOOMSBURY ACADEMIC
NEW YORK • LONDON • OXFORD • NEW DELHI • SYDNEY

BLOOMSBURY ACADEMIC
Bloomsbury Publishing Inc
1385 Broadway, New York, NY 10018, USA
50 Bedford Square, London, WC1B 3DP, UK
29 Earlsfort Terrace, Dublin 2, Ireland

BLOOMSBURY, BLOOMSBURY ACADEMIC and the Diana logo
are trademarks of Bloomsbury Publishing Plc

First published in the United States of America by ABC-CLIO 2015
Paperback edition published by Bloomsbury Academic 2024

Copyright © Bloomsbury Publishing Inc, 2024

For legal purposes the Acknowledgments on p. xv constitute
an extension of this copyright page.

Cover design by Silverander Communications
Cover photos: Vintage black car. (Oleg Saenko/Thinkstock); Undated photo of author
Francis Scott Key Fitzgerald. (AP Photo); Author and playwright Anita Loos poses on the
ship *Olympic* on November 2, 1929. (AP Images); "Teaching An Old Dog New Tricks"
Life Magazine cover by John Held Jr. (John Held Jr./Corbis)

All rights reserved. No part of this publication may be reproduced or
transmitted in any form or by any means, electronic or mechanical,
including photocopying, recording, or any information storage or retrieval
system, without prior permission in writing from the publishers.

Bloomsbury Publishing Inc does not have any control over, or responsibility for,
any third-party websites referred to or in this book. All internet addresses given
in this book were correct at the time of going to press. The author and publisher
regret any inconvenience caused if addresses have changed or sites have
ceased to exist, but can accept no responsibility for any such changes.

Library of Congress Cataloging-in-Publication Data
De Roche, Linda.
The Jazz Age : a historical exploration of literature / Linda De Roche.
pages cm. — (Historical explorations of literature)
Includes bibliographical references and index.
ISBN 978-1-61069-667-8 (hardback) — ISBN 978-1-61069-668-5
1. American literature—20th century—History and criticism.
2. Nineteen twenties. 3. Jazz in literature.
4. Modernism (Aesthetics)—United States. I. Title.
PS223.D4 2015
810.9'0052—dc23 2015022751

ISBN: HB: 978-1-6106-9667-8
PB: 979-8-7651-1595-4
ePDF: 978-1-6106-9668-5
eBook: 979-8-2161-0628-9

Series: Historical Explorations of Literature

To find out more about our authors and books visit www.bloomsbury.com
and sign up for our newsletters.

To Stéphane,
What serendipity!

Contents

Series Foreword, xiii
Acknowledgments, xv
Introduction: The Jazz Age and the Culture of Change, xvii
Chronology of the Jazz Age, xxiii

1   ***Babbitt* (Sinclair Lewis, 1922), 1**

    Synopsis of *Babbitt*, 1

    Historical Background: *Babbitt* and the Perils of Progress and Prosperity, 3

    About Sinclair Lewis: The Man Who Defined Babbittry, 7

    Why We Read *Babbitt*, 10

    Historical Explorations of *Babbitt*, 13

    Documenting *Babbitt*, 22

        The Religion of Business in the Jazz Age, 22

            Document: From "Passing Our Tenth Milestone," Paul P. Harris, 1915, 23

Document: From *The Man Nobody Knows*, Bruce Barton, 1925, 24

Conformity in the Jazz Age, 28

Document: From "Knowledge in Contempt in America, Believe Europeans," H. L. Mencken, 1925, 29

Suggested Readings, 31

2 ***The Great Gatsby* (F. Scott Fitzgerald, 1925), 35**

Synopsis of *The Great Gatsby*, 35

Historical Background: *The Great Gatsby* and the Culture of Contradiction, 37

About F. Scott Fitzgerald: The Man Who Wrote the Jazz Age, 42

Why We Read *The Great Gatsby*, 46

Historical Explorations of *The Great Gatsby*, 50

Documenting *The Great Gatsby*, 60

The Automobile and the Jazz Age, 60

Document: From "How Many American People Can Afford Automobiles?" 1922, 60

Document: From "Your Car and You," 1920, 61

Document: From "On Which Side of the Windshield Do You Do Your Cussing?" H. I. Phillips, 1927, 62

Prohibition and Bootleggers, 65

Document: From The Volstead Act, 1920, 65

Document: From "Nation-Wide Prohibition Ends Fight of 112 Years," 1920, 70

Document: From "Volstead Law Draws Attack of Opponents," 1925, 72

Document: From "Rich Bootleggers Sent to Prison," 1923, 74

Celebrity Culture in the Jazz Age, 76

Document: From "The Secret of Charlie Chaplin's Popularity," St. John Ervine, 1921, 77

Document: From "Chance Writes the Lindbergh Saga," 1927, 80

Document: From "My Friend Babe Ruth," 1924, 83

Suggested Readings, 90

3   *Gentlemen Prefer Blondes* **(Anita Loos, 1925), 93**

Synopsis of *Gentlemen Prefer Blondes*, 93

Historical Background: *Gentlemen Prefer Blondes* and the Gender Politics of the Jazz Age, 96

About Anita Loos: A Life in Words and (Motion) Pictures, 99

Why We Read *Gentlemen Prefer Blondes*, 103

Historical Explorations of *Gentlemen Prefer Blondes*, 106

Documenting *Gentlemen Prefer Blondes*, 114

    The Flapper, 114

       Document: From *The Flapper*, 1922, 115

       Document: From "Flappers Flaunt Fads in Footwear," *The New York Times*, 1922, 116

       Document: From "The Flapper—A New Type," Alfredo Panzini, 1921, 117

       Document: From "Her Eternal Youth," *New York Times*, 1922, 120

    Hollywood and the Motion Picture Revolution, 123

       Document: From "Youth, the Spirit of the Movies," David Wark Griffith, 1921, 123

       Document: From "Flappers Here to Stay, Says Colleen Moore," Gladys Hall, 1922, 124

       Document: From "The Monstrous Movies," Charles Hanson Towne, 1921, 125

       Document: From "Through Hollywood with Gun and Camera," Robert E. Sherwood, 1922, 127

Suggested Readings, 129

4   *The Sun Also Rises* **(Ernest Hemingway, 1926), 131**

Synopsis of *The Sun Also Rises*, 131

Historical Background: Hemingway, Paris, and the Modern Moment, 133

About Ernest Hemingway: The Man Who Wrote the Lost Generation, 137

Why We Read *The Sun Also Rises*, 141

Historical Explorations of *The Sun Also Rises*, 144

Documenting *The Sun Also Rises*, 154

   The Lost Generation, 154

      Document: From *Exile's Return: A Literary Odyssey of the 1920s*, Malcolm Cowley, 1934, 154

      Document: From "American Bohemians in Paris," Ernest Hemingway, 1922, 155

      Document: From *Being Geniuses Together 1920–1930*, Robert McAlmon and Rev. Kay Boyle, 1968, 156

      Document: From *Paris Was Yesterday. 1925–1939*, Janet Flanner, 1972, 158

   The Art of the Bullfight, 160

      Document: From *Being Geniuses Together 1920–1930*, Robert McAlmon and Rev. Kay Boyle, 1968, 160

      Document: From "Bull Fighting a Tragedy," Ernest Hemingway, 1923, 162

      Document: From "Pamplona in July," Ernest Hemingway, 1923, 163

   Race, Ethnicity, and the Ku Klux Klan, 164

      Document: From "For Christian-Jewish Friendship HP," *The Literary Digest*, 1922, 164

      Document: From "New York and the Real Jew," Rollin Lynde Hartt, 1921, 166

      Document: From "The Klan Walks in Washington," *The Literary Digest*, 1925, 169

      Document: From "Klan and Church," Lowell Mellett, 1923, 172

      Document: From "A Judicial Spanking for the Klan," *Literary Digest*, 1928, 180

Suggested Readings, 184

5   *Passing* **(Nella Larsen, 1929), 189**

    Synopsis of *Passing*, 189

    Historical Background: *Passing* and the Harlem Renaissance, 190

    About Nella Larsen: A Life on the Color Line, 193

    Why We Read *Passing*, 196

    Historical Explorations of *Passing*, 199

    Documenting *Passing*, 207

        The Harlem Renaissance, 207

            Document: From *The Big Sea*, Langston Hughes, 1940, 208

            Document: From *Negro Life in New York's Harlem*, Wallace Thurman, 1928, 210

            Document: From " 'Charleston' Dance Sweeps New York City by Storm; Louis Chalif Is Forced to Instruct in Dance That Is Distasteful," Maxine Davis, 1925, 211

        The African American Elite, 213

            Document: From "The Talented Tenth," W. E. B. Du Bois, 1903, 213

            Document: From "The Task of Negro Womanhood," Elise Johnson McDougald, 1925, 215

        Race and the Eugenics Movement in the Jazz Age, 217

            Document: From "Eugenics Seeks to Improve the Natural, Physical, Mental and Temperamental Qualities of the Human Family," Eugenics Record Office, 1927, 218

            Document: From "Fitter Families for Future Firesides," 1924, 220

            Document: From "Body of Woman Shown to Jury," *The Florence* [AL] *Times*, 1925, 222

    Suggested Readings, 223

Index, 227

Series Foreword

The Historical Explorations of Literature series is designed to help students understand key works of American literature by putting them in the context of history, society, and culture through historical context essays, literary analysis, chronologies, primary source documents. Each volume in the series covers four or five canonical works related to a particular area of American literature—significant literary productions of the Jazz Age or the Harlem Renaissance, for example. For each title covered, students will find a brief synopsis of the work; separate essays on the work's historical background and the author's biographical background; an essay on "Why We Read This Work," summarizing the work's enduring value and significance; and a series of thematic "Historical Explorations" that include a selection of related primary documents.

Acknowledgments

I am most pleased to acknowledge the research assistance of Cydnie Flowers, an English major at Wesley College, whose tenacity helped in locating obscure documents and whose knowledge of American literature made her the perfect sounding board for my explorations of these Jazz Age novels. I also wish to thank my editor, Michael Millman, for his patience when life intervened. Without the support of my husband Stéphane, in sickness and in health, this work would have been impossible. For that, and more, he has all my love.

Introduction: The Jazz Age and the Culture of Change

The winds of change were rustling the social and political landscape during the Jazz Age, the name with which its greatest chronicler, the author F. Scott Fitzgerald, christened the decade of the 1920s. Some called it the Roaring Twenties, but "jazz," evoking both a type of modern music that meshed African American with European traditions and a slang term, probably derived from Creole patois referring to strenuous activity, to quick-paced excitement, especially connected to sexual activity, captured precisely the era's tone. Used as a verb—"to jazz up" or "to jazz around"—or as a noun—"all that jazz," bright young things were right on trend. The word flouted conventions and expressed all the self-conscious indifference of a new generation to tired, outmoded standards that a world war and advances in technology had made to seem irrelevant. It was new, it was modern, and to its syncopated rhythms and improvised riffs, the twentieth century would finally spring to life.

The rise of jazz coincided with, contributed to, and represented the social and cultural changes associated with Modernism, a movement that sought to break with the past, and the modern era, which was marked by a general feeling of discontinuity. With its African American origins, jazz should have appealed to a relatively small audience, but the Great Migration of freedmen and women who settled in the nation's Northern cities, in New York, Chicago, Detroit, Philadelphia, exposed it to a white middle class who was hungry for something other than classical music and the measured one, two, three of the waltz and its stately dance steps. This was, after all, the era of the Harlem Renaissance, the first full flowering of African American culture, when all things Negro, as African Americans were then called, became fashionable. In Harlem's Cotton Club, white patrons gyrated to the era's new dances, the Charleston, the Breakaway, and the Lindy Hop, which had also originated in African American culture, and applauded the performances of jazz masters Fletcher Henderson and Duke Ellington. Even those living in the nation's hinterlands could follow the trend, and enjoy one of the era's new technologies, by listening to jazz performances, called "potter palm" concerts, broadcast over the radio airwaves. While jazz may not have significantly advanced race relations in the country, as might have been expected from this fusion of African American traditions and white middle-class ideals, it did at least set the tone and pace of the decade. It also encouraged the rebellion of the nation's youth that had begun in the aftermath of World War I and who were now eager to draw a line beneath the past.

Women were among the groups most eager to embrace the modern. While the New Woman had in fact been evolving since the late nineteenth century, the Jazz Age accelerated her transformation into the flapper, the embodiment of the era's changes. In 1920, after all, with the passage of the Nineteenth Amendment to the U.S. Constitution, women had finally attained the right to vote, and they were increasingly taking their place in the workforce rather than keeping the home fires burning. With their political and economic independence they redefined the gender roles and expectations with which they had grown into adulthood and made a fashion statement to mark the change. They bobbed their hair, raised their hemlines, smoked cigarettes, and drank bootleg liquor in the speakeasies and clubs that flourished during Prohibition. Flouting conventional manners and mores, flappers flirted; they flaunted their sexuality. Petting parties became the rage. The sexual double standard would not deter these young women from asserting their desires and assuming control of their lives. A popular hit of the era, "Ain't We Got Fun," could have been the anthem for the flapper, whose very being signaled a dramatic shift in life as it had been.

No less important to the era's roar than the rise of jazz culture and the invention of the flapper was Prohibition, the noble experiment to eliminate the social and health problems related to alcohol that went into effect seconds after midnight on January 16, 1920. Even before the law that made criminals of the majority of the nation's adult population was reality, enterprising speculators and organized crime bosses, seizing the opportunity to make a fortune, were opening speakeasies and trafficking in bootleg liquor. Others were manufacturing bathtub gin and other intoxicating spirits, many of which were more serious health risks than the whiskey and rum for which they were poor substitutes. At house parties like those hosted by *The Great Gatsby*'s title character, where raucous guests drank pastel cocktails and "champagne was served in glasses bigger than finger-bowls" (Fitzgerald 52), the rich and famous courted celebrity.

The general lawlessness inevitably led to organized crime. In the nation's major cities, men such as Al Capone, Meyer Lansky, Dutch Schultz, and Lucky Luciano ruthlessly dominated the syndicates that controlled the illegal trade, and machine gun fights between rival gangs played out in the streets. In fact, on St. Valentine's Day in 1929, in what the *Chicago Tribune* reported as "the most infamous gangland slaying in America," Capone seized undisputed control of the city's criminal underworld when four of his men, two of whom were dressed as police officers, "pumped . . . ninety bullets from submachine guns, shotguns and a revolver" into seven members of George "Bugs" Moran's rival Irish gang in a perfectly choreographed massacre that revealed just how ineffectual enforcement of Prohibition had become.

Other developments were also driving the transformative changes of the 1920s. The United States, for instance, was no longer a rural nation. The 1920s, in fact, marked the decade in which more Americans lived in the nation's towns and cities than on farms in the countryside. This shift had resulted from rapid industrialization in the late nineteenth century. There were jobs in the cities, promising prosperity to men and women living hard-scrabble lives in rural backwaters and immigrants searching for streets paved with gold, and while the dream of wealth eluded most, urban living offered compensations that most could have neither afforded nor enjoyed in the country, not least of which were those speakeasies and the bustle and pace of a nation at move once again after the frugalities imposed by war.

Indeed, in the decade after World War I, with the nation's factories humming to the tune of consumers' pent-up demand for material goods and a boom in postwar construction, everyone seemed to be prospering. Everyone wanted the radios and telephones, the vacuum sweepers and refrigerators, and, above all, the automobiles that new technologies, chiefly electrification, had made possible, and when Henry Ford developed a process by which to mass-produce his Model T, America's consumer culture shifted into high gear. By the end of the decade, Americans had purchased more than ten million radios, giving birth to a golden age of radio programming funded by the advertising that fueled consumer demand, and nearly twenty-three million, approximately one of every five Americans, owned an automobile. After all, mass production had dropped the price of a Ford from $1,200 in 1909 to $295 in 1928, and the development of the installment plan, like the practice of buying stocks on 10 percent margin, meant that anyone with a stable income could enjoy the freedom of the road. (By buying on margin, they could also play the stock market, with its promise of even greater prosperity, in which more than one million were invested before it crashed on "Black Tuesday," October 29, 1929.) As Calvin Coolidge, one of the three Republican presidents during the 1920s, famously declared, "The chief business of the American people is business." By 1928, that pronouncement rang true, for America had solidified its position as the world's most prosperous nation. Anyone who doubted the power of the new technologies and the possibilities of the modern need only stare up at the sleek, geometric Art Deco forms of New York City's Chrysler Building or follow the flight from New York to Paris of aviator Charles Lindbergh for proof.

In the flush of their unprecedented prosperity, America's consumers also sought outlets for leisure and entertainment. Spectator sports, for instance, soared in popularity. In the 1920s, as Babe Ruth was racking up home runs for the New York Yankees, and becoming a sports icon, baseball, after first regaining its fans' trust in the aftermath of the "Black Sox" scandal of 1919, solidified its hold as America's game, and Jack Dempsey reigned as Heavyweight Champion of the world from 1919 to 1926. College sports also rose to national prominence, the University of Notre Dame's Knute Rockne and its "Four Horsemen," for instance, capturing a new audience for football. Families also gathered round the radio each evening to listen to the latest episode of *Amos 'n Andy*, big-band jazz concerts, and eventually the Grand Ole Opry, as radio programming expanded throughout the decade. Motion pictures, however, vied most competitively for supremacy among the nation's leisure activities. As "talkies" displaced silent films and color enlivened black-and-white pictures, the motion picture industry flourished. Studio magnates constructed glittering movie palaces in major cities to enhance the glamor and excitement of the movie experience; even neighborhood theaters included small-town America in the world of Hollywood dreams. Movie attendance soared in the 1920s, from audiences of fifty million to ninety million a week as the movie star was born.

Indeed, a culture of celebrity flourished during the Jazz Age. The public could not get enough about movie stars such as Charlie Chaplin, Douglas Fairbanks, Mary Pickford, Rudolph Valentino, and the nation's "It" girl, Clara Bow. Their glamor, sophistication, and sex appeal captivated ordinary people living ordinary lives. In the dark of the movie theater they could dream of possibility. Equally fascinating were America's sports icons—Babe Ruth, Ty Cobb, Lou Gehrig, Jack Dempsey—and men and women of achievement, such as the aviators Charles Lindbergh and Amelia Earhart. Even reports of the antics of the writer F. Scott Fitzgerald and his wife Zelda, whose outrageous lifestyle epitomized Jazz Age audacity, filled column inches in the era's new mass-market publications, *Reader's Digest* and *Time*, and its newspaper gossip columns. (The writer, so enamored of his own celebrity, for it was after all a mark of success and not to be scoffed at, clipped his notices and pasted them into his Notebooks.)

Anything seemed possible in the Jazz Age. The economy surged, and with it came prosperity for all but the farmer and those who lived in rural backwaters. Wages increased 30 percent in the decade, and inflation was low. The new technologies transformed social and cultural life and promised to continue to do so into the foreseeable future. Women especially benefited from the changes and used the opportunity to redefine their role in society. The twentieth century, it seemed, had finally managed to throw off the outmoded traditions of previous generations to embrace the new. Yes, indeed, there was some discord. With change there inevitably is. Concerned elders fretted, as always, about the era's bright, young things, and especially its flapper, who had made a verb of the noun "party." They worried too about increasing immigration, radical politics, and the new ideas that were challenging old truths, so the decade that roared also saw the rise of the Ku Klux Klan, a Red Scare, and the Scopes "Monkey" Trial as well as the exodus of many of its Lost Generation, who sought on foreign shores what America could not provide.

Providing a lens on all of these changes were the era's writers. Some, like Ernest Hemingway, about whom Gertrude Stein coined the term, were members of that Lost Generation of young men and women who came of age during World War I and were left disillusioned by its failures and hypocrisies. In his masterpiece, *The Sun Also Rises* (1926), Hemingway captured their stoic resilience and brave determination to find meaning after chaos. Others, like Nella Larsen, a writer of the Harlem Renaissance whose novel *Passing* (1929) explores the subject of racial identity, and Anita Loos, whose novel *Gentlemen Prefer Blondes* (1925) helped define the flapper, examined attitudes toward race and gender in the midst of change. Still others took a more expansive or comprehensive view of the era. In his novel *Babbitt* (1922), for instance, Sinclair Lewis satirized middle-class conformity in the middle of the nation and gave birth to the term that signifies a character type, while in his masterpiece *The Great Gatsby* (1925) F. Scott Fitzgerald defined the era for all time. Jazz Age writers all, these men and women tapped into the spirit of the age. Their novels record an historical moment but are more than social histories, for they capture the rhythms and tone of all the era's contradictions, its boundless sense of possibility and worrisome loss of moorings, its headlong plunge into the modern and fearful retreat into tradition, its eager embrace of change and nostalgic longings for stability. In living the life and recording their impressions of the era, these writers created enduring portraits of the Jazz Age that capture all its complexities.

Chronology of the Jazz Age

1920

January 1	Census figures indicate a U.S. population over 100 million people, a majority of whom live in cities and towns of more than 2,500.
January 2	The Palmer Raids launch a period of intense persecution of radical political dissidents in response to the postwar Red Scare sweeping the nation.
January 10	The League of Nations is established with the Treaty of Versailles, ending World War I. Nine days later the U.S. Senate votes against joining the League.
January 16	Prohibition officially begins.
August 18	Women gain the right to vote with the ratification of the Nineteenth Amendment, known as the Susan B. Anthony Amendment, to the Constitution.
November 2	The Republican Warren G. Harding wins a landslide victory in the first presidential election in which women exercise the vote.

November 2	First commercial radio station, KDKA, broadcasts, Pittsburgh, Pennsylvania.

1921

May 19	Congress passes immigration restrictions that for the first time create immigration quotas for European immigrants to the United States.
September 7–8	Margaret Gorman is crowned the first Miss America in Atlantic City, New Jersey.
October 5–13	Baseball's World Series is broadcast on radio for the first time.
November 10	Margaret Sanger forms the American Birth Control League.

1922

February 5	*Reader's Digest* publishes its first issue.
April 7	The Teapot Dome scandal begins when the U.S. secretary of the interior leases the Teapot Oil Reserves in Wyoming.
May 5	Construction begins on New York City's Yankee Stadium, later dubbed the House That Ruth Built.
May 30	The Lincoln Memorial is dedicated in Washington, D.C. Sinclair Lewis publishes *Babbitt*.

1923

January 1–7	Racially motivated mob atrocity occurs in Rosewood, Florida.
March 2	*Time* magazine publishes its first issue.
April 4	Warner Brothers Pictures is incorporated.
April 15	The first sound motion picture is shown at the Rivoli Theatre in New York City.
August 2	President Warren G. Harding dies in office. He is succeeded by his vice president, Calvin Coolidge.

1924

March 21	National Urban League hosts dinner for a group of African American writers and the white publishers, editors, and critics who can promote their work.

May 10	J. Edgar Hoover is appointed head of the Federal Bureau of Investigation.
November 4	Calvin Coolidge wins election as president of the United States.
	The Ford Motor Company makes its 10 millionth Model T automobile.
	The Charleston, made famous in a 1923 Broadway play, becomes the nation's dance craze.

1925

April 10	F. Scott Fitzgerald publishes *The Great Gatsby*.
April	F. Scott Fitzgerald and Ernest Hemingway meet at the Dingo Bar in Paris.
July 10	The Scopes "Monkey" Trial begins in Dayton, Tennessee, where eight days later a jury will find John T. Scopes guilty of teaching Charles Darwin's evolutionary theory to high school students.
August 8	Forty thousand white hooded Ku Klux Klansmen march down Pennsylvania Avenue in Washington, D.C.
August 16	Charlie Chaplin's silent film classic *The Gold Rush* premiers.
November 28	The Grand Ole Opry transmits its first radio broadcast on WSM.
	Anita Loos publishes *Gentlemen Prefer Blondes*.

1926

October 22	Ernest Hemingway publishes *The Sun Also Rises*.
November 6	The NBC Radio Network is formed by Westinghouse, General Electric, and RCA, opening with twenty-four stations.

1927

May 20	Charles Lindbergh departs Roosevelt Field, New York, on the first transatlantic flight, which he completed thirty-three-and-a-half hours later, landing his aircraft, the "Spirit of St. Louis," at Bourget Field in Paris.
May 26	Henry Ford watches the fifteen millionth Model T roll off the assembly line in his factory in Highland Park, Michigan.

August 23	Nicola Sacco and Bartolomeo Vanzetti, Italian immigrant radicals, are electrocuted after all avenues of appeal have been exhausted.
September 30	New York Yankee star Babe Ruth breaks the home run record he had previously set, hitting his sixtieth of the season.
October 6	*The Jazz Singer*, featuring Al Jolson, the first talking motion picture, or "talkie," debuts in New York City.

1928

May 15	The first appearance of Mickey and Minnie Mouse on film occurs with the release of the animated short film *Plane Crazy*.
June 17	Amelia Earhart becomes the first woman to complete a transatlantic flight.
November 6	Herbert Hoover, the Republican candidate, wins a landslide victory over the Democratic contender from New York, Alfred E. Smith, a Catholic.
November 18	Walt Disney's *Steamboat Willy* premiers, introducing the world to Mickey Mouse.

1929

February 14	In Chicago, gangsters working for Al Capone pull off what is known as the St. Valentine's Day Massacre.
May 16	The first Academy Awards honor *Wings* as Best Picture.
October 11	JC Penney opens store #1252 in Milford, Delaware, the last state in the Union to have one of its retail outlets. The chain's growth indicated the nation's prosperity only two weeks before the stock market crash of 1929.
October 25	The Teapot Dome Scandal comes to an end with the conviction for bribery of Albert B. Fall, the former secretary of the interior.
October 29	Postwar prosperity ends on "Black Tuesday," when the stock market plummets.
	Nella Larsen publishes *Passing*.

1

Babbitt
(Sinclair Lewis, 1922)

SYNOPSIS OF *BABBITT*

For a novel that takes as its central character a most conventional middle-aged, middle-class businessman, the plot of *Babbitt* is highly unconventional. The novel lacks any high drama, any life-shattering epiphanies, any serious confrontations with self or others. Indeed, one contemporary reviewer observed, "Babbitt simply grows two years older as the tale unfolds" (Mencken 138). In those two years, however, Sinclair Lewis captures in a series of chronological events the mundane realities of an average American life, and thus his unconventional plot perfectly mirrors its subject and becomes the ideal strategy by which to render it. The life of a conventional man such as Babbitt, once in motion, the plot suggests, simply moves forward of its own inertia. That seems definitely the case for George F. Babbitt, the forty-six-year-old realtor from the Midwestern metropolis of Zenith.

The novel's first seven chapters record the details of a day in the life of such a conventional man. They introduce readers to Babbitt's family: his devoted wife, Myra, and his three children, Verona, Ted, and Tinka; they enumerate the possessions that provide substance to his existence—his alarm clock, his camp blanket, his Boosters' club button, for instance—as well as the details of his home that contribute to his assurance that he has achieved success; they record the man at work, dictating letters and planning real estate campaigns with his employees, every bit the "Solid Citizen" that he purports to be. Nothing beyond the ordinary worries of an ordinary man—that Verona, for instance, seems too preoccupied with "socialist" ideas, that Ted lacks direction, that a real estate deal may fall through—seems to bother Lewis's ordinary hero, and yet as the novel opens, Babbitt has already begun to dream of a fairy girl who makes him feel confident and young, as if life is starting anew and not winding down into an inevitability. That note of discord in Babbitt's life accounts for all that follows.

In subsequent chapters, Lewis reveals other aspects of Babbitt's life: his memberships in social clubs and professional organizations that help him make valuable business connections and climb the social ladder; the dinner parties that he hosts (and for which he must scramble to purchase bootleg liquor, despite his support of Prohibition). Most important, they record his friendship with his college roommate, Paul Riesling, an even more dissatisfied citizen of Zenith who, unlike Babbitt, is willing to admit the disappointments in his life. Together the friends occasionally escape into the Maine woods, where they can dream of "what might have beens," but they inevitably return to their conventional lives, any thoughts of rebellion temporarily quelled.

Life changes for Babbitt on the day that he is elected vice president of the Boosters' club and discovers that Paul has shot his wife Zilla during another heated argument. When Paul is sentenced to prison for three years, Babbitt loses this important lifeline, and without its steadying influence, he soon finds himself thinking seriously about a fairy girl, someone who will bring change to his routine existence. When he meets an attractive widow, Tanis Judique, Babbitt believes that he has found her.

His affair with Tanis brings Babbitt into contact with her circle of flappers and bohemian friends, and he becomes more and more critical of the conservative views of Zenith's other "solid citizens." In fact, he soon voices support for some of the claims of the laborers who threaten a general strike in the city and espouses the liberal views of the socialist litigator Seneca Doane. These opinions as well as a change in his personal habits—he has begun to stay out late and drink to excess with Tanis's crowd—soon cause him to be ostracized in the community and to lose business. No amount of persuasion on the part of his old friends, however, can convince him to return to his old ways. Only Myra's return to the family home following a temporary absence nursing her sister helps Babbitt recognize that Tanis's circle of friends, "the Bunch," is in its own ways just as conventional as his own circle and to bring him back to his former self.

When Myra falls seriously ill with acute appendicitis, Babbitt nurses his wife to health and, relinquishing all thought of rebellion, rekindles their former intimacy. Soon he has also mended his relationships with his former friends and colleagues and returned to the fold of the Boosters. It is too late, he realizes, for another life. Yet Babbitt's temporary flirtation with his dreams has subtly changed him. When Ted elopes with the neighbor girl, Eunice Littlefield, Babbitt supports his son's plan to drop out of college to pursue his dream of working as a mechanic. Confessing to Ted that he had failed to do what he wanted to do with his life, Babbitt urges his son to resist the pressure to conform to others' expectations and to follow his own path forward. During an era of conformity, such advice from a man whose name would come to signify everything wrong with the utterly conventional must truly have been the most unconventional element of Lewis's novel.

HISTORICAL BACKGROUND: *BABBITT* AND THE PERILS OF PROGRESS AND PROSPERITY

In 1922, when Sinclair Lewis published *Babbitt*, the second of his five decade-defining novels, the nation was already cruising to what another chronicler of the era, F. Scott Fitzgerald, would eventually call the "greatest, gaudiest spree in human history" (*Crack-Up* 87). After a brief, sharp economic downturn in 1920, following the end of World War I, business was booming again in the United States, fueled by the conjunction of historical, economic, and cultural circumstances. That First World War, fought in what was now a devastated Europe, had left strong and intact America's industrial base, and its factories, geared for efficient mass production, were soon manufacturing the automobiles and radios and other consumer goods that its citizens, who were benefiting from full employment and low inflation, were demanding. Those who could not afford to purchase these goods with cash were increasingly willing to exercise their credit and take advantage of the installment plan to enjoy today what they could pay for tomorrow, for it was difficult to resist the siren's songs of the sophisticated new advertisers whose slogans promised such satisfaction from their products. The election of two Republican presidents, moreover, Warren G. Harding, who promised an era of "normalcy," and Calvin

A four-passenger Ford sedan in 1923, by which time the automobile had become a symbol of the nation's prosperity as well as the owner's social status. (Library of Congress)

Coolidge, who in 1925 famously pronounced that "the chief business of the American people is business," effectively signaled the end of government regulation of industry and ushered in an era of laissez-faire economics and an unprecedented boom in the stock market that seemed to be embraced by all. Indeed, even the Teapot Dome scandal that began in 1922 did not provoke much outrage in a nation where so many were profiting from prosperity. Nothing, it seemed, not even its own apprehension about taking the world stage, could have derailed America's political and economic ascendancy in the 1920s.

As if in confirmation of this ascendancy, Lewis created George F. Babbitt, a solid middle-class citizen of Zenith, Winnemac, a fictitious midwestern state adjacent to Ohio, Indiana, Illinois, and Michigan (as the writer elaborated on its location in *Arrowsmith*, his subsequent novel). As its name signifies, Zenith, set deep in the nation's heartland, is the epitome of modernity, the apogee of progress. Indeed, the novel's first seven chapters, which relate the details of a representative day in the life of its title character, offer a compendium of the material items that define the successful realtor, an overview of the activities that comprise his professional and social lives, an introduction to the people with whom he associates, and insight into his opinions and beliefs, his hopes and dreams. From the novel's beginning, Lewis clearly intends that both Babbitt and Zenith be types, representatives of the enterprising American businessman and the progressive American city that his work has created. Equally clear in those first seven chapters is Lewis's satiric intention, for George Babbitt is also a caricature, drawn in broad strokes, a comic counterpoint to the heft of the world that Lewis re-creates in such realistic detail and that created its Babbitts. Something was amiss, in other words, in the Babbitt world, and Sinclair Lewis was determined to expose it.

As a representative of the solid middle class, Babbitt holds all the right ideas and follows all the proper paths, but that, Lewis makes clear, is part of the problem. A firm believer in the gospel of progress, he equates bigger, faster, and newer with all that is right about American society, so he values his alarm clock and electric cigar lighter, symbols of not only cutting-edge technology but also his social status. Driving his automobile gives him a sense of control that soothes away daily tensions: Accelerating from a traffic light, for instance, "he felt superior and powerful, like a shuttle of polished steel darting in a vast machine" (58). He takes pride that his children can get a first-rate education in their local school, which is, after all, "one of the biggest school buildings in the entire country!" (87). His chief satisfaction, however, is Zenith itself.

With its new office buildings, "austere towers of steel and cement and limestone," aspiring to the heavens and "thrusting" the "fretted structures of earlier generations" from its center (1), Zenith has everything, including "zip" and "zest" and "bang," that anyone could desire in a prosperous and growing modern American city. Indeed, "a stranger suddenly dropped into the business-center of Zenith could not have told whether he was in a city of Oregon or Georgia, Ohio or Maine, Oklahoma or Manitoba. But to Babbitt every inch was individual and stirring" (57). The city's very homogeneity in fact inspires Babbitt's confidence, reassures his beliefs, and confirms his self-importance. After all, he exhorts his audience of boosters at the annual meeting of the Zenith Real Estate Board, "Zenith and her sister-cities are producing a new type of civilization," one whose "extraordinary, growing, and sane standardization of stores, offices, streets, hotels, clothes, and newspapers throughout the United States show how strong and enduring a type is ours" (203). Yet this very standardization, Lewis makes clear, is one of the perils of the progress and prosperity that effectively define Babbitt's life.

To achieve this success, Babbitt has had to conform to the values and beliefs of, and cultivate relationships with, the members of his community, whose approval and support will determine his fate. Everything about his life, from the make and model of his automobile to the schools his children attend, from his political affiliation to his choice of church, from his leisure activities to the cut of his coat, is subject to scrutiny and evaluation, so Babbitt chooses the conventional. A member of the Elks, the Boosters' Club, the Zenith Chamber of Commerce, and the Zenith Athletic Club, Babbitt joins all the influential civic organizations, where he enjoys the camaraderie of other like-minded "Good Fellows" and "Solid Citizens." He also attends the Chatham Road Presbyterian Church and votes for Republican Party candidates. These memberships and affiliations as well as the editorial opinions expressed in the *Advocate-Times*, the *Evening Advocate*, and the *Bulletin of the Zenith Chamber of Commerce* are crucial to Babbitt's worldview. Indeed, all of his opinions originate with them, perhaps because his favorite form of art and literature is the comics (83) but more likely because he would not wish to stray from the party line and "until one of [the city's newspapers] had spoken he found it hard to form an original opinion" (83). Babbitt is without doubt a creation of his world, not of the self. Even "the large national advertisers fix the surface of his life, fix what he believed to be his individuality" (105).

The 1920s, with its jazz and flappers, its bathtub gin and speakeasies, was a decade of unprecedented social change, individual freedom, and intellectual rebellion. It was also an era of peace and prosperity that transformed the nation, creating a consumer culture that promised to keep American manufacturing humming. In the nation's Zeniths, however, its Babbitts, its solid citizens and boosters, chiefly representatives of the

In 1927, a flapper supports the repeal of the Eighteenth Amendment authorizing Prohibition, which made illegal the manufacture, transportation, and sale of "intoxicating liquors." The thirteen-year "noble experiment" ended with passage of the Twenty-First Amendment in 1933. (MPI/Getty Images)

business community, were determined that nothing should interfere with their safe and secure and comfortable lives, even if they had to sacrifice their individuality and conform to society's expectations. Sinclair Lewis disclosed this dark underside of progress and prosperity in the Jazz Age, as determined as those boosters that they should see the folly in their sacrifice.

ABOUT SINCLAIR LEWIS: THE MAN WHO DEFINED BABBITTRY

In October 1920, Sinclair Lewis published *Main Street*, the first of five novels published during the decade that exposed the realities of the Jazz Age in Middle America and propelled their author to the Nobel Prize in Literature in 1930, the first American writer to receive such recognition. If his popularity has waned in the intervening years, that was certainly not the case in the 1920s, when *Main Street* sold over one million copies in the two years between its release and the publication of his second major work, *Babbitt*, in 1922, a success that few other writers of the decade would achieve. Born and raised in the Midwest, Lewis clearly understood his native region, the habits of mind and being characteristic of Middle Americans, the quality of the life they lived, and while his re-creation of that world may have dismayed some, it rang true to so many others. Indeed, the writer who created George F. Babbitt added a word to the world's vocabulary as well, for "Babbittry" became synonymous with the materialistic complacency and the mindless conformity of Lewis's most famous character, ensuring Lewis's place in American literary history.

The man who defined "Babbittry" was born Harry Sinclair Lewis on February 7, 1885, in Sauk Centre, Minnesota. Bookish rather than athletic in a region of the country where hunting and fishing and other outdoor pursuits were the standard for young boys, Lewis found it difficult to make friends, and he grew into a lonely and an ungainly young man who dreamed of escaping Sauk Centre. Escape came when his father, a physician, sent him to study at Yale University in New Haven, Connecticut, in 1903, yet even there he remained friendless, a perpetual outsider who, rather ironically, given George Babbitt's propensity for joining, found it difficult, if not impossible, to be one of the gang. At Yale, however, he did find support for his love of literature as well as encouragement for his early literary efforts, poems and short sketches that were published in the *Yale Courant* and the *Yale Magazine*. At Yale, he was also introduced to some radical socialist ideas, meeting the writer Jack London when he visited campus to lecture on socialism, and in 1906, under the influence of Upton Sinclair, briefly abandoning his studies to join Helicon Home Colony, the commune that Sinclair had founded at Englewood, New Jersey. For two months he fired furnaces to contribute to the joint effort and pursued his writing before returning to Yale, where he earned his degree in 1908.

Following graduation, Lewis set about to become a writer, struggling as most writers do for his first success. He traveled the country working low-paying jobs and even selling short story plots to Jack London, who, unlike Lewis, found it difficult to imagine storylines. Eventually he found work in a New York publishing house as a reader, copywriter, and salesman. He also began to sell his stories to *Saturday Evening Post* and to publish a syndicated book page carried in newspapers throughout the country. In 1914, Lewis published his first novel, *Our Mr. Wrenn*, which was well reviewed by the literary establishment. Six years and four minor novels later, he published the work that made him a major voice in American literature, *Main Street* (1920). Set in Gopher Prairie, Minnesota, the novel focused on Carol Kennicott, a sensitive and artistic young woman trapped in a stultifying and provincial small town in America's heartland. Its view of life in that heartland deflated one of the nation's sacred myths, that of the small town, with its industrious and virtuous citizens, its wholesome and nurturing environment, and prompted immediate controversy, propelling the novel to the best-seller list. Lewis's next four novels, all published during the 1920s, made him one of the writers whose name is synonymous with the decade.

Babbitt, published in 1922, extended Lewis's satirical critique of his America to its unbridled faith in business, its passionate embrace of materialism, and its mindless acceptance of the conventional and was as controversial as its predecessor. Lewis followed this success with *Arrowsmith* (1925), a novel that explored the challenges faced by an idealistic doctor and that was awarded the Pulitzer Prize (which Lewis refused to accept). Plunging again into controversy, Lewis published *Elmer Gantry* in 1927. This tale of a hypocritical evangelical minister was denounced by many religious leaders and banned in many cities. Two years later, Lewis closed out the decade with the last of his most important works, *Dodsworth* (1929), in which he examined the lives of the most affluent and influential members of American society and found them as empty and unfulfilling as his Middle Americans'. In five novels Lewis had exposed for all the dark underside of a roaring era.

Lewis continued to write in the years following his decade of success, publishing eleven additional novels, the most famous of which, *It*

Can't Happen Here (1935), imagined the election of a fascist to the American presidency. In the 1940s, he also toured the country with Lewis Browne, a rabbi and popular author, debating such questions as "Has the Modern Woman Made Good?" and "Is the Machine Age Wrecking Civilization?" in crowded lecture halls. But he never reclaimed his previous success, and his personal life was equally disappointing. He had married Grace Livingston Hegger, an editor at *Vogue* magazine, in 1914, just after the publication of his first serious novel, but they had divorced in 1925. Their only child, Wells Lewis, named after the British author H. G. Wells, whose work Lewis greatly admired, was killed in action during World War II. In 1928, Lewis married the journalist Dorothy Thompson, but by 1937, their relationship had soured. They divorced in 1942, and their only child, a son, Michael, died in 1975. Always a heavy drinker, Lewis had battled alcoholism from the late 1930s but was unwilling to give up drinking. On January 10, 1951, in Rome, Italy, Lewis died from the effects on his heart of advanced alcoholism; he was 65 years old.

The first American writer to win the Nobel Prize in Literature, Sinclair Lewis satirized American consumer culture, conformity, and the religion of business in his novels of Middle America. (Library of Congress)

In 1930, when Lewis won the Nobel Prize in Literature, punctuating his decade of achievement, the Swedish Academy praised "his vigorous and graphic art of description and his ability to create, with wit and humor, new types of characters" and specifically cited *Babbitt* in its presentation speech. In his acceptance speech, Lewis praised many of his contemporaries, including Theodore Dreiser, Edith Wharton (to whom he had dedicated *Babbitt*), and Ernest Hemingway and then proceeded to lament that his nation's readers and writers were "still afraid of any literature which is not a glorification of everything American, a glorification of our faults as well as our virtues." In five novels published in the 1920s, Sinclair Lewis had refused to be that kind of writer. He had sought instead to reveal truths about American society, however painful, however unpopular. His Nobel Prize was in part recognition for this achievement.

WHY WE READ *BABBITT*

Babbitt is the perfect antidote to the image of the Jazz Age that exists in the popular imagination. That image, which generally emphasizes the decade's "roar," nearly every aspect of which is associated with Prohibition, from its flappers and jazz cabarets to its bathtub gin and bootleggers and its gangsters and speakeasies, is certainly accurate. It does not, however, represent the whole of the 1920s. Indeed, far more representative of the decade is the title character of Sinclair Lewis's 1922 novel, the genial realtor George F. Babbitt, a forty-six-year-old husband, father, Presbyterian, Republican civic booster in the shining midwestern metropolis of Zenith. He is, as H. L. Mencken asserted in his review of the novel, "America incarnate, exuberant and exquisite" (139), and Lewis renders his physical world, including its social and cultural realities, as well as his inner life (such as it is), including his attitudes toward and beliefs about his world, with such specificity that the 1920s exists in all its complexity and contradictions.

Prohibition, for example, the failed experiment in legislating morality and controlling personal habits, is in 1922 a fact of life, the provisions of the Eighteenth Amendment to the U.S. Constitution having gone into effect just seconds after midnight on January 16, 1920, and Babbitt's attitude about the law is typical of the majority of Americans': "the way it strikes me is that it's a mighty beneficial thing for the poor zob that hasn't got any will-power but for fellows like us, it's an infringement of personal liberty" (154). Preparing to host a dinner party for other solid citizens, Babbitt makes a pleasantly titillating excursion into criminality when he enters a tawdry speakeasy in Zenith's Old Town to purchase a quart of gin (116–119), but he does not own a cocktail shaker, which was "proof of dissipation, the symbol of a Drinker, and Babbitt disliked being known as a Drinker even more than he liked a Drink" (121). Prohibition, Lewis's solid citizens make clear during a discussion of the subject over drinks, was never intended for them, but rather for the irresponsible other guy. They never expected that their support of the law would prevent them from enjoying a convivial glass of wine or beer, and it did not (125–126). Such hypocrisy doomed the "noble experiment" almost from its beginning.

The catalogue of Babbitt's possessions offers further insight into the era's lifestyle and values. The Babbitt house, for example, with its concealed electrical plugs capable of powering the family's electric lamps, electric fan, electric percolator, electric toaster, electric vacuum, and Victrola and decorated in the best of conventional taste, is a perfect example of "Cheerful Modern Houses for Medium Incomes" (116). The Babbitt motor car, moreover, is "poetry and tragedy, love and heroism" to its owner (26), much to the chagrin of his son, who argues the benefits of the new sedans with his more conservative father (80–81). In the modern age, after all, "a family's motor indicated its social rank as precisely as the grades of the peerage determined the rank of an English family," and Ted "aspired to a Packard twin-six and an established position in the motored gentry" (81). New and improved, bigger and better, the material goods of the Jazz Age reflected the public's faith in progress as well as the triumph of consumer culture. If identity were to be represented by one's possessions, then Babbitt, that Jazz Age Everyman, wanted to be certain that he owned all the right things, and he does.

Lewis's depiction of Jazz Age youth culture as well as Babbitt's reaction to it offers additional evidence of the era's contradictions. He worries a bit about Verona, his Bryn Mawr–educated daughter, who thinks vaguely and ineffectually about "doing something worth while" (18) that sounds too much like socialism to her father (18) and in whose reading of "highly irregular poetry" by Vachel Lindsay and "highly improper essays" by H. L. Mencken "he felt a spirit of rebellion against niceness and solid-citizenship" (297). He worries even more, however, about his "motor-mad" son Ted, whose infatuation with the "movie-mad" (248) Eunice Littlefield and flirtation with correspondence courses threaten Babbitt's plans for Ted's own business success (82–95). Eunice, who, Babbitt suspects, smokes cigarettes and wears her hair bobbed and her skirts short and who, according to her father, has "pinned up twenty-one photographs of actors" to her bedroom walls, is clearly a flapper, and Babbitt is "bewildered" by her "worship of new gods" (248), uneasy with provocative behavior. The party Ted throws for his senior class only exacerbates Babbitt's bewilderment and unease.

Babbitt, of course, "had heard stories of what the Athletic Club called 'goings on' at young parties." Ted's party confirms those stories. While none of the girls, all of whom have bobbed hair, wear lipstick and eye makeup, and dress in opulent fabrics, appears to have abandoned her corset in an upstairs dressing room, all seem to have arrived without wearing one, and they "danced cheek to cheek with the boys," provocatively, with Eunice Littlefield a "flying demon" and Ted "maddest of all the boys" (250). Then Babbitt discovers the party's "annex" (250), the dozen cars lining the street outside the house where the guests disappear to smoke and drink and perhaps engage in other immoral behavior. Appalled by the activities of "these children [who] seemed bold to him, and cold" (250), Babbitt and his wife consider their response and, concerned that they could jeopardize Ted's status among his friends, decide to do nothing (251). Jazz Age youth culture was without doubt a sign of the revolution in manners and morals transforming the era, and it seemed to be leaving both young and old without a moral compass.

Babbitt may not have been the kind of experimental work of literary Modernism that the American expatriate poet Ezra Pound exhorted his generation of writers to create with his call to "Make It New." It lacks the technical virtuosity of William Faulkner, the poetic disillusion of F. Scott Fitzgerald, the hard, muscular prose of Ernest Hemingway, the novelists who scholars and critics generally consider the most significant voices of the first half of the twentieth century. In its own way, however, Lewis's satire of Jazz Age America exposes complex truths about the era. His realistic depiction of an average American in Middle America rings so true to the historical record that contemporary readers would have found it hard to dispute his views (although many businessmen and civic boosters valiantly defended its hero). Indeed, it is just the sort of novel that would have made Babbitt uncomfortable (assuming, of course, that he would have read it).

HISTORICAL EXPLORATIONS OF *BABBITT*

Prosperity fueled the roar in the Roaring Twenties. Although the decade began in economic depression (and would end there as well), three consecutive Republican presidents, Warren G. Harding, Calvin Coolidge, and Herbert Hoover, convinced that promoting the country's business interests would result in Hoover's 1928 campaign promise of "A chicken in every pot, and a car in every backyard," set in motion an era of unprecedented prosperity enjoyed by the vast majority of Americans. Granted, the Republicans' laissez-faire policies toward commerce and banking and their series of federal income tax cuts, particularly for the wealthy, did little to alleviate the plight of the farmer, particularly those who grew staple crops such as wheat, corn, and cotton. After all, the nation's dietary habits were changing, and synthetic fabrics such as rayon were transforming the fashion industry. Nor did they ease the depression in coal mining, textile and leather manufacturing, and shipbuilding. But those who worked in the automobile industry and in the various businesses that it spawned, such as gasoline service stations, motels, and diners, or manufactured the latest and most desirable consumer goods, such as the radio, the refrigerator, the washing machine, the telephone, and even cosmetics and cigarettes, suddenly found themselves with the disposable income to purchase these items. According to Frederick Lewis Allen in his groundbreaking history of the 1920s, *Only Yesterday*, "Between 1922 and 1927, the purchasing power of American wages increased at the rate of more than two per cent annually. And during the three years between 1924 and 1927 alone there was a leap from 75 to 283 in the number of Americans who paid taxes on incomes of more than a million dollars a year" (130). In the wake of World War I, business was clearly booming, and life without doubt was improving for nearly everyone in America. For the novelist Sinclair Lewis, conditions were also ripe for a satire of this world.

The primary focus of Lewis's satire was the American businessman, the embodiment of the nation's belief in progress and success and symbol of the triumph of business in the modern era. Whereas previous generations of American leaders had been firmly rooted in the learned professions, especially the law, the pendulum had begun to swing toward bankers, financiers, and industrialists in the aftermath of the Civil War, toward businessmen such as Andrew Mellon, J. P. Morgan, Andrew Carnegie, and John D. Rockefeller, their millions tangible proof of success, their success worthy of emulation and indicative of a shift in attitudes toward what had previously been considered less distinguished professions. Indeed, in 1924 Henry Ford had even been encouraged to run for the presidency. After all, a man who had parlayed ambition, entrepreneurial spirit, and mechanical genius into an automobile empire must surely be capable of leading the nation to even greater prosperity and stability. The founding of The Wharton School for business studies at the University of Pennsylvania in 1881 and the Harvard Business School in 1903 clearly signified the increasing prominence of the businessman in American society.

By the 1920s, many Americans, like Lewis's "Solid Citizen" and successful realtor George F. Babbitt, venerated the nation's business interests. Early in Lewis's novel, for instance, as Babbitt and his auto mechanic, Sylvester Moon, discuss the potential Republican candidates for the forthcoming presidential election, the realtor, repeating the pronouncement of Dr. Howard Littlefield, the "'Great Scholar' of the neighborhood" and "employment-manager and publicity-counsel of the Zenith Street Traction Company" (27), asserts that "what we need first, last, and all the time is a good, sound business administration" (32). If its businesses were booming, after all, everything would surely be right with the nation. Few things, moreover, inspire him more than Zenith's thirty-five-story National Tower, a monument to "integrity" and "strength" and "decision," qualities that move him to a kind of spiritual renewal. In fact, Lewis writes, Babbitt "beheld the tower as a temple-spire of the religion of business a faith passionate, exalted, surpassing common men" (14). While he may have attended Sunday services at the Presbyterian church, with all of the city's other enterprising citizens, Babbitt had put his faith in a secular world and its gospels of success and wealth, and in this faith he was not alone.

Frederick Lewis Allen, in fact, asserts that "the association of business with religion was one of the most significant phenomena of the day" (148) and cites a number of compelling examples to support his point. At an annual convention of the National Association of Credit Men, for instance, Dr. S. Parker Cadman delivered a sermon on "Religion in Business" (148), while the Metropolitan Casualty Insurance Company issued a pamphlet on *Moses, Persuader of Men*, which assured, and reassured its salesmen that "Moses was one of the greatest salesmen and real-estate promoters that ever lived" and that he had conducted "one of the most magnificent selling campaigns that history ever placed upon its pages" (Allen 149). The best-selling nonfiction book of 1925 and 1926, moreover, was the advertising executive Bruce Barton's *The Man Nobody Knows*, which argued that Jesus was "the founder of modern business." After all, Barton observed, "He picked up twelve men from the bottom ranks of business and forged them into an organization that conquered the world," using parables that were "the most powerful advertisements of all time" (Allen 149). An equally compelling example of this conflation of business and religion is *Babbitt*'s Reverend Mike Monday, "the Prophet with a Punch," who sells salvation at "an unprecedented rock-bottom basis." Indeed, according to his most recent report, "He had converted over two hundred thousand lost and priceless souls at an average cost of less than ten dollars a head" (108). Although some of Zenith's solid citizens are at first reluctant to invite Monday, an evocation of the era's famous evangelical preacher Billy Sunday, to preach in their city, when they learn that the evangelist "had turned the minds of workmen from wages and hours to higher things, and thus averted strikes" in other cities where he had erected his tabernacles, they quickly drop all opposition (108). The religion of business reassured all that profit margins and business strategies were sanctioned by a higher power. The businessman was simply part of the plan.

In America's towns and cities, solid citizens like Babbitt channeled their evangelical faith in business through service clubs such as Rotary, Kiwanis, and Lions. Babbitt, for instance, wears in his lapel his Boosters' Club button, which "associated him with Good Fellows, with men who were nice and human, and important in business circles" (10–11), and from his watch chain dangles a "large, yellowish elk's-tooth—proclamation of his membership in the Brotherly and Protective Order of Elks" (10). He is also a member of the Chamber of Commerce and the Zenith Athletic Club, a social organization that marks him as one of the city's distinguished citizens and gives him access to other equally important movers and shakers. Throughout the 1920s, membership in such organizations increased significantly. The Rotary Club, for instance, founded in 1905 and the most famous of the organizations, boasted 150,000 members by 1930 as well as 3,000 clubs in forty-four countries, evidence of its international influence. From 1920 to 1929, the Kiwanis Club, founded in 1915, grew from 205 to 1,800 chapters, and by the end of the decade, the Lions Club, formed in 1917, numbered 1,200 chapters (Allen 147). At weekly breakfasts, luncheons, or dinners members enjoyed good fellowship and made important connections with like-minded business and civic leaders. They also organized charitable events and social programs that confirmed their faith in the religion of business and supported the view of Rotary founder Paul P. Harris that "he profits most who serves best." The Lions Club, for instance, began its work for the blind and visually impaired after Helen Keller addressed its international convention in Cedar Point, Ohio, in 1925, and almost from its inception, the Kiwanis Club focused its efforts on children and youth service. Harris firmly believed that business could be "a redemptive and regenerative influence in the lives of men—and nations" and proclaimed, "Honorable business is an elevating influence, making business men stronger, more straightforward, more sincere and purposeful, more humane and charitable than other men; making business nations more progressive, more enlightened, and less murderous than other nations." In membership to these service clubs, a businessman like Babbitt could thus be assured that he was "the servant of society in the department of finding homes for families and shops for distributors of food" (46). Any profit from such service was merely the reward for vision, a value much admired among the business community (52).

At the forefront of the 1920s religion of business was the salesman and advertising man. American factories may have been churning out all sorts of new products, but their success depended upon the public's willingness to purchase these goods, many of which, despite the new prosperity, were still expensive luxuries. It was left to the advertiser and the salesman to convince the public of the need for an electric washing machine or a radio or anything "new and improved" and of the ease with which they could have it now. What they needed to and did indeed create was a consumer culture, and they relied on increasingly sophisticated methods and the new psychology to achieve their goal.

Until the 1920s, advertising was largely a matter of announcing the availability of a product and informing the consumer of its use and benefits. During the 1920s, however, as mass production and lower prices resulted in an expanded American marketplace and increased competition for consumer dollars, advertisers shifted to persuasive tactics designed to convince the public that they needed and deserved these products. Consequently, as Frederick Lewis Allen observed, "The copywriter was learning to pay less attention to the special qualities and advantages of his product, and more to the study of what the mass of unregenerate mankind wanted—to be young and desirable, to be rich, to keep up with the Joneses, to be envied. The winning method was to associate his product with one or more of these ends, logically or illogically, truthfully or cynically" (142). A 1920s print advertisement for Lux Toilet Soap, for instance, features images of "Clara Bow, Betty Bronson, Janet Gaynor," three famous actresses of the period, and "You," promising in effect that women who washed with Lux would be as lovely as film stars. In other print ads of the period, the baseball hero Babe Ruth endorsed Old Gold cigarettes and claimed that Red Rock Cola was "the finest cola drink I ever tasted!" The appeal of such advertising was psychological, focusing on consumers' unfulfilled desires or needs, and connecting their fulfillment to a specific product. And if that product were connected to a celebrity, so much the better. After all, in the 1920s, when baseball was the national pastime, most men would have been pleased to be compared to Babe Ruth, and in an era that celebrated youth, most women would have been flattered to look like Clara Bow, the nation's "It" girl.

The power of advertising to change public perceptions and habits is perhaps best illustrated by the campaign against the social taboo of women smoking in public engineered by Edward Bernays, the father of public relations and nephew of the psychologist Sigmund Freud, in the late 1920s. Throughout the decade, the American Tobacco Company had sought in its print advertisements to make smoking fashionable for women through images of attractive young women, as well as actresses, smoking Lucky Strikes. In one ad, women were also exhorted "to keep a slender figure . . . Reach for a Lucky." Legitimizing public smoking, and even smoking itself, for women, however, proved a difficult task, so in 1929, Bernays enlisted a group of models to march in the New York City Easter Parade and alerted reporters to expect a unique event. When the models stopped, lit their Lucky Strikes, and openly smoked their "Torches of Freedom," cameras captured their bold assertion of independence, and journalists reported the event to a national audience. Soon enough, resistance to change collapsed, and

Lighting their "Torches of Freedom," women puff at their Lucky Strike cigarettes during the 1929 New York City Easter Parade in a gesture of freedom and absolute equality with men. The demonstration was organized by the "father of public relations," Edward Bernays, for his client, the American Tobacco Company. (Underwood Archives/Getty Images)

women were enjoying yet another male privilege. Such was the power of advertising and public relations to effect social and economic change and thereby create a consumer culture unique to the Jazz Age.

In fact, "consumer culture," according to Liette Gidlow, "was a defining element of public life in the 1920s, and the 1920s were a defining moment in the development of consumer culture. Though consumer goods and advertising, of course, predated the 1920s, a mature consumer society did not" (163). By the end of the decade, however, the American people had developed new attitudes toward material goods and their consumption as well as consumer credit, and "increasingly, American life," according to Laurence B. Glickman, "not just economically but culturally, centered on mass consumption" (16). For many, the more conspicuous the consumption, the better.

Sinclair Lewis spends much of Chapter One of *Babbitt* cataloguing his hero's possessions and his attitude toward them. "A man whose god was Modern Appliances" (5), he is "proud," for instance, of being awakened by "the best of nationally advertised and quantitatively produced alarm-clocks, with all modern attachments, including cathedral chime, intermittent alarm, and a phosphorescent dial" (4). He is also relieved, after admitting to himself that his garage is "the only thing on the place that isn't up-to-date," to survey his "altogether royal bathroom of porcelain and glazed tile and metal sleek as silver," complete with clear glass towel bar set in nickel, a tub "long enough for a Prussian Guard," and a "sensational exhibit of toothbrush holder, shaving-brush holder, soap dish, sponge dish, and medicine-cabinet, so glittering and so ingenious that they resembled an electrical instrument board" (5). After shaving with a new disposable razor blade, he frets that the trousers of his brown suit need pressing and rejects outright his wife's suggestion that he wear the coat of the brown with the trousers of his blue suit. "What do you think I am? A busted bookkeeper?" he rails. His B.V.D. undershirt, however, which distinguishes him from his father-in-law and partner, who wears "tight, long, old-fashioned undergarments" (9), restores his equilibrium, as does the "donning of his spectacles," which transform him into the very image of "the modern business man; one who gave orders to clerks and drove a car and played occasional golf and was scholarly in regard to Salesmanship" (9). By the time he has put on his "well cut, well made, and completely undistinguished" suit (9); transferred the contents of his pockets, about which he feels "earnest" and which include a fountain pen and silver pencil; his "loose-leaf pocket note-book"; and his watch-chain, to which are attached a silver cigar-cutter, seven keys, a yellowish elk's-tooth, and, of course, a good watch, from his brown to his gray suit (10); and stuck in his lapel his Boosters' Club button (11), George Babbitt looks every bit the "Solid Citizen" he believes himself to be (9).

This catalogue of items that defines George Babbitt not only to himself but also for society captures the profound change in the relationship between the individual and material goods that occurred during the Jazz Age. Whereas previous generations had been defined by relatively objective criteria such as race, religion, class, geographical region, and occupation, the new consumer culture prompted people to identify less with the things they produced and more with the goods they purchased. As Kirk Curnutt observes, "The explosion of consumable goods provided individuals with new tools for packaging their personalities in vibrant and captivating ways, which fell under the general rubric of *style*" (91). While Babbitt's style is hardly vibrant or captivating, it does indeed represent him. Everything about his appearance, his house, his car, his amusements and leisure activities, is designed, in fact, to signify his sense of self and confirm his membership in his class, equally important in the 1920s, when success, and especially business success, depended on the individual's willingness to conform to established patterns, customs, and beliefs. Babbitt's elk's-tooth and Boosters' Club button, emblems of his group identity, are thus as important to his selfhood as his purple knitted scarf, "his only frivolity" (9), into which he inserts a "snake-head pin with opal eyes"(10). "Style," as Stuart Ewen defines the term, "was a way of saying who one was, or who one wished to be" (79), and, as Lewis makes clear in his initial description of Babbitt, in a consumer culture identity was increasingly a matter of commodities. Ewen confirms this shift, asserting, "The emerging market in stylized goods provided consumers with a vast palette of symbolic meanings, to be selected and juxtaposed in the assembling of a public self" (79).

Advertisers had done their job well. They had created a demand for consumer goods, a demand rooted not only or even primarily in utility and quality but also equally or even more importantly in personal preference and selfhood. Consumer culture, however, also depended on purchasing power, the ability to pay for desired goods, many of which, including the automobiles and electrical appliances that the era's Babbitts worshipped, were still prohibitively expensive. Granted, wages had risen significantly throughout the twentieth century, increasing the public's disposable income, but Americans traditionally believed in the value of thrift. They did not replace an item simply because manufacturers had released a new and improved model or they had tired of it, and they saved for a rainy day. If consumers were going to be persuaded to buy, they would first have to accept a newly evolving definition of thrift, one that transformed it, according to Lauren Rule Maxwell, into a "form of consumption" (313). Only by erasing the stigma of debt would the nation's business and economic interests make credit and installment buying socially acceptable to the public.

To change the buying habits of the American consumer, the 1920s, according to Curnutt, "witnessed a vilification of financial restraint" (105). Newspapers and magazines published editorials and features that challenged traditional concepts of thrift, calling it the "new menace" and a serious "dilemma" (Curnutt 105) and making saving seem an old-fashioned virtue. Some even suggested that it was a form of hoarding (Glickman 17). Consumers were also encouraged to develop a sense of entitlement about the new products on offer in the marketplace. They had worked hard for their money and should not have to deny themselves the pleasure of ownership, especially when installment buying made it easy to enjoy their purchases as they paid for them. Throughout the decade, Americans experienced what the economist Martha L. Olney calls a "consumer durables revolution" that saw savings fall from 7.1 to 4.4 percent between 1898 to 1916 and 1922 to 1929 ("Advertising" 489–91) and overall consumer debt rise to $7 billion (Curnutt 107). In fact, according to Curnutt, debt had become "a badge of bourgeois pride as securing credit meant that one had not only been deemed a reliable borrower but that one possessed value in the marketplace" (107). By the end of the 1920s, when shopping had for the first time become a type of leisure activity, it was clear that Americans had changed their view of debt (even buying stocks on margin) and that yet another cultural shift had occurred in the nation.

One perhaps unintended consequence of prosperity and the changes that resulted from it was a stultifying conformity among the nation's middle-class majority of which Babbitt was a chief representative. H.L. Mencken, the iconoclastic cultural critic and editor of first the *Smart Set* and then the *American Mercury*, two influential magazines whose audience was distinctively highbrow, coined the term "booboisie" to describe this group of uneducated, uncultured mindless boosters and mediocrities who held sway in the nation, and Sinclair Lewis ridiculed them in *Babbitt*. Having surrendered to the nation's business interests, embraced commodity culture, and profited in doing so, the middle class sought now to consolidate its position and thus saw as threats any person or ideas that challenged their comfortable existence. Any talk of strikes or unionism, for instance, smacked of socialism and challenged the capitalist system on which the nation's prosperity had been built. Any talk of natural selection or evolution, such as John Scopes was teaching to impressionable high school students in Dayton, Tennessee, undermined the Christian teachings on which its system of law and justice was built (as well as man's belief in his superiority). Any failure to contribute to charitable campaigns or join civic organizations was an act of selfish individualism that threatened the good of society. While the 1920s lives in the popular imagination as a "roaring" decade, it was also, rather ironically, an era of social and political conservatism and conformity, of mass consumption and mass culture that some, including Sinclair Lewis, were determined to expose.

Lewis's representative of middle-class conformity, George Babbitt, is simultaneously the embodiment of its critique, and the writer locates the problem in the "standardization of thought" (110), of which his protagonist is also the epitome. While Babbitt is vaguely aware of some dreams and desires unfilled by his personal and professional lives as well as the material possessions that represent him, he seldom thinks clearly or for long about the reasons for his dissatisfaction and probably lacks the facility of judgment to know himself. Woefully ignorant of literature, history, geography, and anything international, he rarely reads a book, preferring instead popular magazines and the local newspapers, where he can find the comic strips, "his favorite literature and art" (83), and takes all his opinions from these publications or trusted authorities such as his neighbor Dr. Littlefield or his minister or fellow boosters. Asked his opinion on a preacher who takes the oath of mayor wearing overalls, for instance, he "searched for an attitude, but neither as a Republican, a Presbyterian, an Elk, nor a real-estate broker did he have any doctrine about preacher-mayors laid down for him, so he grunted and went on" (23). Later, when his son Ted seeks his advice about correspondence courses, Babbitt finds himself "again without a canon which would enable him to speak with authority. Nothing in motoring or real estate had indicated what a Solid Citizen and Regular Fellow ought to think about culture by mail" (87). (Although the slick brochures advertising the courses initially give him pause, he eventually supports conventional public education, for which he is already paying.) Babbitt speaks in clichés and peppers his conversation with slang phrases such as "by gee, by gosh, by jingo" (14) that suggest an inability to frame an original thought. He also holds all the popular views because ultimately what he wants most is to be a hale and hearty good fellow and one of Zenith's respected solid citizens. Tempted for a time to pursue the alternate path of Zenith's few free-thinking bohemians, he feels the weight of the community's approbation and eventually submits to the pressure, grateful to the point of tears when Vergil Gunch invites him to join the Good Citizens' League (421).

In his 1922 *Smart Set* review of *Babbitt*, H.L. Mencken, who shared Lewis's views and sensibility, calling himself "an old professor of Babbittry," praised the novel's realistic portrayal of Jazz Age America and of Babbitt, "the average American of the ruling minority." Babbitt, he declared, was not a character but rather "an archetype," and he represented, so far as Mencken was concerned, everything wrong in the nation: "It is not Babbitt that shines forth most gaudily, but the whole complex of Babbittry, Babbittism, Babbittisimus. . . . His every act is related to the phenomena of [his] society. It is not what he feels and aspires to that moves him primarily; it is what the folks about him will think of him. His politics is communal politics, mob politics, herd politics; his religion is a public rite wholly without subjective significance; his relations to his wife and children are formalized and standardized; even his debaucheries are the orthodox debaucheries of a sound business man. The salient thing about him, in truth, is his complete lack of originality—and that is precisely the salient mark of every American of his class" (139). Babbitt's mindless conformity, his inability to think for himself, as Mencken saw it, compromised every aspect of his and the nation's life, making both inauthentic and fraudulent. It was the underside of the American Dream, the price of prosperity, and Lewis had clearly exposed the truth for all to see.

DOCUMENTING *BABBITT*
The Religion of Business in the Jazz Age

Business was booming in the 1920s, fueling the nation's prosperity. The advent of new consumer goods such as the radio and the electric toaster coincided with an increase in both jobs and wages and the public's pent-up postwar desire for luxuries, or at least modern laborsaving appliances such as the electric vacuum cleaner, to create a consumer-spending spree that reignited America's faith in capitalism. Businessmen such as Henry Ford embodied the American ideal of the self-made man (Ford was even encouraged to run for president), and the economic policies of the decade's three Republican presidents signified that protecting America's business interests was in the best interest of the nation.

Any doubts about those business interests were assuaged by the developing rhetoric of the religion of business. By focusing on the moral and ethical responsibilities of the businessman and engaging the business community in charitable work, business organizations such as the Rotary Club and the Lions Club helped perpetuate the view that the nation's businessmen were as interested in doing good as in making money. By linking religious metaphors to business interests, the gospel of wealth and the ideal of success were no longer associated with materialism but rather with the good life. The businessman was no longer a shyster but a respected member of the community. Capitalism and Christianity were natural allies.

The following documents reveal the veneration of business, and especially the advertising man, that developed during the Jazz Age. The first document finds the founder of the Rotary Club reflecting on the organization's success, which he attributes in part to its melding of business and moral principles. The second, an excerpt from Bruce Barton's The Man Nobody Knows, *which topped the nonfiction best-seller lists in 1925 and 1926, makes clear the connection between business and religion that developed during the Jazz Age by arguing that Jesus was the first advertising man and attributing his success to his salesmanship.*

Document: From "Passing Our Tenth Milestone," Paul P. Harris, 1915

... Big dreams of Rotary are gradually coming true, and encouraged by past performances, we dare to dream again and of even bigger things. I sometimes see, or think I see, Rotary the harbinger of a general world wide philosophy of business and of life, with happiness as its goal. ...

We need in this world a much better and clearer understanding of the worth of some things and of the worthlessness of others.

Rotary has demonstrated its ability to contribute toward the world's supply of happiness by elevating business to a companionable standard. Most of us have to live pretty near to business and it is worth while to have taken a part in the great movements of the day tending toward the idealizing of trade. In this respect the advent of Rotary was particularly opportune. It has often seemed to me that we should stop there, lest our fire become too much scattered to be effective. At other more sanguine moments, it has seemed to me, in view of the heart that has evidenced itself in past endeavors, that it would not be presumptuous, were we to look the entire big job right in the face—Life itself, and rise to the task of undertaking its betterment.

If I improve my mode of living, my business will be very likely to be benefited. Many business successes are the direct consequence of right living, outside of business; and many business failures are directly traceable to wrong living. The business life and the home life are not independent of each other; they are interdependent, one upon the other.

We shall have a Rotarian good book some day, a sort of Rotarian bible; not a disconnected product of many and diverse minds, but a carefully evolved compendium of, not a Rotarian philosophy of the day, but of THE Rotarian philosophy of the day—not the Rotarian philosophy for all time to come, because Rotarian philosophy will always be progressive.

Chapter by chapter, I would love to see the great book built up, not rapidly. In my optimistic moments, I can see it take place among the foremost of the world's productions of its kind. It will fill a long felt want. What a pleasure it will be when we really have something definite to show; when we can hand our book to a friend and say—"There, My Friend, within the covers of that book you will find all that Rotary holds dear. Read it, it will do you good." "Not a Rotarian? Hush man, every one with the love of the world in his heart is a Rotarian; you mean that you are not a member of any Rotary Club; that is different."

Source: Paul P. Harris, "Passing Our Tenth Milestone," *The Rotarian*, February 1915: 15–16.

Document: From *The Man Nobody Knows*, Bruce Barton, 1925

How It Came to Be Written

The little boy sat bolt upright and still in the rough wooden chair, but his mind was very busy.

This was his weekly hour of revolt.

The kindly lady who could never seem to find her glasses would have been terribly shocked if she had known what was going on inside the little boy's mind.

"You must love Jesus," she said every Sunday, "and God."

The little boy did not say anything. He was afraid to say anything; he was almost afraid that something would happen to him because of the things he thought.

Love God? Who was always picking on people for having a good time and sending little boys to hell because they couldn't do better in a world which he had made so hard! Why didn't God take some one his own size?

Love Jesus! The little boy looked up at the picture which hung on the Sunday-school wall. It showed a pale young man with flabby forearms and a sad expression. The young man had red whiskers.

Then the little boy looked across to the other wall. There was Daniel, good old Daniel, standing off the lions. The little boy liked Daniel. He liked David, too, with the trusty sling that landed a stone square on the forehead of Goliath. And Moses, with his rod and his big brass snake. They were winners—those three. He wondered if David could whip Jeffries. Samson could! Say, that would have been a fight!

But Jesus! Jesus was the "lamb of God." The little boy did not know what that meant, but it sounded like Mary's little lamb. Something for girls—sissified. Jesus was also "meek and lowly," a "man of sorrows and acquainted with grief." He went around for three years telling people not to do things.

Sunday was Jesus' day; it was wrong to feel comfortable or laugh on Sunday.

The little boy was glad when the superintendent rang the bell and announced, "We will now sing the closing hymn." One more bad hour was over. For one more week the little boy had got rid of Jesus.

Years went by and the boy grew up and became a business man.

He began to wonder about Jesus.

He said to himself: "Only strong magnetic men inspire great enthusiasm and build great organizations. Yet Jesus built the greatest organization of all. It is extraordinary."

The more sermons the man heard and the more books he read the more mystified he became.

One day he decided to wipe his mind clean of books and sermons.

He said, "I will read what the men who knew Jesus personally said about him. I will read about him as though he were a new historical character, about whom I had never heard anything at all."

The man was amazed.

A physical weakling! Where did they get that idea? Jesus pushed a plane and swung an adze; he was a successful carpenter. He slept outdoors and spent his days walking around his favorite lake. His muscles were so strong that when he drove the money-changers out, nobody dared to oppose him!

A kill-joy! He was the most popular dinner guest in Jerusalem! The criticism which proper people made was that he spent too much time with publicans and sinners (very good fellows, on the whole, the man thought) and enjoyed society too much. They called him a "wine bibber and a gluttonous man."

A failure! He picked up twelve men from the bottom ranks of business and forged them into an organization that conquered the world.

When the man had finished his reading he exclaimed, "This is a man nobody knows!"

"Some day," said he, "someone will write a book about Jesus. Every businessman will read it and send it to his partners and his salesmen. For it will tell the story of the founder of modern business." . . .

Chapter 4: His Method

. . . Surely no one will consider us lacking in reverence if we say that every one of the "principles of modern salesmanship" on which businessmen so much pride themselves are brilliantly exemplified in Jesus' talk and work. . . .

Jesus taught all this without ever teaching it. Every one of his conversations, every contact between his mind and others, is worthy of the attentive study of any sales manager. Passing along the shores of a lake one day, he saw two of the men whom he wanted as disciples. *Their* minds were in motion; their hands were busy with their nets; their conversation was about conditions in the fishing trade, and the prospects of a good market for the day's catch. To have broken in on such thinking with the offer of employment as preachers of a new religion would have been to confuse them and invite a sure rebuff. What was Jesus' approach?

"Come with me," he said, "and I will make you fishers of men."

Fishers . . . that was a word they could understand . . . fishers of men . . . that was a new idea. . . . what was he driving at . . . fishers of men . . . it sounded interesting . . . well, what is it, anyway?"

He sat on a hillside overlooking a fertile country. Many of the crowd who gathered around him were farmers with their wives and sons and daughters. He wanted their interest and attention; it was important to make them understand, at the very outset, that what he had to say was nothing vague or theoretical but of direct and immediate application to their daily lives.

"A sower went forth to sow," he began, "and when he sowed some seeds fell by the wayside and the fowls came and devoured them up . . . " Were they interested . . . *were* they? Every man of them had gone through that experience . . . the thievish crows . . . many a good day's work *they* had spoiled. . . . So this Teacher knew something about the troubles that farmers had to put up with, did he? Fair enough . . . let's hear what he has to say. . . . "

. . . With his very first sentence he put himself in step with [his audience]; it was invariably a thought in line with their own thinking, easy for even the dullest to understand, and shrewdly calculated to awaken an appetite for more.

Chapter 6: The Founder of Modern Business

. . . On one occasion, you recall, he stated his recipe for success. It was on the afternoon when [apostles] James and John came to ask him what promotion they might expect. They were two of the most energetic of the lot, called "Sons of Thunder" by the rest, being noisy and always in the midst of some sort of a storm. They had joined the ranks because they liked him, but with no very definite idea of what it was all about; and now they wanted to know where the enterprise was heading, and just what there would be in it for them.

"Master," they said, "we want to ask what plans you have in mind for us. You're going to need big men around you when you establish your kingdom; our ambition is to sit on either side of you, one on your right hand and the other on your left."

Who can object to that attitude? If a man fails to look after himself, certainly no one will look after him. If you want a big place, go ask for it. That's the way to get ahead.

Jesus answered with a sentence which sounds poetically absurd.

"Whosoever will be great among you, shall be your minister," he said, "and whosoever of you will be the chiefest, shall be servant of all."

A fine piece of rhetoric, now isn't it? Be a good servant and you will be great; be the best possible servant and you will occupy the highest possible place. Nice idealistic talk but utterly impractical; nothing to take seriously in a common sense world. That is just what most men thought for some hundreds of years, and then, quite suddenly, Business woke up to a great discovery. You will hear that discovery proclaimed in every sales convention as something distinctly modern and up to date. It is emblazoned in the advertising pages of every magazine.

Look through these pages.

Here is the advertisement of an automobile company, one of the greatest in the world. And why is it greatest? On what does it base its claim to leadership? On its huge factories and financial strength? They are never mentioned. On its army of workmen or its high salaried executives? You might read its advertisements for years without suspecting that it had either. No. "We are great because of our service," the advertisements cry. "We will crawl under your car oftener and get our backs dirtier than any of our competitors. Drive up to our service stations and ask for anything at all—it will be granted cheerfully. We serve; therefore we grow." . . .

So we have the main points of his business philosophy:

1. Whoever will be great must render service.
2. Whoever will find himself at the top must be willing to lose himself at the bottom.
3. The big rewards come to those who travel the second undemanded mile. . . .

We have quoted some men of conspicuous success, but the same sound principles apply to every walk of life. Great progress will be made in the world when we rid ourselves of the idea that there is a difference between *work* and *religious work*. We have been taught that a man's daily business activities are selfish, and that only the time which he devotes to church meetings and social service activities is consecrated. Ask any ten people what Jesus meant by his "Father's business," and nine of them will answer "preaching." To interpret the words in this narrow sense is to lose the real significance of his life. It was not to preach that he came into the world, nor to teach, nor to heal. These are all departments of his Father's business, but the business itself is far larger, more inclusive. For if human life has any significance, it is this—that God has set going here an experiment to which all His resources are committed. He seeks to develop perfect human beings, superior to circumstance, victorious over Fate. No single kind of human talent or effort can be spared if the experiment is to succeed. The race must be fed and clothed and housed and transported, as well as preached to, and taught and healed. Thus *all* business is his Father's business. All work is worship, all useful service prayer. And whoever works wholeheartedly at any worthy calling is a co-worker with the Almighty in the great enterprise which He has initiated but which he can never finish without the help of men.

Source: Bruce Barton, *The Man Nobody Knows*, Indianapolis, IN: Bobbs-Merrill Company, 1925.

Conformity in the Jazz Age

In the following book review, H. L. Mencken, writer, editor, and one of the era's foremost cultural critics, explores the issue of "standardization" in American society. By "standardization," Mencken effectively means conformity, one of the chief values that Babbitt espouses and that Sinclair Lewis makes clear is detrimental to the nation. Yet during the Jazz Age, Americans felt a tremendous pressure to conform to societal values and attitudes. A Red Scare early in the 1920s, associated with an influx of immigrants from Eastern and Southern Europe, and continued political and labor unrest not only in the United States but also in Europe caused people to fear for the stability of their lives, and the era's rapid pace of change, which is always unsettling, prompted a retreat into old, familiar patterns of behavior and beliefs. Anyone unwilling to conform was looked upon with suspicion and distrust. When Babbitt flirts with socialist ideas, for instance, and associates with Zenith's bohemian crowd, he soon finds himself ostracized from the city's "Solid Citizens" and must pay the consequences for his rebellion by a decline in his business. In a nation that prides itself on independence, conformity was the reality of American culture during the Jazz Age. Mencken's essay reinforces the lessons of Babbitt's rebellion.

Document: From "Knowledge in Contempt in America, Believe Europeans," H. L. Mencken, 1925

When, a few weeks ago, the clans gathered at Berlin to celebrate the sixth anniversary of the German republic, the prat or [sic] of the day reached the climax of his address in the following sentence:

> "We must emancipate ourselves from the mad tendency to permit our national life to become Americanized!"

This remarkable declaration got relatively little attention in the American press; when it was mentioned at all, it was commonly with the declaration that the Germans are still suffering from war wounds, and envy our vast prosperity. But that, I think, was a shallow reading of it. The Germans, as a matter of fact, give very little attention to their war wounds, which, after all, were not fatal; they devote themselves mainly to looking ahead. And our prosperity does not greatly disturb them, for in it they see a guarantee of their own; what we are accomplishing today, with the odds all in our favor, they plan to do tomorrow, with the odds nearly even.

They are, in truth, quite as eager for the dollar as we are, and quite as determined to get it, by fair means or foul. That quest, so nearly universal in the modern world, is not what they have in mind when they speak of the dangers of Americanization. What they think of is something different. It may be described, in general, as the decay of spiritual values that has gone on among us during the past two generations. It may be described, in particular, as our growing impatience with the free play of ideas, our increasing tendency to reduce all virtues to the single one of conformity, our relentless and all pervading standardization. This is what all Europe fears when it contemplates the growing importance and influence of the United States. It hasn't J. P. Morgan in mind, nor even General Pershing; it has Henry Ford. By Americanization it means Fordization—and not only in industry, but also in politics, art and even religion.

II

If you want to see how the United States of today looks to a reflective European you can do no better than get a little book called "Americanization; A World Menace," written by W. T. Colyer. . . .

. . . Mr. Colyer is not blind to what we have accomplished. He sees a wilderness broken to the plow and the flivver. But, he sees also a people broken to the yoke.

It is the merciless ironing out of the individual, indeed, that chiefly arrests his attention, and he offers it as a solemn warning to his own countrymen. Americans have got on in the world, he says, by the simple process of sacrificing everything else to getting on. They began as a nation by setting up a table of inalienable human rights, but one by one those rights have gone by the board. No other nation of today is so rigorously policed. The lust to standardize and regulate extends to the most trivial minutae of private life.

It goes even further, passing beyond acts to thoughts. Such and such an idea is virtuous and "American;" its contrary is full of sin. Mr. Colyer believes that that principle is intolerably dangerous—that it is bound, in the long run, to throttle all intelligence and make for a groveling and ignominious stupidity. More, he believes the people of the United States have already made some progress along that depressing way.

III

. . . Europe sees Americanism, in brief, as a sort of Philistine uprising against the free spirit of man—as a conspiracy of dull and unimaginative men, fortuitously made powerful, against all the ideas and ideals that seem sound to their betters. Henry Ford, with his discovery that history is bunk and science a fraud, seems to it to be the archetypical American. He is, within his own field, a man of great energy and very respectable talents. He has done useful work, and perhaps earned at least a part of his immense reward. But he insists upon leaving his own field for fields that are strange and impenetrable to him, and upon laying down laws therein for the government of their natural inhabitants. This is what Europe understands by Americanism, by Americanization. And this is what it fears.

The trial of the infidel Scopes, I believe, greatly added to those fears. It got more space in the European papers than the election of Coolidge, even more than the death of Harding. They gave it the place of honor for days running. And what was the lesson that they deducted from it? First, that all ordinary intellectual decency had departed from the American people—that they were willing and even eager to flaunt their contempt for all sound knowledge and sound sense before the world. Second, that a nation cherishing such notions and feelings, and with the money and men to enforce them, deserved to be watched very carefully.

IV

Europe hears relatively little about what is being done, often against cruel difficulties, by American artists and scientists, philosophers and publicists. It has its own supply of such men, and it naturally heeds them first. They have a high position over there, unmatched on this side of the ocean. . . . We put such men much lower, and so we have fewer of them, and Europe, having more and better ones at home, hears little about the few we have. But Europe has no Henry Fords, or William Jennings Bryans, or Gimlet-Eye Butlers, or Major Hylans, or Wilbur Volivas, and so it is interested by them, instantly and hugely, when they appear in America. It observes that the American people, or, at all events, the great majority of the American people, take them quite seriously, and it concludes, not without reason, that they accurately represent America. It hears that Bryan was thrice within reach of the White House—and then it hears of him denouncing the theory that man is a mammal. It hears that Butler is an officer wearing the American uniform—and then it hears he is engaged in monkey shines to entertain the Anti-Saloon league. It hears that Ford is the richest man of a country in which riches exceed any other worth—and then it hears him reviling learning like a yokel in a cross roads grocery store.

Such phenomena surprise it—and shock it. They violate all notions of propriety, of decency. It cannot imagine a civilized people suffering them without immediate and angry rebellion. So it concludes that the Americans, despite their vast success in collaring dollars, have yet to go some distance before they are fully civilized. And when it hears talk of Americanization it shivers.

Source: H. L. Mencken, "Knowledge in Contempt in America, Believe Europeans," *Chicago Tribune*, August 30, 1925.

Suggested Readings

Allen, Frederick Lewis. *Only Yesterday. An Informal History of the 1920s*. 1931. New York: Harper Perennial, 1964.

Calder, Lendol G. *Financing the American Dream: A Cultural History of Consumer Credit*. Princeton, NJ: Princeton University Press, 1999.

Curnutt, Kirk. "Fitzgerald's Consumer World." In *A Historical Guide to F. Scott Fitzgerald*. Ed. Kirk Curnutt. Oxford and New York: Oxford University Press, 2004: 85–128.

Dooley, D. J. *The Art of Sinclair Lewis*. Lincoln: University of Nebraska Press, 1967.

Dumenil, Lynn. *The Modern Temper: American Culture and Society in the 1920s*. New York: Hill and Wang, 1995.

Ewen, Stuart. *All Consuming Images: The Politics of Style in Contemporary Culture*. New York: Basic, 1988.

Fitzgerald, F. Scott. *The Crack-Up*. Ed. Edmund Wilson. New York: New Directions, 1945.

Gidlow, Liette. *The Big Vote: Gender, Consumer Culture, and the Politics of Exclusion*. Baltimore: Johns Hopkins University Press, 2004.

Glickman, Lawrence B. "Rethinking Politics: Consumers and the Public Good in the 'Jazz Age.'" *OAH Magazine of History* 21.3(2007): 16–20.

Grebstein, Sheldon Norman. *Sinclair Lewis*. New York: Twayne Publishers, 1962.

Hutchisson, James M. *The Rise of Sinclair Lewis, 1920–1930*. State College: Penn State University Press, 2001.

Lewis, Sinclair. *Babbitt*. 1922. New York: Bantam Classics, 1998.

Light, Martin. *The Quixotic Vision of Sinclair Lewis*. Lafayette, IN: Purdue University Press, 1975.

Lingeman, Richard. *Sinclair Lewis: Rebel from Main Street*. New York: Random House, 2002.

Marchand, Roland. *Advertising the American Dream: Making Way for Modernity, 1920–1940*. Berkeley: University of California Press, 1984.

Maxwell, Lauren Rule. "Consumer Culture and Advertising." In *F. Scott Fitzgerald in Context*. Ed. Bryant Mangum. Cambridge: Cambridge University Press, 2013: 311–320.

Mencken, H. L. "Portrait of an American Citizen." *The Smart Set* 69(October 1922): 138–139.

Olney, Martha L. "Advertising, Consumer Credit, and the 'Consumer Durables Revolution' of the 1920s." *Journal of Economic History* 47.2(1987): 489–491.

Olney, Martha L. *Buy Now, Pay Later: Advertising, Credit, and Consumer Durables in the 1920s*. Chapel Hill: University of North Carolina Press, 1991.

Parrish, Michael E. *Anxious Decades: America in Prosperity and Depression, 1920–1941*. New York: Norton, 1992.

Schorer, Mark. *Sinclair Lewis: An American Life*. New York: McGraw-Hill, 1961.

Schorer, Mark, ed. *Sinclair Lewis: A Collection of Critical Essays*. Englewood Cliffs, NJ: Prentice-Hall, 1962.

Vidal, Gore. "The Romance of Sinclair Lewis." *The New York Review of Books*, October 8, 1992.

2

The Great Gatsby
(F. Scott Fitzgerald, 1925)

SYNOPSIS OF *THE GREAT GATSBY*

The Great Gatsby is a retrospective narrative told primarily from the perspective of its first-person narrator, Nick Carraway, who has retreated to his midwestern home following the tragic events of the summer of 1922, when he had met and befriended a mysterious young man named Jay Gatsby in the fictional village of West Egg on Long Island, New York. A Yale graduate and a World War I veteran, Nick, typical of his generation, hopes to make his fortune in the bond business. He rents a small bungalow located on Gatsby's lavish estate without ever meeting his landlord and observes the celebrated guests who come and go each weekend when Gatsby hosts extravagant parties that he never attends. He also visits his cousin, Daisy Fay Buchanan, and her husband, Tom, who live across the bay from his West Egg home in an exclusive East Egg enclave of landed gentry. There he meets Jordan Baker, a professional golfer, with whom he begins a relationship, and learns from his cousin that Tom is having an affair with Myrtle Wilson, the wife of an automobile mechanic, who lives in the "valley of ashes," an industrial wasteland that lies between West Egg and New York

City. A few days later, Nick accompanies Tom and Myrtle to their Manhattan apartment, where the couple throws a vulgar and bizarre party that culminates in violence when Tom breaks Myrtle's nose because she speaks Daisy's name.

Nick eventually receives an invitation to one of Gatsby's parties and is surprised to discover that his host is not much older than he is and to learn all the rumors and innuendo about his mysterious past. The men strike a friendship of sorts. Gatsby invites him to a luncheon with a business associate, Meyer Wolfsheim, the man who fixed the World Series, on the drive to which Gatsby tells him something of his story. Later, at tea with Jordan Baker, who also knows Gatsby, Nick learns the remainder of his friend's sad and romantic tale: that Gatsby and Daisy had once been in love and engaged to be married; that she had broken their engagement to marry the wealthy Buchanan; that Gatsby has devoted all his efforts to reclaiming Daisy, who represents his ideal of beauty and is the embodiment of his dreams; and that his parties are, in fact, intended to lure Daisy into his life again. She tells him as well that Gatsby hopes that Nick will assist him in reuniting with Daisy, and Nick agrees. After their reunion at Nick's bungalow, in a scene which is the emotional and structural center of the novel, Gatsby and Daisy begin an affair that precipitates the novel's tragic ending.

Discovering his wife's affair, Tom insists that he, Daisy, Nick, Jordan, and Gatsby drive into New York City on one of the hottest days of the summer. There, in the Plaza Hotel, where the party has rented a room and ordered drinks against the enervating late summer heat, Tom proceeds to unmask Gatsby, telling his wife that her lover is a bootlegger and stock-sharper. Daisy, who had previously been appalled by the vulgarity of Gatsby's parties when she finally attended one of them, is horrified by this truth. Tom, having stripped Gatsby of his dream, insists now that Daisy and Gatsby drive home together because he no longer fears Gatsby's power over his wife. On that drive, Daisy, who is at the wheel of Gatsby's automobile, strikes and kills Myrtle Wilson in the valley of ashes and then leaves others to clean up her mess. Several days later, after Tom has insinuated to George Wilson that Gatsby was driving the car that struck Myrtle, the hapless mechanic shoots the romantic dreamer as he floats in his pool, awaiting the fate for which he now hopes. Nick stays for his friend's funeral, which only one other person attends, and then returns disillusioned to the Midwest of his—and Gatsby's—origins. Theirs is a "story of the West, after all" (176). There he hopes to make sense of the tragedy.

HISTORICAL BACKGROUND: *THE GREAT GATSBY* AND THE CULTURE OF CONTRADICTION

F. Scott Fitzgerald's masterpiece, *The Great Gatsby* (1925), is a novel that captures the contradictions of the 1920s. A young man little older than the decade, Fitzgerald had shocked the world in his first novel, *This Side of Paradise* (1920), by revealing the hijinks and habits of its flaming youth culture, and with the publication in 1922 of his second collection of short stories, *Tales of the Jazz Age*, he had christened the era. *The Great Gatsby*, however, like all of his novels part autobiography and part social history, is the work that defines the 1920s, for it probes beneath the glittering surface of the pastel cocktails, raucous dances, and syncopated rhythms with which the decade is synonymous to expose the dark underside of a generation that was moving toward financial bankruptcy because it was already morally bankrupt. Published in 1925, at the midpoint of the Roaring Twenties, *The Great Gatsby* is thus a haunting elegy for all the bright promise of the new.

The decade had in fact begun as an era of progressive reform that promised to improve the quality of life for all. World War I, after all, had ended with the Allies' triumph over the German Kaiser, and a new prosperity was transforming the nation. Advances in technology that seemed to make anything possible fueled consumer demand for the gadgets and machines—the radios, the telephones, the automobiles—associated with the modern era, and jazz music, broadcast over radio airwaves into every home, and motion pictures, projected onto the big screens of movie theaters in every town and city, were democratizing culture. If further evidence that the new millennium had finally arrived were needed, a generation eager for change had only to look for it in the two landmark constitutional amendments that took effect in 1920.

The first, known colloquially as the Volstead Act, for the legislation enabling the passage of the Eighteenth Amendment to the U.S. Constitution, outlawed the manufacture, transportation, import, and sale of "intoxicating liquors" throughout the United States. (It did not, however, restrict the consumption of these liquors, to disastrous effect.) At midnight on January 16, 1920, the law went into effect. Hailed by temperance crusaders as a victory for public morals and health, Prohibition was a noble experiment to reform drinking habits that impoverished families and contributed to violent and disorderly conduct, and it did indeed result in a decrease in alcohol consumption that persisted long after the amendment's repeal in 1933.

As that repeal makes clear, however, Prohibition had its detractors from the time Congress approved the legislation over the veto of President Woodrow Wilson. The nation's "anti-drys," as they were known, found Prohibition an unnecessary intrusion into private life, an effort to impose the Protestant ideals of rural America on a central aspect of urban, immigrant, and Catholic life, which was the changing face of America. After all, the fine, upright white middle-class complained they drank responsibly and did not need government regulation of their behavior, and to be honest, they had never really considered that the law would apply to them as well as the irresponsible working classes and foreigners at whom it was clearly aimed.

Prohibition's unintended consequences soon became its reality. Almost overnight, "speakeasies," private establishments also known as "blind pigs" and "blind tigers" for the consumption of illegal alcohol, sprang up in cities and towns across the nation, for as historian Daniel Okrent has noted, "It didn't take much more than a bottle and two chairs to make a speakeasy" (208). Operated primarily by organized syndicates with the resources to bribe law enforcers and to purchase the bootleg liquor from the West Indies stored safely on boats moored in international waters or transported by sled across the Canadian border, speakeasies catered to a democratic clientele of men and women of different race and class, inadvertently hastening the era's social and cultural changes. They also contributed to the era's lawlessness. Prohibition had, after all, made criminals of the majority of Americans, many of whom had stockpiled liquor in the year between passage and ratification of the amendment, others of whom took to brewing their own "bathtub gin" and other intoxicants, however poisonous they might have been. Moreover, gangsters such as Al Capone and Lucky Luciano headed the syndicates running the trade, and the brutal competition for business led to gunfights, assassinations, and gang warfare in the nation's urban centers.

Prohibition dominated the era as no other development would. Rivaling its influence, however, was the flapper, the embodiment of female emancipation signified by the ratification of the Nineteenth Amendment to the U.S. Constitution giving women the right to vote on August 18, 1920, the second of the decade's progressive reforms. The flapper, like her counterpart the New Woman of the late nineteenth century, redefined notions of womanhood for the modern era by pushing the boundaries of gender identity and claiming sexual and economic freedoms that had been previously reserved for men. Unwilling to be constrained by the conventions of the past, she signified her independence in her fashion style and lifestyle. She

Historical Background: *The Great Gatsby* and the Culture of Contradiction

In January 1930, when Prohibition was still the law of the land, police in Queens, New York, seize 25-gallon stills in which bootleggers were manufacturing "intoxicating liquor" for their thirsty customers. Three years later, the "noble experiment" to regulate the nation's drinking habits would end with the repeal of the Eighteenth Amendment. (Bettmann/Corbis)

bobbed her hair, raised her hemlines, and discarded the restrictive corsets of previous decades for the Symington Side Lacer that gave her the boyish, athletic figure envied by all. She smoked cigarettes, enjoyed a cocktail—or two, engaged in premarital sex and used birth control, and increasingly competed with men in the world of work outside the home. And she now voted. A controversial figure, the flapper mounted a challenge to the manners and mores and expectations of a previous generation and so was right on trend during the Jazz Age.

Despite the spirit of reform represented by these constitutional amendments and the social and cultural changes they ushered into being, many Americans were suspicious of, and skeptical about, the changes that were transforming the nation. It was one thing to embrace the technology that was eliminating the drudgery and expanding the entertainment and recreational activities of daily life. It was another to accept the waves of new immigrants from eastern and southern Europe, many of whom had been displaced by poverty and revolution in their homelands and were now agitating for improved working conditions and increased pay for workers in their adopted country. In an era of big business and xenophobic nationalism fueled by World War I and the Russian Revolution, such radical ideas sparked a Red Scare in 1919–1920. When the May Day Riots of 1920 that Attorney General William Palmer predicted for the nation's major cities never materialized, the Red Scare was essentially ended, although two Italian-born anarchists, Nicola Sacco and Bartolomeo Vanzetti, who were executed on August 23, 1927, more for their ethnicity and political beliefs than the crime for which they had been convicted, might have disagreed. In 1924, Congress passed another in a series of Immigration Acts restricting the influx of foreign nationals to the United States, evidence that the nation's citizens remained anxious about and fearful of aliens and their radical ideas that were threatening to overturn American society.

The rise and expansion of the Ku Klux Klan into regions beyond its traditional Southern base provides additional evidence of the conservative reaction to change that gripped the nation's citizens in the 1920s. Begun as a secret vigilante movement that thrived in the Southern states during the 1860s and 1870s to ensure white supremacy, the Klan was revived in 1915, following the release of D. W. Griffith's film *The Birth of a Nation*, which mythologized and glorified the Klan's first incarnation. Its second was no less racist, but its structure and scope were vastly expanded. Organized as formal fraternal associations with national and state bureaucracies, Klan membership advanced into the Midwest and Western states as well as urban centers, where the Great Migration of African Americans from the South following the Civil War and the influx of immigrants from eastern and southern Europe, all of whom were considered inferior to the nation's original Anglo-Saxon Protestant settlers, had given rise to the social tensions of urban industrialization.

The Klan of the 1920s was anti-immigrant, anti-Catholic, anti-Semitic, and Prohibitionist. Its goal, as its leader William J. Simmons announced in a 1917 pamphlet titled *ABC of the Invisible Empire*, was "to shield the sanctity of the home and the chastity of womanhood; to maintain white supremacy; to teach and faithfully inculcate a high spiritual philosophy through an exalted ritualism, and by a practical devotedness to conserve, protect and maintain the distinctive institutions, rights, privileges, principles and ideals of a pure Americanism." It sought, in other words, to uphold its version of American values and Christian morality and preached a doctrine of "One Hundred Percent Americanism." It even had a women's auxiliary organization. By the mid-1920s, Indiana was the Klan's stronghold, and more than 15 percent of the nation's eligible population, four–six million men, were members. Although white-robed Klansmen still conducted their cross-burnings under cover of darkness, the Klan was no longer a secret society. In fact, its members marched through the streets of

Washington, D.C., in 1925 in a show of strength, the significance of which could not be ignored among the symbols of American democracy.

The 1925 Scopes Trial offers further evidence of the cultural conflicts that characterized the roaring decade. For eight days in 1925 Americans listened intently to radio transmissions from a courthouse in Dayton, Tennessee, as two of the nation's most distinguished and controversial lawyers battled in a show trial engineered by the American Civil Liberties Union to challenge the state's Butler Act, a law that prohibited the teaching of evolutionary theory in public schools. Prosecuting the case against substitute teacher John T. Scopes, who had agreed to be the defendant in the test case, was William Jennings Bryan, a three-time candidate for president of the United States. Defending the case was Clarence Darrow, a celebrated champion of liberty and liberal causes. At issue for the millions who followed the proceedings was the veracity of the Bible, the foundation of Christianity, and the authority of science, increasingly the source of truth in the twentieth century. For a nation founded on Christian beliefs and ideals, the outcome mattered.

Science, after all, was responsible for so many of the technological advances that were modernizing the century, but it was also undermining received notions and deeply held beliefs about humanity's place in the universe, none more so than the origins of humans themselves. Charles Darwin may not have intended to challenge Christian beliefs when he published *Origin of Species* in 1859, but that unintended consequence was undermining the moral authority of the Church, or at least that was how the behaviors and activities, the manners and mores, of the new generation appeared to fundamentalist believers who shared the despair of Bryan when he bemoaned the notion that humans had been descended "not even from monkeys, but from old world monkeys." After deliberating the evidence for nine minutes, the jury returned its guilty verdict and fined Scopes $100 for his crime. Yet for eight days, the Monkey Trial, as H. L. Mencken, the journalist for the *Baltimore Sun*, labeled it, had exposed the deep chasm between modern thought and conservative belief that complicated life in the 1920s.

F. Scott Fitzgerald understood these conflicts and complications. He was born in 1896, at the end of the nineteenth century, and had been influenced as a young boy by the values and attitudes of its genteel tradition, but he had grown into adulthood during World War I, an event that forever altered the world's social and political landscape and ushered in the modern era. In *The Great Gatsby*, his masterpiece, Fitzgerald captured the tensions of this world in flux. Nick Carraway, for instance, the novel's narrator, may, like its title character Jay Gatsby, have come east to participate in the nation's new prosperity and achieve his dreams, but by the novel's end, he has retreated to the Midwest, where he knows he will find "the world to be in uniform and at a sort of moral attention forever" (8), and Daisy Buchanan, its flapper heroine, will choose instead of the self-invented Gatsby the man whose privileged background will protect her from scandal. The contradictions of the Jazz Age, the novel made clear, were inherent in and from the beginning.

ABOUT F. SCOTT FITZGERALD: THE MAN WHO WROTE THE JAZZ AGE

The man who wrote the Jazz Age lived it as well. Born on September 24, 1896, in St. Paul, Minnesota, Francis Scott Key Fitzgerald, whose father claimed distant kinship with the composer of "The Star Spangled Banner," came of age during World War I and established his literary career and early married life during a decade that roared, and he roared with it.

F. Scott Fitzgerald (1896–1940) coined the phrase "the Jazz Age" for the 1920s. (Corbis)

Indeed, the yearning midwestern boy developed into a man whose life epitomized the gay and carefree excesses of the period and its tragic collapse, for it followed the trajectory of the era, beginning with bright promise and ending with tarnished dreams. Thus, he became its ideal chronicler.

Formed by his midwestern background, his Irish-Catholic heritage, and a mother who was socially ambitious for her bright, handsome son, Fitzgerald moved in St. Paul's elite society, among the country club set, and was educated at Newman Academy, a Roman Catholic preparatory school in New Jersey, and Princeton University, from which he failed to graduate. He was ever aware, however, of the precarious nature of his social position, for his father, who was seldom able to support his family by his own efforts, relied on his wife's inheritance to sustain them, making economies necessary to preserve their livelihood. Fitzgerald's social standing was thus to some extent a matter of posturing. He seemed, in fact, to develop into a handsome and clever but insecure young man whose longing for position and privilege was ever thwarted, rather like the protagonists of many of his short stories and novels, including *The Great Gatsby*.

Possessed of a keen intellect and a fine sensibility, Fitzgerald pursued from an early age his literary talent, encouraged at the Newman School by his mentor Father Cyril Sigourney Webster Fay and by his successes writing features and stories for Princeton's *Nassau Literary Magazine* and its humor magazine, *The Tiger*, as well as musical comedies and light operetta for its prestigious clubs. But these literary and social successes came at the expense of his academic career. As Fitzgerald later recalled, "I spent my entire freshman year writing an operetta for the Triangle Club. I failed in Algebra, trigonometry, coordinate geometry and hygiene, but the Triangle Club accepted my show, and by tutoring all through a stuffy August I managed to come back a sophomore and act in it as a chorus girl" (*F. Scott Fitzgerald: In His Own Time* 269). When he returned to Princeton in the fall of 1917, it was merely to await his twenty-first birthday, when he could accept his commission as second lieutenant in the regular army, the exam for which he had successfully sat the previous summer.

World War I may have been raging in 1917, but little patriotic fervor fueled Fitzgerald's military career. Indeed, it was as undistinguished as his academic career, for once again it interfered with his literary efforts. When he should have been studying infantry tactics in preparation for assuming command on the battlefields of Europe, he was instead revising the manuscript of what would become his first novel, *This Side of Paradise* (1920), begun during his Princeton days, concealing his notebook behind the covers of his military manuals. Although the war ended before Fitzgerald was posted to Europe, he could count himself doubly fortunate for his military service. Not only did he complete his first novel, which he then called "The Romantic Egotists," during this time, but he also met the woman he loved for the remainder of his life, Zelda Sayre.

A thoroughly modern new woman, Zelda was the pampered daughter of a prominent Montgomery, Alabama, family when Fitzgerald met the eighteen-year-old at a country club dance in 1918. By the spring of 1919, he was engaged to this dream girl who flouted convention at every opportunity and relied on the Sayre prestige and respectability to protect her from the condemnation that her outrageous reputation for sexual promiscuity should have warranted. Wary, however, of Fitzgerald's ability to support her lifestyle, Zelda broke off their engagement as the struggling writer sought a publisher for his manuscript and labored discontentedly producing copy for a New York advertising agency. Eight days after *This Side of Paradise* was published to both critical acclaim and commercial and popular success, however, on April 3, 1920, Scott Fitzgerald and Zelda Sayre married in the rectory of St. Patrick's Cathedral in New York City and began their career as the decade's quintessential couple.

In the flush of first success and the glow of early married life, the Fitzgeralds stormed New York. Their alcohol-fueled pranks made them notorious. Ejected from the Biltmore Hotel for disturbing other guests, they announced their arrival at the Commodore Hotel by spinning through the revolving doors for a half hour, for example. They were also famous for jumping into the fountains in New York City's Union Square and the Plaza Hotel. Their reputation for outrageous behavior and incessant partying soon made them symbolic of the excesses of the 1920s, which Fitzgerald chronicled in his stories and novels. Settling nowhere and living in a series of hotels, apartments, and rental houses, they established a nomadic pattern for their lives that persisted even after the birth of their only child, a daughter, born on October 26, 1921, and named Frances Scott Fitzgerald but always called Scottie.

Their extravagant lifestyle plunged them soon into debt. In a 1924 magazine piece titled "How to Live on $36,000 a Year" (nearly twenty times the average American income), Fitzgerald joked about the effort to live up to his new prosperity, but the crisis in his bank account was real. Although his second novel, *The Beautiful and Damned*, published to critical and commercial success in 1922, had cemented his reputation and temporarily eased the family's financial situation, Fitzgerald increasingly found himself writing for the short story market rather than crafting the serious fiction that he felt worthy of his talent. He also attempted to write for the theater, but when he finally secured the financial backing to mount a production of his play *The Vegetable*, a political satire inspired by the scandal-ridden administration of President Warren G. Harding at the beginning of the decade, it was a colossal failure, closing in tryouts before ever opening on Broadway. Fitzgerald was so mortified by the hostile reception to his play that he spent the second and third acts in a bar. The failure prompted him to realize that he was squandering his talent in drink and excess. By March 1924, having written himself out of debt by plying the short story trade, he and his family set sail for France, joining the exodus of other American expatriate writers and artists, members of the Lost Generation who sought a different sort of life in Europe. There, in an alien culture for which Fitzgerald had no great love or deep understanding and about which he cared little to learn, he and his family would spend most of the remainder of the decade.

Settling primarily in a villa on the Riviera, an area in the south of France that he helped make fashionable as a playground for the rich and avant-garde, Fitzgerald worked with difficulty to complete his masterpiece, *The Great Gatsby* (1925), for the early years of excess were beginning to take their toll on his life and marriage. Bored and restless, Zelda had a brief affair with a French aviator, and then, frustrated by a desire for an artistic identity of her own, threw herself into ballet lessons, determined, at the age of twenty-six, to become a professional. She also wrote a novel, *Save Me the Waltz* (1932), that Fitzgerald considered a betrayal because it mined the same territory that he was excavating in his fourth novel, *Tender Is the Night* (1934). Fitzgerald turned increasingly to alcohol to ease his insecurities and frustrations, which ended inevitably in drunken rows. Neither he nor Zelda thrived on foreign shores, and as she slipped into the schizophrenia that would send her from one sanitarium to another in search of a cure until her death in a fire at the Highland Hospital in Asheville, North Carolina, on March 10, 1948, Fitzgerald battled his alcoholism and suffered his

F. Scott Fitzgerald, his wife Zelda, and their daughter Frances, "Scottie," motor in Italy during the 1920s, when he and other members of the Lost Generation could live cheaply in Europe among a community of writers, artists, and intellectuals. (Bettmann/Corbis)

own "crack-up." Their gay, gaudy spree crashed to its end, like the roaring decade, as the Great Depression tightened its grip on the world.

By 1937, Fitzgerald had recovered sufficiently to begin again. Deeply in debt and faced with the expense of Zelda's extended care and Scottie's schooling, he sought to recoup his credit and self-worth by returning to the only activity that he valued—his work. Although he had failed on two previous visits to Hollywood to find success as a screenwriter, Fitzgerald now accepted a six-month contract with MGM for $1,000 a week, hoping to revive his career. Chafing under the industry's artistic control, however, he earned only one screen credit, for the film *Three Comrades*, during his eighteen months under contract. Yet the experience also provided the material for his seventeen Pat Hobby stories and for *The Love of the Last Tycoon* (1941), the novel that he would leave unfinished when he suffered a fatal heart attack on December 21, 1940, at the age of forty-four. In Hollywood, a city of false hopes and broken dreams to so many aspiring men and women, Fitzgerald, too, found it again impossible to be the kind of writer he wanted to be.

In death, Fitzgerald nearly fell victim to his Jazz Age image, for many of his obituaries emphasized his life rather than his work and suggested that he had squandered his talent and failed to achieve his potential during the gay, gaudy spree of the 1920s. In 1941, however, the writer and critic Edmund Wilson, who had been Fitzgerald's friend since their Princeton days, rescued the writer's reputation by editing *The Last Tycoon* for publication and compiling *The Crack-Up* (1945), a collection of Fitzgerald's essays, letters, and notebook entries as well as critical appreciations of his work by other prominent writers. Since that time, Fitzgerald's stature as a major twentieth-century American novelist has rested secure. He is, after all, the writer who defined an era in his first novel, *This Side of Paradise*, and then exposed its dark underside as well as the dreams and illusions of a nation in a tale that many consider *the* American novel, *The Great Gatsby*. If he had written nothing more, that achievement would have been sufficient for greatness.

WHY WE READ *THE GREAT GATSBY*

In the final elegiac paragraphs of *The Great Gatsby*, F. Scott Fitzgerald shifts his tale of the Jazz Age from the topical to the mythic, claiming as his subject the American Dream that beckoned settlers to the New World's shores even before the nation's founding. While its meaning has evolved over time, the Dream has ever been a promise of possibility, of new beginnings and boundless opportunities, a foundational myth that has sustained the hopes and beliefs of generations, even into the twenty-first century. Like those before him, James Gatz believed in this dream, so he reinvented himself and as Jay Gatsby set off to attain it. His quest, however, fails because what begins as an ideal becomes fettered to the material, and such a dream is merely counterfeit. It can never satisfy. Inherent in Gatsby's failure is a critique of the American Dream, the national myth. It, too, began as an ideal, but evolved into something far less ambitious. It, too, was conceived in greatness, but delivered less than it promised. In *The Great Gatsby*, Fitzgerald articulated these truths and in so doing created an American masterpiece, perhaps *the* American novel, for he captured the contradictions at the heart of the nation, the contradictions that keep it always and still from achieving its vision of all it could be.

As an ideal, the American Dream is a vision of being and becoming, a dream of self, and it established a belief in the exceptional nature of the New World. Fitzgerald evokes that ideal when Nick imagines the Dutch sailors who first set eyes on the "fresh green breast of the new world" that would one day become New York (187). "For a transitory enchanted moment," Nick thinks, "man must have held his breath in the presence of this continent, compelled into an aesthetic contemplation he neither understood nor desired, face to face for the last time in history with something commensurate to his capacity for wonder" (187–188). The New World's vast, empty landscape was an awe-inspiring opportunity to create a "new heaven, new earth," as the Puritan settlers of New England envisioned it. Indeed, a central aspect of the American Dream is the belief in Edenic possibility, the hope that paradise could be re-created not in the next world and not out of time, but in the here and now of a new continent, a New World. Europeans from the time of its first settlement saw America as a land of hope and freedom, a place where men and women could escape the Old World's poverty, misery, and corruption and begin anew in a land undefiled. In this New World they would establish a New Eden, a model for all other nations of the world.

This New Eden would inevitably give rise to a New Adam who, unfettered from the corrupting influences of European society, would become his best self by living close to nature and, rather than conforming to artificial hierarchies, following the natural order of life. The New Adam, as R. W. B. Lewis describes him in his seminal study *The American Adam*, is "a radically new personality, the hero of the new adventure: an individual emancipated from history, happily bereft of ancestry, untouched and undefiled by the usual inheritances of family and race; an individual standing alone, self-reliant and self-propelling, ready to confront whatever awaited him with the aid of his own unique and inherent resources" (5). James Fenimore Cooper's Natty Bumppo in his series of Leatherstocking novels is the frontier version of this hero. His civilized counterpart is the Self-Made Man, the hero of a later definition of the American Dream—the Dream of Success. This hero is a direct descendent of Benjamin Franklin, who arrived in Philadelphia with little more than wit, ingenuity, and the will to succeed and through pluck, luck, and the cultivation of some key virtues rose from rags to riches to dine with kings, three, to be exact, he reminds his readers. Horatio Alger's nineteenth-century hero Ragged Dick is another exemplar. So, too, is Fitzgerald's Jay Gatsby.

Guided by his "Schedule" and list of "general Resolves" recorded on the flyleaf of his tattered copy of *Hopalong Cassidy* (179–180), another American icon, James Gatz transforms himself into Jay Gatsby, following the footsteps of Franklin, the mythic American hero who first articulates the American Dream of Success. Motivated by an ideal embodied in Daisy, who represents the good, the true, and the beautiful to him and to whom he has "forever wed his unutterable dreams" (118), Gatsby has amassed a fortune to attain her. That achievement affirms the continued vitality of the myth in American cultural life more than two hundred years after the original appeared. Yet the Self-Made Man of the American Dream of Success is far different from the New Adam of the New Eden, and the difference speaks to a profound shift in values that, Fitzgerald's novel makes clear, has diminished the meaning of America.

When the dream of self became the dream of success, when the opportunity to be became the opportunity to be rich, and when the goal of life became the acquisition of goods that signify economic success rather than self-fulfillment, the bright promise of that "fresh green breast of the new world" was forever tarnished by the corrupting power of money. In fact, Daisy's "voice is full of money," Gatsby tells Nick (126), and its seductive power corrupts his dream just as surely as the sirens' song of easy money ringing out from the stock market corrupts the dreams of countless Americans. From a dog leash of leather and braided silver to a life of ease and a new identity, money can buy anything. Even Daisy was for sale for Tom's $350,000 pearl necklace. Money, Gatsby's tragedy makes clear, has changed the nature of the American Dream; it has destroyed its finest conception. Gatsby may have invested his dreams and hopes in Daisy, but he tainted them by purchasing a mansion, a Rolls Royce, a rainbow array of custom-made shirts with which to bedazzle her. What he wins instead is merely an illusion, for he has served "a vast, vulgar, and meretricious beauty" (105) from the moment he "sprang from his Platonic conception of himself" (105). Gatsby's death thus suggests the bankruptcy of the American Dream of Success, for a dream based on the material, which is, after all, both transient and mutable, provides no firm foundation and will inevitably collapse of its own lack of substance.

When a chastened Nick Carraway, in the final paragraphs of *The Great Gatsby*, reflects on the meaning of his experience in the East and finds it in the connection between Gatsby's story and the national myth of the American Dream, F. Scott Fitzgerald lifted his novel from what many reviewers derided as little more than a tabloid tale of a sordid murder among the smart set to a profound meditation on the nation itself. Behind *The Great Gatsby* world lie remnants of the new world that had "flowered once for Dutch sailors' eyes" (187). Those sailors, like Gatsby, had gazed on possibility and been awed by it. For Gatsby and those sailors, the enormity of the challenge—to imagine a world equal to its promise—was beyond human capability, so even at the moment of discovery, that bright new promise had already disappeared. Bound by time to mutability and loss, each generation struggles, nevertheless, to dream a world of perfection into existence again. That effort, that dream, is both the hope and the tragedy of the human experience and the American myth. In the heyday of the Jazz Age, when anything seemed possible, *The Great Gatsby* cautioned readers, and cautions them still, against the false hopes and corrupted dreams that could transform an ideal into crass reality. That insight expressed the underside of an era as well as a nation and makes *The Great Gatsby* still one of the greatest American novels of all time.

HISTORICAL EXPLORATIONS OF *THE GREAT GATSBY*

Glimmering, gleaming roadsters, their polished exteriors refracting the opulence and splendor of unprecedented prosperity, the stuff of which dreams are made, hum down the roads in F. Scott Fitzgerald's Jazz Age masterpiece *The Great Gatsby*. In movement frenzied and frenetic the modern era, to the accompaniment of a jazz soundtrack, was springing to life, replacing comfortable certainties with stimulating possibilities. Women had attained the vote, and Prohibition had unintentionally resulted in seismic social and cultural shifts. Fitzgerald's primary symbol, the automobile, perfectly captured the moment. The embodiment of the new technologies that were transforming American society, it enabled movement, not just movement but individual movement, on one's own terms, at one's own time and pace. From the humble Model T to the stately Pierce Arrow, it also announced its owner's social class, and in an era of celebrity and consumption, including conspicuous consumption, differences mattered. Radio may have been democratizing the nation, and speakeasies may have erased some racial and gender boundaries. Fitzgerald, however, recognized the underside of these and all the era's changes, perhaps because he lived them, and wrote them into the general consciousness in a novel that takes as its subject nothing less than the national myth of success. In *The Great Gatsby*, the automobile, as it was in American life, is the vehicle of that change, the register of that success.

Until the 1920s, the price of an automobile limited ownership primarily to the wealthy, but Henry Ford's development of the assembly line, which made possible mass production and reduced costs, opened the market to the middle class, who were just as eager to know the freedom of the road as the nation's elite. Stripped of frills and available in any color, Ford famously observed, "so long as it was black," the Model T, also known as the "Tin Lizzie," fit the bill. Indeed, it was a catalyst for the social, cultural, and economic changes that transformed the nation. In 1920, there were approximately eight million registered vehicles on the road. By the end of the decade that number had increased to twenty-three million. There was approximately one car on the road for every five Americans by 1929, and the majority was driving the Model T.

Ford's effort to democratize automobile ownership was a shrewd business decision. So, too, was the rise in wages that he paid his workers, from $2 to $5 for an eight-hour day, which provided them the means to purchase their Tin Lizzies, if not outright, then on the payment plan that Ford's more

Factory workers in a Ford Motor Company assembly line in April 1924. By 1925, Ford was producing a car every ten seconds. (Library of Congress)

than 10,000 dealerships extended to their customers. To meet the motoring needs of these new drivers, service stations began to hug the berms of the new highways that were quickly being constructed to link them to their destinations. Motoring and touring soon became popular leisure activities, prompting the construction of diners and motels for the comfort of weary travelers. The manufacturing sector as well as small businesses thrived on the public's appetite for the automobile, fueling the era's prosperity.

A new phenomenon, traffic jams, testified to the ubiquity of the automobile in the 1920s, but it was the roadsters cruising between Manhattan and Long Island in the summer of 1922 that most interested F. Scott Fitzgerald in *The Great Gatsby*. From Gatsby's "gorgeous" yellow Rolls Royce, with its "three-noted horn" (69)' to Tom's "easy-going blue coupé" (131) and the steady stream of limousines making their way to the weekly parties at Gatsby's mansion, these automobiles were the symbols of the nation's real prosperity. Owned by movers and shakers, these automobiles were a source of longing for working-class men such as George Wilson, who had their own dreams of joining that elite. The reckless abandon with which their drivers operated these vehicles was a clear sign of their privilege. The proliferation of the automobile, in other words, had not erased the nation's class divisions, one of *The Great Gatsby*'s primary subjects.

George Wilson, for instance, who operates a garage located in the bleak, gray valley of ashes that separates New York's dazzling possibilities from East and West Eggs' landed gentry, spends his days servicing the automobiles of the elite. The job makes clear the distance between his life and theirs. On a hot July day early in the novel, Nick Carraway, the first-person narrator, travels by train to New York with Tom Buchanan, the haughty representative of East Egg's hereditary elite, when their train pauses on the tracks near a "foul river" (29) and Tom insists they jump off to see his mistress, George's wife Myrtle. Making their way quickly to one of three shops located in a nondescript yellow brick building, Tom introduces Nick to George, a "blond, spiritless man" whose "anaemic" (31) pallor matches the "cement color of the walls" (32). Although the sign outside the garage indicates that George buys, sells, and repairs automobiles, within its "unprosperous and bare" interior is only one vehicle, a "dust-covered wreck of a Ford" (30). George obviously does not earn much of a living from his business. Indeed, only the prospect that Tom will sell him his car, which he hopes to sell on for a profit, ignites any spark of life in this ghost of a man for whom Tom has nothing but disdain and whose own wife treats him as an inconvenience.

On this occasion, Tom toys with George as only a man with certain knowledge of his advantage can do, threatening to sell his car to another dealer if George becomes too demanding (31), and George, ever conscious of the divide that separates them, quickly retracts his offending remarks (although they are nothing more than a query about the vehicle) and assumes his appropriately subservient role, even carrying chairs into the garage at Myrtle's command. Late in the novel, only the desperateness of George's position has changed. On the day that Tom exposes Gatsby's past to his wife Daisy, George telephones Tom to enquire again about purchasing his coupé. Angered by the intrusion, and likely the presumption, of a tradesman entering his personal space, Tom upbraids the hapless man and withdraws his offer to sell. A few hours later, however, when Tom, Nick, and their friend Jordan Baker, the professional golfer, stop to fill the gas tank as they motor into the city, he seemingly relents, offering to sell him the car he is driving, Gatsby's yellow car, when he sees the man's broken state. Aware now of his wife's infidelity (but ignorant of her lover's identity), a sick and "hollow-eyed" (129) George fails to recognize that Tom once again is merely exercising his privilege and presses him about selling his coupé. He needs the money, he confesses to Tom, to move west with his wife for a new beginning. In one of his few human gestures in the novel, Tom promises to send the coupé the next day. He has, after all, just stared into the face of a man who could be his double, if he did not have the means, in this case, the automobile, with which to escape his circumstances. But he does. Indeed, within minutes of departing the garage, he is careening down the highway at fifty miles an hour "with the double purpose of overtaking Daisy," who rides with Gatsby in Tom's blue coupé, "and leaving Wilson behind" (131). Later that day, in the aftermath of the hit-and-run accident that kills his lover, Tom distances himself even further from the unfortunate Wilson, making certain that George knows that the yellow car was never his.

Class issues are key to Fitzgerald's treatment of the automobile. George Wilson trades in cars but seems not to own one, unless it is that dilapidated Ford cowering in the corner of his garage. He understands fully, however, the freedom and authority such ownership signifies. So, too, does his wife Myrtle, who, on the day that she, Tom, and Nick travel into New York for an impromptu party, waves off four taxis until she finds just the right one, "lavender-colored with grey upholstery" (33), that suits her sense of luxury and sophistication. She is, after all, a woman who aspires to the life of her lover, a woman who makes lists of all the items she wants and needs to possess, she believes, to secure her place in his world, and while the paucity of her vision of that world may undermine her aspirations, it cannot erase the poignancy that arises from Nick's brief "glimpse of Mrs. Wilson straining at the garage pump with panting vitality" (74) on the day that Gatsby drives him into town for lunch. Like her husband, she seems destined to serve the rich rather than join them. Fitzgerald makes her fate even more poignant by following that glimpse of Myrtle pumping gas with Nick's hearty chuckle at a passing limousine, "driven by a white chauffeur, in which sat three modish negroes" staring out "in haughty rivalry" (75). While "Anything can happen," Nick thinks, "now that we've slid over this bridge," (75), the example of the Wilsons suggests otherwise.

So, too, does Gatsby's Rolls Royce. Like the lavender taxi that represented Myrtle's vision of glamor and sophistication, its magnificence symbolizes its owner's mistaken understanding of wealth and privilege. "A rich cream color, bright with nickel, swollen here and there in its monstrous length with triumphant hat-boxes and supper-boxes and tool-boxes," the singular vehicle is "terraced with a labyrinth of wind-shields that mirrored a dozen suns. Sitting down behind [its] many layers of glass," Nick felt as if he were in a "green leather conservatory" (70). Magnificent as it may have seemed to Gatsby, the car is gaudy and ostentatious. A "circus wagon," Tom sneers at it (127), voicing the natural superciliousness of a man born to wealth for the anxious assertions of the parvenu. Gatsby's automobile is the sign of a man who is trying too hard to become what the man who belongs is already, a fact that everyone but Gatsby (and those like him) seems to understand.

Any doubt about the class issues that differentiate Gatsby's gaudy vehicle from Tom's understated coupé Fitzgerald clarifies through development of one of the novel's central metaphors, carelessness. The proliferation of automobiles on the nation's roads, especially before speed limits and uniform traffic signals, led to a significant rise in traffic accidents and deaths. Everyone drove as if he or she owned the roads, but especially those with the means to pay for their carelessness, to use Fitzgerald's term. *The Great Gatsby* is filled with such people.

A shiny new coupé, for instance, "violently shorn of one wheel" and sitting miraculously upright in a ditch, punctuates the first of Gatsby's parties that Nick attends. The vehicle's driver is so drunk that when he crawls from the wreckage he insists that he will back out of the ditch as "a dozen men, some of them a little better off than he was" (62), try to make him understand the situation. The novel, moreover, ends with the hit-and-run accident, the very equivalent of carelessness, in which Daisy kills Myrtle. Protected by Gatsby, on the one hand, who takes responsibility for her crime, and Tom, on the other, whose impeccable credentials and vast family fortune insulate her from suspicion, Daisy effectively gets away with murder. Earlier in the novel, when Nick accuses the "incurably dishonest" (64) Jordan of being a "careless" driver, she breezily assures him that she relies on "other people" being "careful" (65) for her. By the end of the novel, Nick has come to understand exactly what Jordan's assertion means, sadly observing, "They were careless people, Tom and Daisy—they smashed up things and creatures and then retreated back into their money or their vast carelessness, or whatever it was that kept them together, and let other people clean up the mess they had made" (186). Gatsby, the poor boy from the Midwest who had ventured east to reinvent himself and make his fortune in pursuit of the girl who embodies his dreams, has never understood the assumptions of the rich. He has failed to see that Daisy is not as impressed as he is by the "celebrated people" (97) who come to his parties, that, lacking her pedigree, they are all merely inhabitants along a shortcut from "nothing to nothing" (114), that he is himself one of the "other people," and so he plays his part. He is careful for Daisy and thus falls victim to her carelessness. In the scheme of things, it could not have been any different.

If Fitzgerald's primary symbol, the automobile, conveys the class divisions typical of the era, so, too, does his Jazz Age setting, the era of Prohibition. *The Great Gatsby* is awash in cocktails and champagne, whiskey and gin. Its background characters, the celebrated people who attend Gatsby's parties as well as the gatecrashers, generally carry a concealed bottle of spirits for their spirits. Fitzgerald's novel, set two years after Prohibition, the noble experiment to reform the nation's drinking habits and improve the quality of life for women and children, the primary victims of drunkenness, gives ample evidence of its failure. Indeed, except for its use of coded language, "drug-stores," "cellar," "bootlegger," it would be impossible to tell that virtually everyone in the novel is a criminal, but then none of them sees themselves as one. After all, Prohibition was primarily intended to regulate the behavior of immigrants whose customs did not conform to the ethos of a Protestant nation and the working class whose irresponsible drunkenness cost employers in absences and productivity. The nation's elite and its solid middle class, for whom a glass of wine with a celebratory dinner defined their drinking habits, needed no such regulation. From its inception, in other words, Prohibition had been grounded in class consciousness, no matter what its advocates maintained.

Fitzgerald's novel brings vividly to life the realities of Prohibition. It may have been illegal to manufacture, transport, and sell "intoxicating spirits," but demand for them had merely diminished, not disappeared. Consequently, the trade went underground, to the speakeasy or blind pig, where the fashionable drink was the cocktail because it disguised the taste of the spirits, which were generally diluted with other forms of alcohol. When Nick and Gatsby, for instance, meet Meyer Wolfsheim, the man who fixed the 1919 World Series, for lunch at a "well-fanned Forty-second Street cellar" (75), they order highballs with their hash: such an establishment would have replaced the saloons and bars where typical business luncheons would previously have taken place, and beer, difficult to brew and transport, was seldom available. Late in the novel, moreover, all the talk of Gatsby's "drug-stores" culminates in Tom's triumphant revelation that the mysterious title character is indeed a bootlegger (140): those "drug-stores," after all, are simply outlets for the "legal" purchase of medicinal whiskey, which had not been outlawed during Prohibition. (Nor, by the way, had Communion wine, prompting an increase in church attendance during the era.) Needless to say, the nation saw a dramatic rise in "dryitis" throughout the 1920s as those suffering from the condition sought treatment for its relief, a prescription from an obliging physician, perhaps for a fee. "Drug-stores" thus became fronts for the bootlegger. In New York alone more than 3,000 enterprising "pharmacists" quickly sought licenses to meet the needs of the state's "patients," and the Walgreen's chain of drugstores increased from 20 to nearly 500 outlets during the decade, its management accounting for the expansion by the introduction of the milkshake in 1922 (Okrent 197).

Prohibition would seem to have been a great leveler. Speakeasies, after all, opened their doors to anyone who knocked, including women, whereas saloons and bars had previously been male bastions, and everyone, of course, was drinking illegal liquor. The quality of that liquor, however, varied greatly, and wealth and connections mattered. Prior to January 1920, when Prohibition went into effect, those with the resources stockpiled liquor for their personal use in anticipation of the event. So, too, did private clubs that catered to the elite. The Yale Club, for instance, had stocked a fourteen-year supply of liquor that lasted beyond Prohibition's repeal in 1933 (Dumenil 233). Throughout the era, moreover, bootleggers always had a ready supply of good Caribbean rum stored on boats moored in international waters three miles beyond the Eastern seaboard and premium Canadian whiskey transported across the Great Lakes and the nation's long, unguarded Northern border ready for purchase by those who could afford the real thing. The guests at Gatsby's parties, for instance, who drink champagne from "glasses bigger than finger-bowls" (53), enjoy the privilege of being served from a bar "stocked with gins and liquors and with cordials so long forgotten that most of his female guests were too young to know one from another" (46). Gatsby, of course, can afford to serve the real thing (and is anxious enough about his social position to do so).

Most people, however, were reduced to drinking "bathtub gin," "moonshine," and other easily distilled synthetic spirits, many of which were manufactured from highly toxic wood alcohol or industrial methanol as well as "canned heat," or sterno. Drunkenness was the least of the consequences these drinkers faced. Paralysis, blindness, and even death often resulted from imbibing these versions of the real thing. Even the government contributed to the danger when it ordered the poisoning of denatured alcohol without the public's knowledge.

At the center of the trade, for all, were the bootleggers, who quickly acquired the kind of wealth that should have gained them entry to elite society (and in some cases did). That was certainly what Gatsby believed, and plenty of examples seemed to prove his assumption true. Samuel Bronfman, for instance, the founder of Distillers Corporation Limited in Montreal, Canada, earned enough from the illegal border trade to purchase the Seagram's Distillery in 1928 and build an empire on which to rise to philanthropic prominence, and George Remus, known as the King of the Bootleggers, used the fortune he amassed not only to purchase more than one hundred distilleries, including Fleischmann's, but also to stage spectacular parties complete with diamond watches and Pontiacs as party favors for Cincinnati's elite. (Fitzgerald would clearly not have needed to invent Gatsby, for he already existed.) Nevertheless, a whiff of the underworld trailed them. Meyer Wolfsheim, for instance, Gatsby's associate, wears cufflinks made of human molars and tells Nick the sad tale of Rosy Rosenthal, gunned down in what is clearly a gangland shooting. Moreover, Wolfsheim's presence (and his sad tale) makes clear that organized crime bosses were increasingly dominating the trade in illegal spirits during the era. Indeed, by Prohibition's repeal, Al Capone, who controlled the trade from Chicago to Florida, had become a celebrity, despite the fact that trailing him was the scent of death. In the end, bootleggers were criminals, and although they thrived because they served other criminals, all the nation's illegal drinkers, they would always, like Gatsby, remain "Mr. Nobody from Nowhere" (136).

In fact, Tom's damning judgment of Gatsby highlights the contradictions at the center of so many of the era's social and cultural developments. Gatsby, as the discovery of his battered copy of *Hopalong Cassidy* makes clear, believed in the American Dream of success. On the flyleaf a young James Gatz, in the tradition of Benjamin Franklin, whose *Autobiography* served as a primer for the self-made man, had recorded his "general Resolves" and developed a schedule to ensure that he made productive use of his day. Through industry and initiative and the development of personal qualities such as "poise" (180), he intended to rise from his humble beginnings to a position of privilege and power, but in its treatment of the era's celebrity culture, *The Great Gatsby* makes patently clear the obstacles that impede his efforts.

The technological developments that created the Jazz Age's consumer culture contributed to its celebrity culture as well. Motion pictures had made stars of Douglas Fairbanks and Mary Pickford, Buster Keaton and Charlie Chaplin, Tallulah Bankhead and Clara Bow, and, of course, Rudolph Valentino, whose death at the age of thirty-one in 1926 prompted long lines of heart-broken fans to pass by his embalmed body. Equally intriguing were the nation's new sports heroes, Babe Ruth, Ty Cobb, Lou Gehrig, Jack Dempsey, and those of singular talents and accomplishments, Harry Houdini, Charles Lindbergh, Amelia Earhart, and even the F. Scott Fitzgeralds. Fans clamored to read about their glamorous lives and lavish lifestyles on the pages of *Town Topics*, which styled itself a "Journal of Society" but was little more than a scandal sheet, the sort of publication that Myrtle Wilson purchases when she arrives in New York City with Tom and Nick, old copies of which are strewn about her tawdry love nest, and which Fitzgerald lampoons as "Town Tattle" (35).

Celebrities constituted a new upper class in the Jazz Age. Their remarkable achievements, extraordinary creativity, and relentless pursuit of their dreams exemplified the spirit of an age in which anything seemed possible. Many of these celebrities, moreover, even those from the criminal underworld, embodied the dream of success that was the promise of America and thereby won the hearts of a nation. Fitzgerald captures their raw yearning in Gatsby, the "elegant young roughneck" whose smile has the "quality of eternal reassurance" (54), and his riotous parties, with their cacophony of sounds, their "swirls and eddies of people" (47), their general hilarity exacerbated by the never-ending cocktails and punctuated by an undertone of violence on the verge of eruption. When Nick, for instance, attends his first Gatsby party, he vibrates to the liberating exhilaration of the 1920s and finds himself captivated by his host. But a sense of "unpleasantness" complicates his second experience of Gatsby's hospitality. The "same many-colored, many-keyed commotion" (111) now seems chaotic and desperate, in danger of spinning out of control. He recognized that he has come to see the Gatsby-world of West Egg as "complete in itself, with its own standards and its own great figures, second to nothing because it had no consciousness of being so" (111). These contradictions also represent the spirit of the age, and they, too, are part of celebrity culture.

By 1922, the year in which Fitzgerald sets *The Great Gatsby*, celebrities, especially those from the entertainment industry, were increasingly aligning themselves with the landed gentry on Long Island, settling across the narrow inlet from their stately mansions in a migration that prompted *Town Topics* to report that "Great Neck is becoming known as 'the Hollywood of the East'" (Churchwell 56). Fitzgerald confirms the report in his creation of East Egg and West Egg. East Egg, where the Buchanans' "cheerful red-and-white Georgian Colonial mansion" (12) is deeply rooted, is associated with hereditary wealth and pedigree. Those from East Egg who attend Gatsby's parties hold themselves aloof from the general hilarity, "[preserving] a dignified homogeneity, . . . and representing the staid nobility of the countryside" (51). West Egg, where Gatsby's palatial mansion sits in "factual imitation of some Hôtel de Ville in Normandy" (11), exists in crude imitation of its neighbor across the water. Money and power have elevated the producers and directors and "theatrical people" (68) who have settled there, but Daisy, representing her class, cannot help but be "appalled" by "this unprecedented 'place' that Broadway had begotten upon a Long Island fishing village—appalled by its raw vigor that chafed under the old euphemisms" (114) but chiefly by the failure of these rowdy upstarts to realize that money and power cannot purchase acceptance. East Egg may drink Gatsby's cocktails, but it condescends to do so. Celebrity makes them interesting, but it does not make them "one of us."

Something about celebrity culture, Fitzgerald makes clear, is amiss. Granted, the denizens of East Egg have their flaws, the least of which is hypocrisy. After all, their names appear alongside those from West Egg on the railway timetable on which Nick lists those who attended Gatsby's parties that summer. Certainty of their position in the social hierarchy, moreover, makes easy their disapproval of the Gatsby-world of West Egg. Yet that disapproval implies a self-awareness that seems to have eluded West Egg's celebrities, many of whom, like Gatsby, have reinvented themselves and are thus enacting a part. East Egg may play by outmoded rules, but West Egg seems to play without any rules, which results in the chaos that is Gatsby's parties, the chaos of the modern, which is all a bit disconcerting, however promising it may seem. In his depiction of celebrity culture, Fitzgerald thereby captures once again the contradictions inherent in the Jazz Age.

The Great Gatsby captures the spirit of the Jazz Age like no other novel of its time. The modern era had finally come. America was roaring. Change was happening, and with it came a sense of possibility. As Nick recognizes on the day that the chauffeur-driven "modish negroes" pass him and Gatsby on the Queensboro Bridge linking Long Island to New York, completely reversing traditional hierarchies, "Anything can happen now . . .; anything at all. . . . Even Gatsby could happen, without any particular wonder" (75). Everything about the old order seemed in flux—gender roles and expectations, racial boundaries, class barriers. Prosperity and new technologies were redefining ways of living for all. Fitzgerald's Jazz Age novel is a record of all these changes as well as a reaction to them. By its end, both Myrtle Wilson and Jay Gatsby, mirror images of aspiration no matter the difference in scale of their conceptions of greatness, are murdered, their common fate suggesting that change has its limits. Nick, moreover, has retreated to the certainties of the Midwest (even if they are somewhat reactionary) to recover his moral bearings. In 1925, the year of *The Great Gatsby*'s publication, Fitzgerald could not have known that the gay, gaudy decade would come crashing to its end in October 1929, but the novel certainly anticipates its fall. Fitzgerald clearly understood the complexities of change. Indeed, *The Great Gatsby* is his elegy to romantic possibility, for a generation's longing for what could never be.

DOCUMENTING *THE GREAT GATSBY*

The Automobile and the Jazz Age

The automobile, more than any other technological advancement of the twentieth century, was the vehicle of change in the 1920s. The Great Gatsby *certainly provides evidence of that fact. Its characters cruise in and out of Manhattan in sleek roadsters and garish coupés, and an automobile accident catapults the plot to its resolution. The following sources provide additional evidence of its importance to and influence on American culture. The first article demonstrates both the appeal and the popularity of the automobile among all classes of citizens. The second speaks to the influence of the automobile on the nation. The third documents, in comic style, the habits of the era's drivers.*

Document: From "How Many American People Can Afford Automobiles?" 1922

The family skeleton in the closet of the motor makers, kept for private inspection only, is the "saturation point" of the market. The ghost thus far has kept in retirement, for, in spite of frequent predictions that the time is about due for it to walk abroad, the public's buying ability has been continually advanced and the appearance of the spook has always been indefinitely postponed. Time was when it was thought that the use of pleasure cars would never extend beyond the 15,000 families whose incomes exceed $10,000. That it would be seriously considered by the 200,000 families with incomes of from $5,000 to $10,000 was gravely doubted; and at an early stage of development the suggestion that 400,000 households with incomes of from $3,000 to $5,000 could buy and support cars was "conclusively proved to be impossible." Yet look at the registration figures in the United States to-day—in excess of 7,000,000 cars!

Taking the most carefully estimated figures available, families with incomes of from $2,000 and upwards number some three million units. It is apparent, therefore, that we must locate over one-half of the motor cars with families of individuals whose estimated cash income is $2,000 or less. This, as Park Mathewson, vice-president of the New York Business Bourse, observes, in *Forbes*, opens up possibilities of auto sales running into very high figures, especially with an increasing ratio of earnings per family.

Figures show that possibly 80 per cent of all cars made are produced by seven of the popular-price manufacturers—Ford, Willys-Overland,

Chevrolet, Dodge, Buick, Studebaker, Maxwell. Hence, from present indications it appears that, for some time to come, the "higher priced" cars will not be produced in sufficient quantity to saturate their market, even tho it be limited to a comparatively small proportion of the auto-buying public. Altho the problem of the higher-priced car is well worth considering, it is declared to be of no such importance as that of the popular-priced car.

The overshadowing problem in the motor industry is that of demand, supply and saturation point in the field covered by the pleasure cars whose price appeals to the masses. In this class one manufacturer alone advertises his capacity as a million cars a year, which is about one-seventh of the number of all automobiles in use in this country. It is suggested that, "allowing an average yearly production of three million cars for the next ten years, and giving the cheap ones an average life of six years, the hypothetical market would not be saturated in a decade, even if wealth and population stood still."

Figures compiled by one of the large trust companies showed that during the war the three family groups enjoying incomes of from $1,000 to $4,000 could contribute, in one year, to the purchase of Liberty Bonds as follows: Group one, $209; group two, $516; group three, $931. On the basis of the same investment per annum in a motor car and its up-keep, if payments were extended over a four-year period, it is evident to the *Forbes* statistician that an individual in these groups might buy an automobile costing $700, $1,200 or $2,000 each. Assuming that these groups consist in 1920 of the same number of families, they could, on the same reckoning, buy over sixteen million autos at between $600 and $700 and half a million machines at around $2,000.

Source: "How Many American People Can Afford Automobiles?" *Current Opinion* 72, February 1922.

Document: From "Your Car and You," 1920

This is the most active part of the year in the motor world, both for manufacturers and for those who are interested in automobiles from a buying or scientific standpoint. Great thought and great publicity are given to the new styles in body designs and in the new features introduced into the chassis construction. But very few people, even in the industry itself, realize the really important part the automobile has taken in the daily life of our country and its people.

The village smithy is no more. In the place of that interesting relic of a bygone day, there stands a substantial concrete building marked "Garage".

This garage may not be all that we desire in the way of efficiency, honesty, courtesy or personnel, but the thing that it represents has become the most omnipresent and revolutionizing factor in our existence in the short space of twenty-five years. Indeed, the motor car has become so commonplace that we regard it rather in the light of a piece of household equipment, scolding about its shortcomings and seldom, if ever, giving thought to the fact that here, in exchange for a comparatively few dollars, we have come into possession of the most perfect saver of time, money, energy and ennui ever produced by the mind of man.

A congressional investigator has stated that in this country we waste $500,000,000 a year in the inefficient transportation of food and that of every dollar expended for food 66¢ are expended in its distribution. It is in relieving this situation that the automobile, as typified by the truck, is going to be the greatest element in reducing the present excessive high cost of living.

One-third of the passenger automobiles in this country, or approximately 2,300,000, are owned by farmers. Seventy-eight per cent of their mileage is for business and a recent canvass of farm owners showed that they had increased their productivity sixty-eight per cent through the use of the automobile. It will take but little time for this condition to assert itself in the lowering scale of living costs. On account of the relief given to the more or less inefficiently handled railroads by motor transportation and the opening up of new territory which has no rail communication the motor car has become pre-eminent in the building up of the country.

Source: "Your Car and You," *Vanity Fair*, 1920.

Document: From "On Which Side of the Windshield Do You Do Your Cussing?" H. I. Phillips, 1927

Are automobilists people?

Can a man be a motorist, and still be himself?

Is it possible for a person to drive an automobile, and remain a human being?

Do gasoline and courtesy mix?

Why is it that Casper M. V. Bluegills, the mildest, gentlest man in the neighborhood when afoot, becomes a Terrible-Tempered Mr. Bang the moment you put a steering wheel into his hands?

How comes it that Chester X. Y. Oohms, the well-poised bank clerk, will ride all day in a stuffy day coach and show only mild irritation if the train is held up by cows on the track ten times during a 55-mile run, yet becomes a profane and infuriated madman if, when driving his coupé around the block to get a pack of cigarettes, he is delayed forty-five seconds by a traffic cop directing a bewildered old lady to an emergency hospital?

How do you explain that Artemus V. Beedeez, passenger on a twelve-day boat to Europe, will force a smile and say philosophically, "Well, we'll have to make the best of it," when the ship is delayed nine hours by a fog, but become apoplectic with rage, and bellow, "It's a blankety-blank outrage!" whenever he is out in his fireless cooker and is held up two minutes by a hard-smoking coal-truck driver trying to back up to the curb and unload?

Why is Luther Q. Brighteyes, efficiency expert, psychologist, and author of the stirring pamphlet "The Importance of Patience and Self-Control in Business," one of the first men to fly off the handle when a little boy, hurrying home from the delicatessen store with a pound of potato salad and a dozen eggs, tries to cross the street unaccompanied by the state militia?

Can you tell me why Otis Throckmorton Whoozies, secretary of the Golden Rule Society, will smile graciously, lift his hat, and say sweetly, "I beg your pardon. I'm really awfully sorry. Please excuse me," when he accidentally steps on a strange woman's foot in a theatre lobby, yet will lean out and make faces at his own grandmother if she fails to slow up her flivver and allow him to "cut in" on a congested highway? It's all over my head. I haven't got the right answers.

Possibly there's something about a windshield that distorts a man's outlook on life.

I'm not preaching. As a matter of fact, I'm in the same boat with the rest of the Occasionally Human Race. I believe in graciousness. I think courtesy and consideration two great virtues. I have no patience with the gruff, ill-mannered person who has no sense of fair play. Ordinarily, I keep my temper and rarely do I wax profane. But I'd hate to be held strictly accountable for all that I do, say, or think when driving an automobile.

Once the smell of gasoline gets into my nostrils, I become a different man. And how!

Few things that the other fellow does seem right to me. I denounce traffic policemen as dumb-bells, brand truck drivers as idiots, classify women drivers as nitwits, howl out little children as crazy numb-skulls, and dismiss pedestrians as a whole with the scornful, "The big louts! Can you beat 'em?"

I become overbearing, disdainful, superior. I become, as it were, an hauteur-mobilist.

Now, I'm not that way under other conditions. Subway tie-ups I regard as unavoidable. When one occurs, I read my paper for fifteen or twenty minutes, and then, if the train isn't ready to move, I walk out and grab a taxi. If the taxi gets tied up in traffic, it nettles me somewhat, but I don't tear my hair, glare out the window, and use language not permitted in the fourth-best families.

If I go to the theatre and the curtain, scheduled to rise at eight-thirty, does not rise until nine I get somewhat peeved. I shuffle my feet a bit and mutter a little, but I don't blow a horn vociferously at the producer and make grimaces at the usherettes.

Even on the telephone I am under better control than in an automobile. I give "central" an even break, at least. She always gets a minute for rebuttal.

But in the gasoline rickshaw—that's something else again! Once aboard the motor lugger and I'm the whole nine reels of D. H. Griffiths's [sic] "Intolerance." And I'd be awfully upset about it and conscience-stricken if I didn't know from observation that ninety-nine out of one hundred men are the same the minute they step on a self-starter or let in a clutch.

Is the craze for speed so predominant a characteristic of the people of the United States that, once it is given an opportunity to express itself, it submerges all other traits? That may be it.

One touch of gasoline, possibly, makes the whole world spin.

Give a man a chassis, four tires, a map box, and a horn, and he immediately wants to become the Vanishing American.

From that time on he believes in the survival of the fleetest.

He has two mottoes. They are:

1. Fright makes right.
2. The other fellow is always wrong.

The speed mania is no respecter of persons. Last summer I was all but sideswiped by a big rumbling limousine that tore out of a side street with absolutely no warning. My amazement at the performance was eclipsed by the recognition of the driver as a beloved priest, well over sixty and widely known for his generous ways and inherent kindliness. He probably didn't know what a different picture he made with his foot on an accelerator. One of the most careless drivers in my home town was a bishop. Any place but at the wheel of his runabout he was a cautious, slow-moving, extremely considerate gentleman. But once in his petrol-barouche, and he was more of an insurance risk than the fire-chief.

For some years, I was secretary of an automobile club in my home town. Its slogan was "Safety First!" and its board of directors, meeting once a week, issued a flood of bulletins emphasizing the need of cautious driving, and urging all motorists to consider the rights of others. One of the officers was arrested one day while carrying some "Go Slow" signs into the suburbs!

After nailing up one "Go Slow" sign, he had violated the speed laws in his rush to put up the others! At another time, the club, aroused by a series of accidents, appealed to the public to report to the club any persons observed driving recklessly. When the complaints were opened at a later meeting, one of the first read was against the president of the club. . . .

It's in the blood. The man on the way to a notions store to buy a spool of thread for his wife drives just as heedlessly as the chairman of the reception committee clearing the way for a channel swimmer, a golf champion, or the Prince of Wales.

The motto of both is, "Don't stop until you see the whites of their eyes!" And that—let's be honest about it—is mine, too. . . .

Source: H. I. Phillips, "On Which Side of the Windshield Do You Do Your Cussing?" *The American Magazine*, May 1927.

Prohibition and Bootleggers

Readers of The Great Gatsby *might be surprised to learn that the manufacture, importation, transportation, and selling of alcohol were illegal during the time of the novel, for Gatsby's parties are infamous for the rainbow-colored cocktails that flow to excess well into the early hours of the morning. Prohibition, however, the "noble experiment" of the 1920s, dominated American culture in the Jazz Age, and the following documents reveal its wide-ranging effect on the nation. The first document is an excerpt from the law that enabled the enforcement of the Eighteenth Amendment that outlawed intoxicating spirits in the nation. Its provisions suggest some of the reasons for the experiment's failure thirteen years later. The second provides a brief history of the "dry" movement in the United States that culminated in Prohibition. The third reports the results of a survey of drinking habits five years into Prohibition. The fourth focuses on a sensational criminal case against bootleggers in the Northeast and reveals much about the public's attitude toward Prohibition and those who violated its intent and provisions.*

Document: From The Volstead Act, 1920

An Act to prohibit intoxicating beverages, and to regulate the manufacture, production, use, and sale of high-proof spirits for other than beverage purposes, and to insure an ample supply of alcohol and promote its use in scientific research and in the development of fuel, dye, and other lawful industries.

Be it enacted by the Senate and House of Representatives of the United States of America in Congress assembled, That the short title of this Act shall be the "National Prohibition Act."

Title II
Prohibition of Intoxicating Beverages

Sec. 1. When used in Title II and Title III of this Act (1) The word "liquor" or the phrase "intoxicating liquor" shall be construed to include alcohol, brandy, whisky, rum, gin, beer, ale, porter, and wine, and in addition thereto any spirituous, vinous, malt or fermented liquor, liquids, and compounds, whether medicated, proprietary, patented, or not, and by whatever name called, containing one-half of 1 per centum or more of alcohol by volume which are fit for use for beverage purposes: Provided, That the foregoing definition shall not extend to dealcoholized wine nor to any beverage or liquid produced by the process by which beer, ale, porter or wine is produced, if it contains less than one-half of 1 per centum of alcohol by volume, and is made as prescribed in section 37 of this title, and is otherwise denominated than as beer, ale, or porter, and is contained and sold in, or from, such sealed and labeled bottles, casks, or containers as the commissioner may by regulation prescribe. . . .

Sec. 3. No person shall on or after the date when the eighteenth amendment to the Constitution of the United States goes into effect, manufacture, sell, barter, transport, import, export, deliver, furnish or possess any intoxicating liquor except as authorized in this Act, and all the provisions of this Act shall be liberally construed to the end that the use of intoxicating liquor as a beverage may be prevented.

Liquor for nonbeverage purposes and wine for sacramental purposes may be manufactured, purchased, sold, bartered, transported, imported, exported, delivered, furnished and possessed, but only as therein provided, and the commissioner may, upon application, issue permits therefore. . . .

Sec. 4. The articles enumerated in this section shall not, after having been manufactured and prepared for the market, be subject to the provisions of this Act if they correspond with the following descriptions and limitations, namely:

(a) Denatured alcohol or denatured rum produced and used as provided by laws and regulations now or hereafter in force.

(b) Medicinal preparations manufactured in accordance with formulas prescribed by the United States Pharmacopoeia, National Formulary or the American Institute of Homeopathy that are unfit for use for beverage purposes.
(c) Patented, patent, and proprietary medicines that are unfit for use for beverage purposes.
(d) Toilet, medicinal, and antiseptic preparations and solutions that are unfit for use for beverage purposes.
(e) Flavoring extracts and syrups that are unfit for use as a beverage, or for intoxicating beverage purposes.
(f) Vinegar and preserved sweet cider.

A person who manufactures any of the articles mentioned in this section may purchase and possess liquor for that purpose, but he shall secure permits to manufacture such articles and to purchase such liquor, give the bonds, keep the records, and make the reports specified in this Act and as directed by the commissioner. No such manufacturer shall sell, use, or dispose of any liquor otherwise than as an ingredient of the articles authorized to be manufactured therefrom. No more alcohol shall be used in the manufacture of any extract, syrup, or the articles named in paragraphs b, c, and d of this section which may be used for beverage purposes than the quantity necessary for extraction or solution of the elements contained therein and for the preservation of the article. . . .

Sec. 6. No one shall manufacture, sell, purchase, transport, or prescribe any liquor without first obtaining a permit from the commissioner so to do, except that a person may, without a permit, purchase and use liquor for medicinal purposes when prescribed by a physician as herein provided, and except that any person who in the opinion of the commissioner is conducting a bona fide hospital or sanatorium engaged in the treatment of persons suffering from alcoholism, may, under such rules, regulations, and conditions as the commissioner shall prescribe, purchase and use, in accordance with the methods in use in such institution, liquor, to be administered to the patients of such institution under the direction of a duly qualified physician employed by such institution. . . .

Nothing in this title shall be held to apply to the manufacture, sale, transportation, importation, possession, or distribution of wine for sacramental purposes, or like religious rites, except section 6 (save as the same requires a permit to purchase) and section 10 hereof, and the provisions of this Act prescribing penalties for the violation of either of said sections. No person to whom a permit may be issued to manufacture, transport, import, or sell wines for sacramental purposes or like religious rites shall sell, barter, exchange, or furnish any such to any person not a rabbi, minister of the gospel, priest, or any officer duly authorized for the purpose by any church or congregation, nor to any such except upon an application duly subscribed by him, which application, authenticated as regulations may prescribe, shall be filed and preserved by the seller. The head of any conference or diocese or other ecclesiastical jurisdiction may designate any rabbi, minister, or priest to supervise the manufacture of wine to be used for the purposes and rites in this section mentioned, and the person so designated may, in the discretion of the commissioner, be granted a permit to supervise such manufacture.

Sec. 7. No one but a physician holding a permit to prescribe liquor shall issue any prescription for liquor. And no physician shall prescribe liquor unless after careful physical examination of the person for whom such prescription is sought, or if such examination is found impracticable, then upon the best information obtainable, he in good faith believes that the use of such liquor as a medicine by such person is necessary and will afford relief to him from some known ailment. Not more than a pint of spirituous liquor to be taken internally shall be prescribed for use by the same person within any period of ten days and no prescription shall be filled more than once. Any pharmacist filling a prescription shall at the time indorse upon it over his own signature the word "canceled," together with the date when the liquor was delivered, and then make the same a part of the record that he is required to keep as herein provided.

Every physician who issues a prescription for liquor shall keep a record, alphabetically arranged in a book prescribed by the commissioner, which shall show the date of issue, amount prescribed, to whom issued, the purpose or ailment for which it is to be used and directions for use, stating the amount and frequency of the dose.

Sec. 8. The commissioner shall cause to be printed blanks for the prescriptions herein required, and he shall furnish the same, free of cost, to physicians holding permits to prescribe. The prescription blanks shall be printed in a book form and shall be numbered consecutively from one to one hundred, and each book shall carry the same numbers as and be copies of the prescriptions. The books containing such stubs shall be returned to the commissioner when the prescription blanks have been used, or sooner, if directed by the commissioner. All unused, mutilated, or defaced blanks shall be returned with the book. No physician shall prescribe and no pharmacist shall fill any prescription for liquor except on blanks so provided, except in cases of emergency, in which event a record and report shall be made and kept as in other cases. . . .

Sec. 12. All persons manufacturing liquor for sale under the provisions of this title shall securely and permanently attach to every container thereof, as the same is manufactured, a label stating name of manufacturer, kind and quantity of liquor contained therein, and the date of its manufacture, together with the number of the permit authorizing the manufacture thereof; and all persons possessing such liquor in wholesale quantities shall securely keep and maintain such label therein; and all persons selling at wholesale shall attach to every package of liquor, when sold, a label setting for the kind and quantity of liquor contained therein, by whom manufactured, the date of sale, and the person to whom sold; which label shall likewise be kept and maintained thereon until the liquor is used for the purpose for which such sale was authorized. . . .

Sec. 17. It shall be unlawful to advertise anywhere, or by any means or method, liquor, or the manufacture, sale, keeping for sale or furnishing of the same, or where, how, from whom, or at what price the same may be obtained. No one shall permit any sign or billboard containing such advertisement to remain upon one's premises. But nothing herein shall prohibit manufacturers and wholesale druggists holding permits to sell liquor from furnishing price lists, with description of liquor for sale, to persons permitted to purchase liquor, or from advertising alcohol in business publications or trade journals circulating generally among manufacturers of lawful alcoholic perfumes, toilet preparations, flavoring extracts, medicinal preparations, and like articles. . . .

Sec. 18. It shall be unlawful to advertise, manufacture, sell, or possess for sale any utensil, contrivance, machine, preparation, compound, tablet, substance, formula direction, or recipe advertised, designed, or intended for use in the unlawful manufacture of intoxicating liquor. . . .

Sec. 21. Any room, house, building, boat, vehicle, structure, or place where intoxicating liquor is manufactured, sold, kept, or bartered in violation of this title, and all intoxicating liquor and property kept and used in maintaining the same, is hereby declared to be a common nuisance, and any person who maintains such a common nuisance shall be guilty of a misdemeanor and upon conviction thereof shall be fined not more than $1,000 or be imprisoned for not more than one year or both. If a person has knowledge or reason to believe that this room, house, building, boat, vehicle, structure, or place is occupied or used for the manufacture or sale of liquor contrary to the provision of this title, and suffers the same to be so occupied or used, such room, house, building, boat, vehicle, structure, or place shall be subject to a lien for and may be sold to pay all fines and costs assessed against the person guilty of such nuisance for such violation, and any such lien may be enforced by action in any court having jurisdiction. . . .

Sec. 29. Any person who manufactures or sells liquor in violation of this title shall for a first offense be fined not more than $1,000 or imprisoned not exceeding six months, and for a second or subsequent offense shall be fined not less than $200 nor more than $2,000 and be imprisoned not less than one month nor more than five years. . . .

Sec. 33. After February 1, 1920, the possession of liquors by any person not legally permitted under this title to possess liquor shall be a prima facie evidence that such liquor is kept for the purpose of being sold, bartered, exchanged, given away, furnished, or otherwise disposed of in violation of the provisions of this title. Every person legally permitted under this title to have liquor shall report to the commissioner within ten days after the date when the eighteenth amendment of the Constitution of the United States goes into effect, the kind and amount of intoxicating liquors in his possession. But it shall not be unlawful to possess liquors in one's private dwelling while the same is occupied and used by him at his dwelling only and such liquor need not be reported, provided such liquors are for use only for the personal consumption of the owner thereof and his family residing in such dwelling and of his bona fide guests when entertained by him therein; and the burden of proof shall be upon the possessor in any action concerning the same to prove that such liquor was lawfully acquired, possessed, and used. . . .

Source: The Volstead Act, Public Law 66–66. 83, 41. Washington D.C: *U.S. Statutes at Large* 305–323 (1920).

Document: From "Nation-Wide Prohibition Ends Fight of 112 Years," 1920

War on John Barley Corn Begun by Women in Little Ohio Town Finally Caused Abolishment of Strong Drink for Entire Nation.

National prohibition in the United States, under a specific constitutional provision, is the fruition of a movement which had its beginning in America 112 years ago. Efforts to check the use of ardent spirits were started in this country in 1808. It grew steadily, evolving into a demand for prohibition rather than regulation as far back as 1847. The question was taken into politics through the organization of the Prohibition party in convention at Chicago, September 1, 1869.

The war of women on liquor began with the organization of the Women's Christian Temperance Union in Ohio during the "crusade" during 1873 and 1874.

Maine was the first state to declare for prohibition. It went "dry" in 1851. Prohibition was made a part of its constitution in 1884. Kansas was the second state to embrace prohibition. That was in 1880. North Dakota was third, in 1889.

But the prohibition wave which has swept the liquor business entirely out of the country began with the action of the Georgia State Legislature in 1907. By their own acts, in a steady procession, thirty-three states followed suit. In twenty-one prohibition was decreed by popular vote and in twelve by act of the legislatures.

Webb-Kenyon Act

Prohibition made its first big advance nationally when Congress passed on March 1, 1913, the Webb-Kenyon law forbidding the shipment of liquor from "wet" to "dry" territory. . . .

The [18th] amendment was submitted by the House, 28 to 128, and by the Senate, 65 to 20.

When Congress submitted the amendment, December 19, 1917, it attempted a restriction, limiting the time for ratification to seven years. Instead, the necessary thirty-six states ratified Constitutional prohibition within thirteen months, the thirty-sixth registering its approval January 16, 1919. The last to ratify was Pennsylvania, and the next to last New York. . . .

Liquor Men Too Confident

Except for starting small and easily handled backfires the liquor people made no effort to counter the progress of prohibition until the passage of the Webb-Kenyon law. The only movement within the trade to meet some of the most potent arguments of the "Drys" was represented by the Model License League, an organization that received comparatively little support from the saloon interests, which never for a moment believed that their power in politics could be entirely overborne.

That this attitude has persisted to the last is indicated by the fact that the liquor interests hoisted prices to almost prohibitive altitudes last July, and retained huge stocks in warehouses. These same stocks, which now constitute a problem for the government officials, who must guard them in bonded warehouses until some means are found for disposing of them without violating the law which forbids export, import and possession of liquor anywhere but in private homes.

Millions of gallons were held, in spite of the fact that other millions were exports, apparently in anticipation of a time when a reaction from absolute prohibition would afford an outlet at huge profits. The hoped-for reaction failed to materialize during the period of war-time prohibition, and under the rigid provisions of the constitutional amendment modification is all the more difficult, though the liquor interests are hoping now that the government, to solve the problem of the stored liquor, will agree to buy it.

Proclaimed on January 29, 1919

The prohibition amendment was proclaimed January 29, 1919, the proclamation fixing January 16, 1920, twelve months after ratification by the thirty-sixth state, as the date for its going into effect.

Congress went to work on enforcement legislation, and the law produced is regarded as drastic enough to dry up all reserve sources of liquor, according to official estimates, in five or six years. By 1925, it is stated, the United States will be a desert with entirely exhausted cellars.

The United States not only loses a revenue of $500,000,000 a year through prohibition, but will require millions, during the first years at least, to enforce the provisions of the law putting the amendment into effect.

Daniel C. Roper, Commissioner of Internal Revenue, has delegated enforcement to a special prohibition bureau under John F. Kremer, of Mansfield, Ohio. Mr. Kremer has divided the country into nine districts, each with a supervisor. Each state has a director, and the bureau will have at hand a large corps of enforcement agents who will be shifted from state to state at periods frequent enough to prevent the forming of friendships or alliances and consequent interference with the administration of the law in letter as well as in spirit.

Source: "Nation-Wide Prohibition Ends Fight of 112 Years," *New York Tribune*, January 17, 1920: 3.

Document: From "Volstead Law Draws Attack of Opponents," 1925

Moderation League Declares Drunkenness is on Increase. Claimed Young Drinking More. Wheeler Characterizes Statement as Being Inaccurate One.

New York

Results of one of the most sweeping surveys of prohibition ever made, showing according to statistics that drunkenness was as prevalent in 1914 as in 1924, were made public by the Moderation League here today.

The Moderation League, seeking restriction in sale of liquor but opposed to bone-dry prohibition, on its board of directors leading professional and business men of the nation.

These include, Elihu Root, former secretary of state; Kermit Roosevelt; Right-Reverend Charles Fiske, bishop of Central New York; William N. Dykman, president of the New York Bar association; Newcomb Carlton, president of the Western Union Telegraph company; William C. Bedford, former secretary of commerce; William B. Parsons, president of the board of trustees, Columbia university.

The chairman of the board is Austen G. Fox, New York attorney.

The report is based on a canvass of police departments in cities over 5,000 on the number of arrests for drunkenness.

A chart illustrates graphically the history of America's drinking population. During 1914–1915, before the war boom got underway, arrests for drunkenness remained practically stationary. During 1916 and 1917, war boom years, there was a marked increase.

Drunkenness, during 1918 and 1919, when emergency war-time restrictions on the sale of liquors were in effect, took a remarkable drop. The lowest level reached, the chart shows, just before prohibition went into effect in 1920. In succeeding years, drunkenness has climbed steadily back to the 1914 level, according to the chart.

Commenting on the statistics, the Moderation League says:

"When we consider that drunkenness has already increased to the pre-prohibition level, and that drunken drivers and drunken children have increased far above anything ever known before in this country, we cannot escape the fact that the Volstead act has utterly failed to do what it was intended to do, namely, promote temperance and sobriety.

"Moreover since conditions have become worse, not better each year, and with the next generation drinking as never before, there seems to be no hope that the Volstead act in its present drastic form will accomplish its purpose in the long run."

Pointing to the figures from 1918 and 1919 when partial restriction on the sale and consumption of liquor was in effect, the statement continues:

"We believe that a greater degree of temperance can be obtained by a wise restrictive law than by a bone-dry law which does not command the respect of a large part of the people."

"We are also of the firm conviction," the statement adds, "that such a policy of wise restriction could have the incidental advantage of eliminating almost entirely the scandalous corruption and bribery of public officials, would stop the growth of the bootlegging millionaire class, would check disrespect for law, and would in addition produce a handsome national revenue."

Startling figures are given showing the increase of drunkenness among "children" and also the increase in the number of arrests of intoxicated motor car drivers.

"To be exact," the league states, "motor vehicles in the United States increased from 1919 to 1924 132 percent, whereas drunken drivers increased in the same period about 354 percent on the average. The difference of 222 percent is clearly attributable to the Volstead act."

One of the interesting things disclosed by the survey is that while conditions in former "wet" states are now about the same as in 1914, while in former "dry" states which had some form of state prohibition or semi-prohibition law before the 18th amendment was adopted, conditions are worse today under the bone-dry Volstead act than they formerly were under their own state dry laws. . . .

Source: "Volstead Law Draws Attack of Opponents." *The Florence* [AL] *Times*, November 23, 1925.

Document: From "Rich Bootleggers Sent to Prison," 1923

Bootlegging is not a game for polo or racquet players, or other "sprigs of society," concludes the Providence *News* after reading of the prison sentence of the four La Montagne brothers, of New York, for "conspiracy to violate the Volstead Act," and fines of $2,000 each for three of the brothers. These young men, prominent socially, composed the firm of E. La Montagne's Sons, whisky and wine merchants. Rene La Montagne, one of them, is known internationally as a polo player. Last year, we read in the New York *Evening Post*, Government agents spent months investigating a scheme of systematized bootlegging through which some of the most exclusive clubs in the city were said to receive plenty of liquors of all sorts. Later came the indictment of the brothers, and an offer of immunity if they would involve others "lower down," in this instance. But all four refused to "tell on" their confederates and friends, altho they confessed in court to their own sins.

"This sentence by Judge Winslow in the Federal District Court is the Government's warning to all bootleggers, whether in society or in the underworld, that violation of the Prohibition Law will be prosecuted relentlessly," declares the New York *American*. It is also an indication to the Springfield *Republican* that "the Government is beginning to learn the technique in fighting rum runners, bootleggers, and their allies." "Certainly," observes the New York *Times*, "it is the first time that men of the standing of the La Montagnes have been sentenced to prison under the Volstead Law."

The plea for leniency made by several well-known lawyers on the ground of the social prominence of the accused, was "pitiable and foolish," in the opinion of the New York *Globe*. In fact, the Philadelphia *Bulletin* derives considerable satisfaction from the infliction of punishment "on those 'high up' where it too infrequently is applied." As we are told in *The Times*:

> "What the counsel for the prisoners forgot to say was that these men, having inherited a business which nobody of sensibilities at all delicate would follow, had been content to take its profits for many years, tho the taking of those profits involved the acceptance of a moral responsibility exactly the same as that carried by liquor dealers and barkeepers in general, and that the 'high society' in which they moved was composed of persons who drew no line against men who lived by serving the vices and weaknesses of their neighbors. One thing the counsel did not do in these last appeals—they did not repeat the grotesque absurdity of claiming that the wholesale bootlegging had been done without the knowledge of the four partners. The judge was spared that, if nothing else.
>
> "Over the mishap that has befallen the brothers concerned there need be, and should be, no special exultation. Their guilt was exactly that of several thousand other criminals, some of whom have been punished with more severity and others—probably the majority—with less. If they had been entirely inconspicuous bootleggers, the chances are that they would have escaped more easily.
>
> "One can not help noticing, however, that what troubles these brothers—and their friends—is not their guilt, but their conviction, and not their conviction so much as that they must go to jail. Of repentance no word has been said—none of admission that laws, as laws, either should be observed or else fought through exercise of the inalienable right of open rebellion with full acceptance of its consequences. These men did exactly what burglars and pickpockets do—they broke the law in secret and evidently, if they had not been found out, would have continued to do so indefinitely or as long as there was any money in it. Their claim to be sportsmen is not well founded."

"If there is to be a Prohibition Law on the statute books it must be enforced," continues *The Bulletin*, "and the bootlegger to society must be brought to book as well as the bartender." In the opinion of the Philadelphia *Public Ledger*:

> "This strange notion that 'social prominence'—whatever that may mean—ought to give those who possess it immunity from punishment or crime is

unfortunately too familiar to those who watch the habitual administration of justice in the court." . . .

In summing up his case, which had been prepared by an assistant, the United States District Attorney said:

"To allow these defendants to escape with a fine, it seems to me, would be a travesty of justice and a mockery of the majesty of the law. It would announce to the public that even the Federal Judges were complaisant toward the wide-spread reign of alcoholic anarchy in New York City. It would mean that equality before the law had disappeared, and would justify the belief that men of great wealth or influence or power are above the law."

Source: "Rich Bootleggers Sent to Prison," *The Literary Digest*, February 24, 1923.

Celebrity Culture in the Jazz Age

Celebrity culture developed in the Jazz Age, at least in part because the advent of the radio and motion pictures popularized the exploits of exceptional men and women throughout the nation. Baseball, for instance, "America's game," was now broadcast over the radio waves, and fans from New York to San Francisco could listen to the play-by-play of sportsmen such as Babe Ruth and Ty Cobb, making them national heroes. The stars of the silver screen, such as Mary Pickford, Douglas Fairbanks, Rudolph Valentino, and Charlie Chaplin, were endlessly fascinating to moviegoers who dreamed of living the lives they enacted. Indeed, among the many purchases that Myrtle Wilson makes on her trip to New York City in The Great Gatsby *are magazines filled with gossip about the rich and famous whose lives she wishes to emulate. The exploits of men and women of achievement were now the subject not only of newspaper and magazine articles but also newsreels at the local movie palace, breathing life into the trans-Atlantic flight of Charles Lindbergh, for instance, and the daring-do of Amelia Earhart.*

The sources that follow provide evidence of the Jazz Age interest in celebrities. The first article seeks to define the reasons for Charlie Chaplin's popularity. The second captures the high drama of Charles Lindbergh's flight, making clear that it was a carefully orchestrated performance designed to capture the public's imagination. The third article, about Babe Ruth, the King of Swat, would certainly have fulfilled Myrtle's desire for gossip, for its author, one of the Babe's closest friends, reveals much about the player's private life, including the fact that he liked to hunt frogs. These articles make clear that the public interest in stars and celebrities knew no bounds during the Jazz Age.

Document: From "The Secret of Charlie Chaplin's Popularity," St. John Ervine, 1921

Why Is It That Both Highbrows and Lowbrows Pay Tribute to the Great Comedian of the Screen? . . .

An International Comedian

The arrival of Charlie Chaplin in England prompts me to discourse on the subject [of comedy]. He is the first of the great international comedians whose dominion of the civilized world has been made possible by the cinema, and his dominion is based on the extraordinary skill with which he exploits the mechanical in human affairs.

Thoughtful laughter, as understood by Meredith, can never, I suppose, be universal in character, partly because it is cramped by conditions of language and education, but chiefly because the thought which causes mirth in one man may cause wrath in another. The difference between a Republic and a Dominion may be so slight as to excite one man's derision, but so great as to send another man gladly to his grave. All thought is impermanent—only the instincts are everlasting—and the idea which was the deliverance of one generation may be the death-warrant of the next.

Mr. Chaplin has conquered the world because he has remained in the world. Report says that he aspired to be a tragedian, and probably report is true, for most of the great comedians have had this aspiration; but if he had set out to be as great a tragedian as he is a comedian, he could only have done so by travelling along very much the same sort of road which has led him to his present high position. Epigrams are local in their effect, but the slapstick is universal; and a man will win wider suffrages by wearing a wreath of cabbages than he will ever win by wearing a wreath of laurels. Virtue is its own reward; it is also its own punishment; and those who strive to get beyond the elementals must put up with the consequences, the disregard, even the contempt, of the mass of mankind. Mr. Chaplin has publicly stated that he is tired of hitting people in the face with custard-pies. He will do well not to let his fatigue prevent him from continuing to hit people in the face with custard-pies, for most of us would much rather see a man covered with custard than covered with glory.

I spent an hour in a private movie-theatre last week, looking at films in which Mr. Chaplin figures. Whenever Mr. Chaplin kicked a man in the stomach or smashed a custard-pie in his face, or did some grievous and seemingly permanent injury to him, I rocked with laughter. I hurt myself laughing when he jabbed a man's posterior with a large sword, and hit a pugilist a terrific smack on the jaw with a boxing-glove in which he had carelessly concealed a horse-shoe. When I had recovered from the almost hysterical state into which Mr. Chaplin's antics had precipitated me, my neighbor began to discourse on the cause of Mr. Chaplin's popularity. Why has this one man, among so many film-actors of ability, seized and held the world's regard? What is there in him which makes men and women and children of every sort, gentle and simple, highbrow and lowbrow, pay tribute to him? Personally, I would go a long way to see Mr. Chaplin in a film, but I do not think I would put myself out to much extent to see any one else, and I have met many persons in similar case to myself.

Chaplin's Inventiveness

Mr. Chaplin is certainly, as some one pointed out to me, very fertile in invention, and a film in which he figures will be full of totally unexpected incidents. In one of the pictures, entitled, I think, *Champion Charlie*, he engages in a prizefight with a famous bruiser. In eluding the pugilist's blows, he hurls himself against the ropes of the ring, and then occurs one of those unexpected inventions which are remarkably comic. He suddenly does the sort of tight-wire walk along the lower rope, while holding on with both hands to the upper one, which every boy in the world has done some time or other on seeing a wirefence or rails where such a performance is possible. That incident lasts for a moment, but in effect is immediate and provocative of laughter. I do not believe that it is entirely explicable by M. Bergson's dogma that laughter is caused when the "mechanical is encrusted on the living," although, no doubt, that goes a long way towards explaining it.

But there is something profounder than the comicality of seeing the mechanical imposed upon the living in the laughter provoked by this one of many similar incidents in Mr. Chaplin's repertoire. The spontaneity of the act seems irreconcilable with the theory of mechanics, but whether that be so or not, surely the basic fact in the promotion of this laughter is the memory it stimulates. All of us, highbrow and lowbrow, have tried to emulate Blondin on a tight-rope. I remember trying to do it on a bed-rail one morning, and falling with such violence on the floor that I nearly went through into the kitchen. Mr. Chaplin builds his movies on the things which enthralled and amused us when we were children, and he keeps us who are adult continually entertained because he takes the secret aspirations of children, together with their cruelties and fears and vanities and adventures, and puts them into the circumstances of men. And since man is never so universal in character as he is in his childhood, it follows that the laughter which Mr. Chaplin excites can be shared by the whole world. We do not love the stars the less because all men can see them: we are not any the less amused by Mr. Chaplin because he can make an old man laugh as heartily as he can make a child.

The Small Boy's Heart

Mr. Chaplin is the small boy realizing his ambitions. He has fierce fights with big men, and always wins them. When he meets a policeman, instantly he reveals the small boy's heart. Observe the sudden look of dismay that comes over Mr. Chaplin's face as he turns quickly and finds a policeman at his elbow. It is not the dismay of a criminal, but the dismay of the child in contact with authority. There is a little twitch of nervousness, followed by a disarming smile and a futile effort to appear unconcerned and detached. You can almost hear the small boy's heart thumping as he tries to pretend that he had nothing whatever to do with the unfortunate affair now engaging a policeman's attention. And then comes the triumph when authority is humbled and defeated. The policeman dives towards the terrified small boy—and misses him, for Mr. Chaplin, fulfilling the small boy's secret desire to be a proficient acrobat and to flout authority, leaps through the policemen's distent legs and gallops up the street with the humiliated bobby vainly following. The boy who sauced a "peeler" in Ireland, when he becomes a ratepayer and an elector, may not feel much sympathy with ratepayers and electors, if there are such, in the Balearic Islands, but he has immediate kinship with them when he identifies them as boys who sauced policemen, even as he sauced them. And it is the great gift of Mr. Chaplin, as it is also his privilege, to make men recognize their identities. He has taken Englishmen and Irishmen, Spaniards and Russians, Frenchmen and Germans, Americans and Japanese, and reduced them all to their elements; and in so doing has achieved very largely what the more sober Dr. Wilson failed to do at Paris.

Source: St. John Ervine, "The Secret of Charlie Chaplin's Popularity." *Vanity Fair*, December 1921.

Document: From "Chance Writes the Lindbergh Saga," 1927

"Truth is stranger than fiction is an old writer's saw that the pen plodders know and the general reader doubts. But that truth and fiction may be one and the same thing comes to light in the story of Lindbergh's flight. No fiction writer could have contrived a story more perfect and right in its details. "Every experienced fiction writer and dramatist has marveled at the dramatic unrolling of the events leading up to this climax, as interest and suspense have steadily been driven up to higher levels." So writes W. D. Kennedy, editor of *The Writer* (Boston), a magazine that teaches the art that is practiced by perhaps every fifth one among us. The writer here stops just short of claiming that the ultimate purpose of the Lindbergh flight was to teach fiction writers their business. What he does claim is that "never in modern history has it been so clearly revealed that accident or chance may write a connected story beyond the powers of the imagination of the greatest artist." The order and tempo of the events, we are reminded, have wrung "every last drop of possible dramatic interest, intoxicating the imagination of the world as only once before in the memories of living men: in the World War." "The Lindbergh story stands alone as the supreme news story of modern times." Let us reconstruct it stage by stage.

"The story begins with the offering of a prize of twenty-five thousand dollars for a non-stop trip from New York to Paris. A desultory public interest develops in the plans of various individuals to make the attempt. The difficulties of the flight are suggested in the discussion of experts. Interest begins to rise slightly. Captain Fenck's plane is wrecked and burned at the take-off. Two men die. Two American aviators perish on the test flight in a plane that they were to use in an attempt to make the flight. Then two of the world's greatest aviators take off from Paris. They are lost. Up to this time the real hero has not made his entrance. We are not yet in the body of the story, but the situation is being driven home to the reader slowly, laboriously, painstakingly, and impressively. He is being made to see two things: first, the worth-whileness of the thing that is to be accomplished; and second, the difficulties which must be overcome to accomplish it.

"Why is the flight worth making? The winner will receive twenty-five thousand dollars, but that is only a symbol, as it were, of the real accomplishment of him who succeeds in making the flight. Before the public can be intensely interested, it must be persuaded that there is something much far more than money involved. Yet the larger objective is almost indefinable. The *Journal des Debats* of Paris attempts it: "What is the value of this flight," may be asked by certain obstinate minds.

"Firstly, noble gestures, even seemingly without utility, must always be honored because they are equivalent to works of high art, making for man the finest aspirations and qualities of the race. Lindbergh's feat, in a certain sense, is comparable to a great monument or a great book. It is a masterpiece, deserving admiration. And besides, from the viewpoint of athletics or sport, it is a magnificent record."

"The worth-whileness of the objective, since it is in the higher realms of the imagination, can not [*sic*] be absolutely defined. That gives it its great power over the imagination. Six men have died in futile attempts to accomplish it. We are convinced of the nobility of the objective even tho—perhaps because—it transcends any liberal, commonplace view of the comparative value of life and death.

"Not only is the nobility of the objective brought home to us in the preliminary exposition to the real story, but the forces antagonistic to accomplishment are forcefully portrayed as vast and menacing. They are clearly illustrated in the fate of Nungesser and Coli. Difficulties of the takeoff, the hazards of weather, possible mechanical weakness of the plane, and that greatest of all dangers, arising from human frailty, sleep. Any one [*sic*] who has read the newspapers has now a perfect background for a complete understanding of the action which is to follow.

"Now the minor characters of the drama are shown. A spirit of rivalry develops. Two planes are ready for the hop, one commanded by a man who has been much in the public eye for his flight over the North Pole. Then the hero enters. It is a superb entrance. No one could have planned it better because it could not have been a more complete surprise. He literally drops from the skies, unheralded and unknown, after spanning the continent in two long jumps. The real story begins. But he does not take flight at once—weather interferes. It raises a hindrance to the action. This delay, for curious reasons, heightens rather than lowers the suspense. If he had hopped off the next day, the interest in the outcome would not have been one-tenth as keen. If he had waited too long, it would have flagged. Higher and higher it mounts as the search for the lost Frenchmen emphasizes the power of the opposing forces. During the delay, swiftly, definitely, the hero is characterized. We see his mother, a school-teacher in Detroit. We hear of his past exploits. Four times he has had to jump with a parachute from burning planes. He finds a kitten asleep in his cockpit and adopts it as a mascot, but he will not take it with him because he fears that it will freeze to death. We see his picture and we like his face. His little actions reveal him as silent, modest, independent, and brave. In bold contrast to squabbling and wrangling in a rival camp, he works quietly and alone, saying little as he prepares his plane. There is a beautiful restraint in the action which saves it from melodrama and makes it purely heroic. His mother comes to say good-by, and departs quietly, refusing to kiss him for the newspaper photographers. In all this action building up to the climax, I am reminded of a line from Thoreau, 'The little that is said is eked out by implication of the truth that was done.' The truth is so superbly artistic that even the merest dub of a newspaper reporter can't spoil it. The moving hand of fact is writing surely and gracefully.

"Then the climax, the grand scene. It comes, like the entrance of the hero, a thunder-clap of surprise. Altho we have had reason to expect it, we have not been quite sure. With swift decision he climbs into the cockpit. The machine takes off. Disaster looms for a moment, but he is finally in the air. The last set has begun. The fine, bold figure of Byrd stands there, frustrated in an attempt to convoy him part way. His mother goes on with her work of teaching chemistry. Her children anxiously refrain from mentioning the flight in her hearing. Squabbling goes on among the rivals. The weather clears—but we remember that he has had only two hours of sleep during the night before.

"Bulletins begin to come in. In a few short days an unknown lad has become the hero of the world. His name is on the lips of more people than any under the sun. His face etched in more minds than any living human. The narrative question of the story, 'Will he make it?' is on everybody's lips, from President to beggar."

The "real story" has already been told. "No matter what happens next," says the school-master of fiction, the story is a truly great one. And that, he tells us, "is where so many young writers go wrong":

"If you draw from this the lesson that people like to read about trans-ocean flights for a prize, you have failed to grasp the significance of one of the finest examples of narrative technique that you will ever read. Be honest with yourself. Would you have written the story this way? Would you have dared write with such restraint? Would you have shown so carefully the thing to be accomplished and the opposing forces to accomplishment so clearly and artistically? Would you have made your readers cry aloud for the answer to the narrative question as the world was crying on May 21? Or would you have started your story with the take-off and assumed that the reader would be interested in what happened thereafter just because you were writing the story? When you have proved to yourself why so many people were asking themselves so intensely 'Will he make it?' when Lindbergh took the air, you have learned the first lesson of narrative technique.

"Lindbergh's flight is a perfect example, too, of what most writers need to learn: hold your suspense, make them wait. If it were a matter of a few hours, the public wouldn't have been so intensely interested. But, for two long days, sketchy bulletins kept our suspense alive and drove it steadily to higher levels. Thus, the wild panorama of the happy ending."

For finally, and curiously enough, this story has a "happy ending"—something disdained by the "arty" writer. Make 'em weep, not laugh: that's more artistic. But is it?

"Hundreds who read this are failing to reach the public to which their talents recommend them simply because they hold to this as a sincere belief. To them, I say this: I would not for worlds destroy your artistic standards. But won't you recall and analyze your feelings when you heard that Lindbergh had landed. Did you laugh? Or was there a stinging sensation in your eyes? Would you have been any closer to tears if you had read that he had fallen in flames over the English Channel? No! A thousand times, no! It is in the story itself that artistry lies, not in the ending, and most of all is the part of the story that is written long before Paris rose in her emotional might to acclaim the hero."

Source: "Chance Writes the Lindbergh Saga." *Literary Digest*, June 18, 1927.

Document: From "My Friend Babe Ruth," 1924

For some years I have enjoyed a peculiarly intimate friendship with Babe Ruth. I have traveled with him as a New York newspaperman, lived with him in and out of the baseball season, and helped him write his newspaper articles.

We have developed, totally apart from business relations, a friendship which has thrown us together in a sort of Boswell-Johnson capacity. We have been trainmates and playmates on trips around the big circuit, in the baseball hinterland, and in the obscurity of private life.

To the alternately idolatrous and jeering millions who have watched this modern Beowulf at bat, driving out his smashes, it may have appeared that he was just a thick-skinned ballplayer, schooled to deafness on the field.

The skin of my friend Babe Ruth is not thick. I have seen hundreds of men, women, and hero-worshiping boys get under it. Like me, they discovered that Ruth, in the raw, is as likable as a human being as he is interesting and fascinating as a ball player and psychological study.

For ten years, I have done widely diversified newspaper work in New York, meeting all kinds of characters in and out of sport, on and off Broadway, around and about the country, but never have I met one who has sustained my interest from day to day and year to year as has Babe Ruth.

He has very few secrets from me. And knowing all his faults I am genuinely helpless in my affection for him. In short, I like him and often apologize for him; at other times, it is impossible even to apologize. He is a human being apart from all others of the species. He is more than unique; he is really a phenomenon. And I like him.

What manner of man is that Gargantuan sporting character that only two or three people really know?

Whereto do his private life and private mannerisms, habits, and customs differ from the public impression?

How does he look and act and sum up under the X-ray of close and constant scrutiny?

Mrs. Ruth calls him George, and it is of George Ruth, mainly, that I write, the Ruth that neither the public, nor the newspapermen, nor even his fellow players know.

He has a gruff manner about him. He deals profusely in horse-play. He is something of a physical clown—a good-natured personification of Brute Force. But he is ever so gentle and tender, too. I have seen him in a boxing match with Mrs. Ruth in the room of a Boston hotel at which only one other person and myself were spectators—a match in which he allowed himself to be decisively outpointed and slightly wounded. I have also seen him wrestled to the floor by his blond-haired three-year-old daughter, Dorothy. I myself have tapped him on the head with a golf club without any serious aftermath.

But just as he is a success even when he fails on the baseball field—that is, a sensation and a source of dramatic interest even when he strikes out—so is he equally interesting in Pullman trains and in hotels on the road.

Often he travels with a little portable phonograph and gives concerts in the baggage-rooms of some wayside railroad station while waiting for a train. At such time he will sing bass in a quartet and do quite well indeed with his favorite song, "My Darling Lou," and not as well with others. He has a special fondness for the ukulele and likes to dance. He plays bridge, stud poker, and draw poker the way he hits a baseball—wildly, freely, forcefully; and more often than not he loses.

And How He Does Eat!

He eats as very few men can. He eats often—preferably on an average of ten times a day. Railroad engines consume an enormous amount of fuel.

So does he, and it is a wonder that he manages to survive the amount and sort of food he eats.

He is a little temperamental. He has a deep, abiding suspicion that he always suffers from stomach trouble. Before almost every game he complains to the club trainer about this and then devours huge quantities of bicarbonate of soda. I don't believe there is another human being alive in all the world who has actually eaten so much sod and chewed so much tobacco as Ruth.

He reads very little but is amazingly well informed on baseball statistics. Of all the big-league players I know I don't think there is a one who [possesses] a keener analysis of the records statistics. And I know of no player who is so fundamentally well-liked by his team-mates or is so genuinely considerate of them.

He does not wear underwear, winter or summer. One of his favorite diversions is bull-frog hunting at night with lights attached to the front sites of the rifles. He is immaculately groomed and always has his barbering done in his hotel room. He is manicured frequently and pays high for everything. A Texas barber once charged him $1.80 for a haircut and a few wet towels.

And, as you might expect, he is superstitious. . . .

He does more autographing of souvenirs than probably the ten most pertinent movie stars combined. He writes an enormous number of letters to his fans all over the country, and no "celebrity" ever received such queer requests—from get-rich-quick promoters, than charitable organizations, from strangers who want to share in the richest attribute to him, and from clubs, schools, and churches—asking him to various functions or possibly make a little speech. Incidentally, the Babe is an astonishingly good after-dinner talker. He has perfect poise and presence and a free flow of talk.

Consider his superstitions. The sight of a white or yellow butterfly on the field of play will either terrify him with forebodings of ill luck or exalt him with a plane of ineffable anticipation of assured good fortune on the diamond.

On the road, a few years ago, he pitched to the Yankees at batting practice following the loss of a few important games, and that day the Yankees, then engaged in the thick of a pennant fight, won. The next day and every day thereafter until the Yankees lost again he pitched to the players in batting practice because he was convinced it was lucky.

When they lost he tried warming up the pitcher before the game—for luck—and found that successful. He kept on warming up the pitchers until the Yanks again lost, and then he tried hitting fungoes to the outfield. When all other expedients failed he went out on the coaching lines.

These are his special superstitions; but with Miller Huggins, the Yankee manager, he shares another. If the team wins, he returns to the hotel and goes through the same door that he used on his way out. If it loses he tries another door. And in common with most ball players he believes that a load of empty barrels, seen on the way to the ball park, is a sign of certain victory.

He rarely answers letters but sometimes the thoughts of his correspondents stick out in his mind. Fans tell him he has a right stance or a wrong stance or a bad swing for a curve ball. "I guess," he says, "that most of the baseball scientists sit in the bleachers."

He is solicited by vaudeville agents, who offer attractive tours; . . . by committees of fraternal organizations who want him to appear on the coast in exhibition games. To these requests Babe turns the cold ear of a business man. He'd be foolish if he didn't. An athlete's productive life is short.

But there are innumerable requests to which the Babe does not turn a cold, businesslike ear. They come in shoals. Daily, when the team is at home. Christy Walsh, who syndicates his newspaper articles, carries to the Yankee Stadium loads of balls and bats—all for the bold and legible signature of the recognized Sultan of Swat. Out in Los Angeles there is a high school league. It means something in the lives of the winning team if each member receives as a trophy of victory a bat signed by Babe Ruth.

In Indiana the Knights of Columbus, of which the Babe is a member, are building a school for delinquent boys. Baseballs signed by the Home Run King can be sold to advantage for the home. In Nebraska the Elks, and in Oklahoma the Masons, have similar charities, and balls and bats similarly signed have added market value. Or a ladies' organization desires him to attend a bazarre in some town where he is scheduled to play, and will he make a talk and sign souvenir programs? He will and does, gladly. By mid-July, this year, Ruth had signed eleven hundred bats and three times that number of balls.

Newspaper editors throughout the country use him and his name to stimulate circulation and attract interest in their papers. It is advertised that on such and such a day at a certain time the Babe will throw several dozen autographed baseballs out of a window in the offices of a newspaper, and long before the appointed hour the streets are jammed with thousands of boys and grown-ups eager and ready to scramble for the balls.

Baseball leagues for boys bearing his name are organized by newspapers. Some youngsters in a hospital would like to see and meet the Babe in the flesh; newspapers arrange that, and the Babe is happy to oblige.

And what is the significance of all this? It's this—Babe Ruth to-day is a milestone in the progress of American life—yes, even a vital economic and social force and factor. The Yankee Stadium cost several millions and is appropriately called, "The House That Ruth Built." He has drawn more people to baseball than any player in the history of the game. Everywhere larger ball parks have been built simply because of the interest he has attracted to the game. And baseball salaries have gone up because of him.

No sporting figure has ever received the publicity he has. He is before the public, as a player, one hundred and fifty-four days a year. But there are some stories concerning him that have never been told. The one that follows, told here for the first time, involves the most dramatic moment I have ever shared with the Babe.

It was somewhere in Texas, on the special train in which the Yankees were making their spring training trip north from New Orleans, playing exhibition games en route.

My friend the Babe was suffering from an attack of "The Misery" which was critically and alarmingly acute. "The Misery" is peculiarly a baseball disease. It is a compound of all the ailments known to the ball player. It includes a long and concerous [sic] batting slump and general debility. In short, it is a Terrible Thing.

Physically the Babe was in better shape than he had ever been. He had spent the winter on the farm at Sudbury, Mass., chopping wood, building hen-houses, hunting and plowing through miles of snow-covered roads. He had gone back to nature and to wide open spaces to forget and live down his colossal failure in the world series against the Giants in '22; and he reported for training at New Orleans weighing only 200 pounds—a weight which presumably attuned his tremendous bulk to the celebrated "pink of condition."

The newspaper correspondents with the Yankees said he would have his greatest year. Then The Misery attacked him, feeding at first upon the memory of his failure in the world series and then gnawing at his inability of the moment to hit a baseball with anything approximating his former violence and consistency.

Day after day the Babe went without making a hit; a week passed and he made no homers. Another week of pitiful effort. The king—the Home Run King—was tottering on his throne.

He brooded almost insanely. Huggins diagnosed his condition and case over and over again, and finally arrived at a decision in his drawing-room in the special train in which they were touring the South and Southwest.

The Babe, Huggins, and myself were the only ones in the room.

"Babe," Huggins said, "I want to tell you something. I think you ought to know. I have been in baseball for more than twenty years. I have seen ball players come and go. No man lasts forever. This slump that you have been having is no ordinary thing. I have been trying to figure out what is the matter with you. Apparently you swing the bat the way you used to. Apparently nothing is the matter with your eyes. Physically you're in great shape. But for a month you have looked worse than the bushiest bush-leaguer in the outfit.

"The symptoms are all familiar. There are times when dying men should be told the truth. Babe, I don't like to say it but I think it is best that I should. Babe, you're slipping! You've seen your best days. You're just about through. Make up your mind to it—you're just about *through*!"

A strange, fugitive look came into the Babe's eyes. He did not gasp but his huge body stiffened almost imperceptibly at the shock. He glanced incisively at Huggins. Then, almost savagely he growled, "Hug, you're crazy!"

But the manner in which he spoke indicated he believed that Huggins *might* be right. For several minutes he sat there silently, staring out of the window into the dark shadows of night, alternately puffing on a cigar that was not lit and chewing tobacco.

Huggins said nothing. I said nothing. The situation was funereally oppressive. Babe Ruth—the Home Run King—the greatest and most picturesque figure baseball had ever known—was dying and had been told so! The public, through the news bulletins issued daily by observing and expert baseball writers, knew that the Babe was ailing and had "The Misery," but the public did not know just how seriously indisposed he was. Even the baseball writers themselves didn't know.

The next day the Babe struck out a few times. He acted like a man who had been told he was dying. But he also acted as a man who said over and over again, "I won't die—I won't die—I won't die; I'm not slipping—*I'm not through*." And toward the end of the game, in overwhelming ultimate desperation, he reached out with the big bat for a ball that was wide and high of the plate—virtually a wild pitch—and made one of the longest home runs I have ever seen him hit. He caught the ball two or three inches from the end of his bat, swung the full force of his great shoulders and back behind it and drove the ball high and far above and beyond the roof of the distant bleachers—accomplishing a feat which had never even been approximated before. That home run was oxygen to the dying Home Run King.

In 1921 the Babe made his record of fifty-nine home runs. Every baseball fan in the country followed the sensational composition of his record from day to day. Newspapers in tiny, obscure towns carried telegraphic, ball-by-ball descriptions of his turns at bat, at great expense. Millions and millions of words were written about him. . . . He was becoming a Great American Idol, followed everywhere by crowds, worshiped by boys and besieged by all kinds of promoters and schemers.

One day Huggins went to him and said, "Babe, you've got this country goofy. You're drawing the biggest crowds that ever went to baseball games. You have been doing some things you shouldn't do—things that other players do not do. So long as you keep doing well I don't mind. But that isn't the point. I'm thinking now of you. You're fat. You have been keeping bad hours. All this success may spoil you, turn your head and ruin your career when it's just starting. Let's get organized right, Babe. Cut out the fast living. Go to bed early. Be careful of what you eat and drink. Take off twenty-five pounds and you'll get more base hits; your eye will be clearer: you'll get more home runs. You'll do better every way. What do you say?"

That night the Babe went to bed at nine o'clock. The next day he failed to get a home run, to say nothing of a measly little ordinary base hit. But again he went to bed early, and once more he had the same experience. He did this twice again, with the same result, and finally he exploded. For a greater love of home runs and base hits hath no baseball player; and the Babe could not tolerate an abstinence from them.

Ping Bodie, his room-mate, came to me in Detroit and said, "Come on. We're going out. The Babe is in an uproar. The panic is on." So out we went. Then we came back and played cards all night. Virtue alone was not a satisfying reward. The Babe simply could not sleep.

In between he ate probably fourteen sirloin and hamburger steak sandwiches, with some odds and ends thrown in. And I know it to be absolute fact that he did not get more than two hours' sleep. But what happened?

What happened illustrates precisely the utter freakishness of the man. Where for four days he had gone to bed early and gone hitless and home-runless he now went to the ball park visibly affected by the change of habit and drove out two home runs in one game—one of them over the scoreboard in deepest center field; something that had never been done before!

That fall he defied Judge Landis and was suspended for the first six weeks of the 1922 season. But in the intervening months and until the end of the year he earned about $250,000—and spent most of it.

He went to the race tracks and gambled high, betting as much as $26,000 on a single race. In Cuba, following a disastrous experience with book-makers, he found himself about "broke" and in an awkward situation. He owed $65,000 to the racetrack hawks and vultures. He had transportation for himself and Mrs. Ruth back to the States but he had that obligation of $65,000 to take care of, and what little money he had left was tied up in investments which Mrs. Ruth had made for him.

Finally he was compelled to take Mrs. Ruth into his confidence. "We'll have to cancel our passage," he said, "until I can dig up that sixty-five grand."

But they did nothing of the kind. Mrs. Ruth calls the Babe "Hon".

"Hon," she said, "here's a check for $65,000. Go out and pay your debts."

And the Babe did, after an almost miraculous recovery from the shock of discovering his wife had somehow managed to save $65,000 from the wild wreckage of his first year's great successes. And since then Babe Ruth has learned many things—and failed to learn a few others.

It was necessary, following this, to protect him from himself and the attacks of the army of confidence men and women which constantly intrigued against him. So detectives employed by the Yankee owners and by the powers that be in baseball began to watch him and those who insinuated themselves upon him.

But that—as they say—is another story, spun of the fabric of an old-fashioned dime novel and equally as thrilling in its melodramatic developments.

Source: Arthur Robinson, "My Friend Babe Ruth." *Collier's*, September 26, 1924.

Suggested Readings

Batchelor, Bob. *Gatsby. The Cultural History of a Great American Novel*. Lanham, MD: Rowman & Littlefield, 2014.

Behr, Edward. *Prohibition. Thirteen Years That Changed America*. New York: Arcade, 1996.

Bruccoli, Matthew J., ed. *New Essays on* The Great Gatsby. Cambridge: Cambridge University Press, 1985.

Callahan, John F. *The Illusions of a Nation: Myth and History in the Novels of F. Scott Fitzgerald*. Urbana: University of Illinois Press, 1972.

Churchwell, Sarah. *Careless People. Murder, Mayhem, and the Invention of* The Great Gatsby. New York: Penguin Press, 2014.

Corrigan, Maureen. *So We Read On: How* The Great Gatsby *Came to Be and Why It Endures*. New York: Little, Brown and Company, 2014.

Cowley, Malcolm, and Robert Cowley, eds. *Fitzgerald and the Jazz Age*. New York: Charles Scribner's Sons, 1966.

Curnutt, Kirk, ed. *A Historical Guide to F. Scott Fitzgerald*. Oxford and New York: Oxford University Press, 2004.

Donaldson, Scott, ed. *Critical Essays on F. Scott Fitzgerald's* The Great Gatsby. Boston: G. K. Hall, 1984.

Donaldson, Scott, ed. *Fool for Love*. New York: Congdon & Weed, 1983.

Drowne, Kathleen. *Spirits of Defiance: National Prohibition and Jazz Age Literature, 1920–1933*. Columbus: Ohio State University Press, 2005.

Dumenil, Lynn. *The Modern Temper: American Culture and Society in the 1920s*. New York: Hill and Wang, 1995.

F. Scott Fitzgerald: In His Own Time: A Miscellany. Eds. Matthew J. Bruccoli and Jackson R. Bryer. Kent, OH: Kent State University Press, 1971.

Fitzgerald, F. Scott. *The Great Gatsby*. New York: Charles Scribner's Sons, 1925; Scribner Paperback Fiction, 1995.

Fryer, Sarah Beebe. *Fitzgerald's New Women. Harbingers of Change*. Ann Arbor and London: UMI Research Press, 1988.

Gray, W. Russel. "Corinthian Crooks Are Not Like You and Me: Mystery, Detection and Crime in *The Great Gatsby*." *Clues* 16(1995): 35–45.

Latham, Aaron. *Crazy Sundays: F. Scott Fitzgerald in Hollywood*. New York: Viking, 1971.

Leuders, Edward. "Revisiting Babylon: Fitzgerald and the 1920s." *Western Humanities Review* 29(1975): 285–291.

Lewis, R. W. B. *The American Adam. Innocence, Tragedy, and Tradition in the Nineteenth-Century*. 1955. Chicago and London: University of Chicago Press, 1968.

Long, Robert Emmet. *The Achieving of "The Great Gatsby": F. Scott Fitzgerald, 1920–1925*. Lewisburg, PA: Bucknell University Press, 1979.

Mackrell, Judith. *Flappers: Six Women of a Dangerous Generation*. New York: Sarah Crichton Books. Farrar, Straus and Giroux, 2013.

Mangum, Bryant, ed. *F. Scott Fitzgerald in Context*. Cambridge: Cambridge University Press, 2013.

Mayfield, Sara. *Exiles from Paradise: Scott and Zelda Fitzgerald*. New York: Delacorte Press, 1971.

Mellow, James R. *Invented Lives: F. Scott and Zelda Fitzgerald*. New York: Ballantine Books, 1984.

Meyers, Jeffrey. *Scott Fitzgerald: A Biography*. New York: HarperCollins, 1994.

Okrent, Daniel. *Last Call: The Rise and Fall of Prohibition*. New York: Scribner, 2010.

Pelzer, Linda C. *Student Companion to F. Scott Fitzgerald*. Westport, CT: Greenwood Press, 2000.

Piper, Henry Dan. *F. Scott Fitzgerald: A Critical Portrait*. New York: Holt, 1965.

Simmons, W. J. *ABC of the Invisible Empire*. Atlanta: Knights of the Ku Klux Klan, 1917.

Sklar, Robert. *F. Scott Fitzgerald: The Last Laocoön*. New York: Oxford University Press, 1967.

Stern, Milton. *The Golden Moment: The Novels of F. Scott Fitzgerald*. Urbana: University of Illinois Press, 1970.

Turnbull, Andrew. *Scott Fitzgerald*. New York: Charles Scribner's Sons, 1962.

Weston, Elizabeth A. *The International Theme in F. Scott Fitzgerald's Literature*. New York: Peter Lang, 1995.

Whitley, John S. "'A Touch of Disaster': Fitzgerald, Spengler, and the Decline of the West." In *Scott Fitzgerald: The Promises of Life*. Ed. Robert A. Lee. New York: St. Martin's, 1989: 157–180.

3

Gentlemen Prefer Blondes (Anita Loos, 1925)

SYNOPSIS OF *GENTLEMEN PREFER BLONDES*

Lorelei Lee's "Illuminating Diary," as it claims to be in the subtitle to *Gentlemen Prefer Blondes*, bears all the hallmarks of that form: misspellings and grammatical errors, uncensored opinions and observations, personal revelations, and unself-conscious voice. Lorelei tells her reader that she is recording the details of her life because a male friend had suggested that her thoughts would make for lively reading. In *Gentlemen Prefer Blondes*, Lorelei certainly delivers on that expectation.

As the novel begins, Lorelei is living comfortably in New York City, in an apartment for which Mr. Gus Eisman, a button manufacturer from Chicago, pays the rent. When she met "the Button King," Lorelei had been working in the movies in Hollywood, but he insisted that Hollywood was no place for a "girl like I" and moved her across country where he could visit whenever he was in town to "educate" her. He spends a fortune keeping her in gowns and jewelry and flowers and taking her to dinner at the Ritz and lively parties. During one of his many absences, Lorelei meets an English novelist, Gerald Lamson, who disapproves of her relationship with Eisman. He, too, plans to "educate" the young woman and, much to her disappointment, sends a gift of books rather than the diamonds that she prefers. He also promises to marry her after he secures a divorce from his wife. Fearing the scandal that would be attached to her reputation if she were to marry Gerry (who rather bores her) and reluctant to deny herself the pleasure of the trip to Europe that Mr. Eisman has promised her, Lorelei packs her bags for the Continent and sets off for adventure with her friend Dorothy.

Aboard the ocean liner *Majestic*, Lorelei encounters a gentleman from her past and is soon confiding her secrets to the sympathetic Major Falcon, who, like all her male acquaintances, has taken great interest in her. Lorelei confesses that when she was a girl in Arkansas, her father had sent her to secretarial school in Little Rock, where a lawyer offered her a position even before she had completed her course of study. One evening when she went to "pay a call" on him at his apartment, she found another woman visiting. When she awoke from a fit of hysterics prompted by the shock, she discovered that she had shot her employer with her tiny revolver. In court, the jury of twelve men, moved by her story of betrayal, quickly acquitted her of all charges, but the judge suggested that she might want to begin again in Hollywood, where her talents might be better suited. He also supplied her with her screen name. Until she met Mr. Eisman, Lorelei seemed destined for stardom.

Docking in England, Lorelei and Dorothy make their way to London, where their European adventure begins. There they tour the historic city, which fails to impress them, and meet members of the aristocracy, who seem to be selling their family jewels to wealthy Americans, as well as the Prince of Wales, to whom Dorothy teaches some American slang. When she meets Mrs. Weeks, Lorelei determines that she simply must have the diamond tiara that this aristocratic woman is selling for ten thousand pounds and casts her eye about the room for a wealthy gentleman who will purchase it for her. Settling on Sir Francis Beekman, whom she calls "Piggie," Lorelei, who has been warned that he is a miser, musters all her charms to flatter the old man into buying it for her. She then sets sail for Paris, the next stop on her grand tour.

Lorelei finds Paris "devine" and is especially impressed with Coty, Cartier, and the "Eyeful" Tower, but the French viscount with whom she spends her time and who spends hardly any money on her leads Lorelei to conclude that a kiss on the hand may make her feel special but a diamond tiara lasts forever. Her tiara, however, is suddenly in jeopardy, for the wife of Sir Francis, having learned that her husband purchased the object for

Lorelei, descends on her rival to demand its return. After all, Sir Francis had never, in thirty-five years of marriage, given her such a gift, indeed had never given her any gifts. The next morning, Lady Beekman's lawyer, Robert Broussard, bursts into Lorelei's room and rants at her and Dorothy in French. Through a French waiter who speaks English, the women learn that the Broussards, father and son, Louis, plan to show them the sights of Paris, charging the expenses to Lady Beekman, while awaiting an opportunity to steal the tiara for their employer. They visit the Fontainebleau, the Folies Bergère, and the Palace of Versailles. Meanwhile Lorelei orders a paste copy of the tiara and manages to keep the real one by outmaneuvering them all.

After Mr. Eisman joins Lorelei and Dorothy in Paris (and Lorelei finally makes those shopping trips that have been the true objective of her visit), he books the travelers on the Orient Express for Vienna, where they will meet him again. On the journey, Lorelei meets Henry Spofford, who hails from one of the most prestigious and wealthy families in Philadelphia. Spofford, a staunch Presbyterian and prohibitionist, spends his days watching the moving pictures in order to censor everything objectionable in them—and he finds much that is objectionable. Because Lorelei is trying to reform Dorothy, whose bad habits include taking an interest in the wrong sort of men (because they lack the resources to treat her lavishly), she feels a connection with the reformist Spofford, who takes an interest in her.

After a brief stop in Munich, Lorelei, who is unimpressed by the city's cultural attractions and disgusted by the Germans' eating habits, arrives in Vienna, where, at Spofford's request, she visits "Dr. Froyd"—Sigmund Freud—who advises her to cultivate some inhibitions because she has none. At the Demel Restaurant, Lorelei sees Henry's mother with her companion Miss Chapman, who is cautioning her about Lorelei's influence on her son. Fearing that Mrs. Spofford's disapproval might cause Henry to end their relationship, Lorelei tells him the story of her past, casting it much like a Puritan spiritual autobiography of reform and redemption and moving Henry to tears. He subsequently arranges a meeting with his mother, and by its end, Lorelei has her drinking champagne and has cut her hair into a fashionable bob.

In Budapest, the final stop on her grand tour with Mr. Eisman, Lorelei receives a letter from Henry proposing marriage. Although she is not attracted to him, she is fully aware of his wealth, so she agrees to the proposal (although she can barely conceal her disappointment with the engagement ring—his college ring—that he presents her on her arrival in New York). Now, of course, Lorelei feels that she must make her debut into polite society, so she hosts a debutante ball that lasts for three days. Among the guests are society sports club members as well as bootleggers, and the rowdy celebration even leads to police intervention.

Still uncertain about the marriage, Lorelei goes on a shopping spree, charging all her expenses to Henry, to discourage his love. She also meets a movie scenario writer, Gilbertson Montrose, who rekindles her interest in Hollywood. Plotting her escape, Lorelei enlists Dorothy's help: she convinces her friend to fill Henry's mind with all sorts of lies about Lorelei—that she intends to purchase the Russian crown jewels, that her family has a history of mental illness, that her extravagance knows no bounds. Meanwhile, Montrose is devastated to discover her ploy because, he tells her, he had hoped that Henry would finance his new movie—in which he intended Lorelei to star. Determined now to marry Henry but fearing that she has ruined her chance, Lorelei rushes to Penn Station and tells him that Dorothy's stories were false, that the jewels she purchased were paste, and that everything had been a test of his love and devotion, which he had failed. A remorseful Henry vows to marry Lorelei and to finance Montrose's movie, and the novel ends with Lorelei achieving all her desires by confessing that she has only ever wanted to make others happy.

HISTORICAL BACKGROUND: *GENTLEMEN PREFER BLONDES* AND THE GENDER POLITICS OF THE JAZZ AGE

In 1924, as Anita Loos was traveling aboard the *Santa Fé Chief* from New York to Los Angeles with a party of coworkers in the film industry, she found herself pondering the reason that one of the group, a young woman no more attractive than she, no older than she, and certainly no more intelligent than she, should have been "waited on, catered to and cajoled by the entire male assemblage" while she, who was clearly more petite than the other young woman, "was allowed to lug heavy suitcases from their racks" by her oblivious male travelling companions (Loos xxxvii). Their only difference, she determined, was their hair color: Loos was a brunette, the young woman a blonde. "Could her strength," she wondered, "be rooted (like that of Samson) in her hair?" (xxxvii–xxxviii). Her conclusion, she thought as she considered her various blonde acquaintances, would certainly explain another anomaly: how "one of the keenest minds of our era—H.L. Mencken"—could have been "bewitched" by "the dumbest blonde of all" (xxxviii). Taking up pen and paper, Loos began to write the sketches that some months later, and at the bemused urging of Mencken himself, would be published serially in *Harper's Bazaar* and then, as *Gentlemen Prefer Blondes: The Illuminating Diary of a Professional Lady*, become the surprise best-seller of 1925.

Lorelei Lee's diary, complete with misspellings and grammatical errors, was a hit not only with readers of popular fiction but also with the era's literary lions. Edith Wharton called *Gentlemen Prefer Blondes* "the great American novel," and William Faulkner wrote to Loos, "I wish I had thought of Dorothy first" (Carey 108). His eyesight failing, the Irish novelist James Joyce, Loos was told, had selected *Gentlemen Prefer Blondes* as one of the few current novels he would read (Carey 98).

H. L. Mencken (1880–1956), American journalist, satirist, cultural critic, and publisher, was known as "the sage of Baltimore." His infatuation with a "dumb blonde" prompted Anita Loos to write *Gentlemen Prefer Blondes*. (Bettmann/Corbis)

She may have been little more than a caricature, but Lorelei, as well as her friend Dorothy, had clearly exposed truths about the era, especially about its gender politics, that resonated with its readers. In a novel filled with topical references that made it thoroughly modern, they helped fashion the image of the Jazz Age flapper, who was herself thoroughly modern. Indeed, these irreverent good-time girls, who are far more astute than anyone suspects, are in process of dismantling the world that made them.

Against the backdrop of the Jazz Age's inherent contradictions, Lorelei Lee determines to make a place for herself in a society where her class and her gender put her at a distinct disadvantage. Born and raised in Arkansas, the state that Mencken had proclaimed "the Sahara of the Beaux Arts"— and which he spelled *Bozarts* (Loos xl), Mabel Minnow, who has little but her blonde good looks to recommend her, is attending business college in Little Rock at her father's insistence because he "did not like a gentleman who used to pay calls on me in the park" (*Blondes* 24). A week after she begins her course, a lawyer, Mr. Jennings, offers to employ her. One evening about a year later, when Mabel "went to pay a call on him at his apartment" (24) and finds a notorious young woman visiting already, she realizes that Mr. Jennings is not a nice man, falls into a trance, and, when she recovers her senses, discovers that she has shot him. Three minutes after the jury begins deliberations at her trial, the men, all of whom had been reduced to tears by her sad tale of betrayal by a sexual predator, acquit her of any crime, after which the judge gives her a name, Lorelei, that suits her personality (26) and purchases a ticket to Hollywood for her.

"A girl like I," (93), as Lorelei would say, should never have managed to marry into a prominent Philadelphia "Prespyterian" family. After all, she is woefully undereducated, entirely without inhibitions, as "Dr. Froyd" tells her after a consultation in Vienna, and, as the references to her male acquaintances imply, of questionable morality. Focused almost entirely on having a good time and acquiring the diamonds and emeralds that truly make a girl feel appreciated, Lorelei is hardly the type who belongs in the Social Register, and yet as she knows, and proves time and again, the society people on the list are no different from her. Indeed, at the conclusion to *But Gentlemen Marry Brunettes*, Loos's 1928 sequel to *Gentlemen Prefer Blondes* that continues Lorelei's adventures and relates Dorothy's story, the audacious heroine observes, "I really believe that I shall be the next one to get into the Social Register, because the way they are having to put Society people out of it, somebody or other has got to take their place, and it will probably be me. And when I get in, I am going to try to get Dorothy in to" (*Brunettes* 243). In an era of excess, when manners and mores were in flux, when men had too much money and too much time, when women were in process of change, when Prohibition had demolished class and race and gender barriers, Lorelei was essentially an agent of change. As she and Dorothy expose the hypocrisy, the pretentiousness, the vapidity and ennui of a class that believes not only in its own entitlement but also in others' insignificance, they make their presence felt, using their female charms to achieve the power denied them by a social and economic system based on patriarchal authority. After all, men who can so easily be manipulated by "a girl like I" are far less powerful than they believe themselves to be.

Loos's satire of the Jazz Age cuts deep and wide. From the men who are willing and eager to educate Lorelei to the women who are quick to condemn her, from Britain's aristocracy to America's patricians, from intellectuals to the purveyors of popular culture, nobody is immune to Lorelei's charms, nor is anyone or anything exempt from her unique perspective, which her life on the periphery of polite society has shaped. Moreover, because everyone thinks he knows her or sees in her what he wants to see, because she is, in other words, a "dumb blonde" or a "gold-digger" or a "flapper," a stereotype rather than a person to those who rotate into her orbit, everyone underestimates her nature and misconstrues her actions. Consequently, she is the perfect vehicle for delivering Loos's barbed humor, for nobody suspects that she sees so clearly the true nature of her world.

In her introduction to a 1963 edition of *Gentlemen Prefer Blondes*, Anita Loos confessed, "I have always considered grown-ups to be figures of fun, as children generally do, and have never been deceived by their hypocrisies" (xxxviii). Neither was her greatest creation, Lorelei Lee, whose philosophy of life was "Smile, smile, smile" (27). And whereas her contemporaries, she noted, such as Sherwood Anderson, Theodore Dreiser, William Faulkner, and Ernest Hemingway, would have been provoked to "massive indignation" by Lorelei's world while F. Scott Fitzgerald would have "shed bittersweet tears over such sad eventualities" (xxxix), both Loos and Lorelei find nothing but foolishness. As women, after all, who have always been marginalized, they harbor no illusions about the social order. These different responses speak to the gender politics of the Jazz Age that provide the foundation of *Gentlemen Prefer Blondes*.

ABOUT ANITA LOOS: A LIFE IN WORDS AND (MOTION) PICTURES

Like Lorelei Lee, her most famous creation, Anita Loos understood the temper of her times and expressed it with disarming candor. Indeed, the respected screenwriter, best-selling novelist, and talented playwright, who proclaimed that "gentlemen prefer blondes" and advised those gentlemen that "kissing [a girl's] hand may make [her] feel very very good but a diamond and safire bracelet lasts forever" (55), was, like her heroine, the embodiment of the Jazz Age flapper, and she remained thoroughly modern throughout her long life. When she died, in fact, at the age of ninety-three, on August 18, 1981, Loos, a born storyteller and acerbic wit who could not be deceived by celebrity and social pretense, had not yet become irrelevant, as the full-page obituary published in the *New York Times* testified. Hers was a life in words and motion pictures

Looking every bit the flapper, novelist, screenwriter, and playwright Anita Loos poses on the ship *Olympic* on November 2, 1929. (AP Photo)

that epitomized as well as revolutionized an era's popular culture. Without Loos, the Jazz Age would certainly have been without some of its roar.

Corinne Anita Loos was born in April 1888 at her maternal grandparents' home in Etna, California, to a charming ne'er-do-well dreamer, R. Beers Loos, and Minnie Smith, the daughter of a successful cattle rancher. Four years later, the family, which included Loos's elder brother Clifford and younger sister Gladys, moved to San Francisco, the city that Loos would always consider her hometown. When R. Beers, as he was known, failed to make a success of the tabloid paper of which he was editor, Minnie sold the family home she had purchased with an inheritance from her father, and the family settled in San Diego, where R. Beers managed a vaudeville theater (when he was not carousing with friends on "fishing trips" to a neighboring town, on one of which eight-year-old Gladys died of appendicitis and was buried before his return). An adoring Loos loved her father despite his shortcomings and was pleased to please him by going on stage in San Francisco as a young girl to help pay the rent and winning the audience's applause. Had she known that she was establishing a pattern for her relationships with men, Loos might have been less eager to please.

The motion picture industry was in its infancy at the turn of the twentieth century, but it had already captured the interest of the clever young woman who had grown up watching the one-reel films that were screened between the live acts at the San Diego theater her father managed. Convinced that she could invent story lines for these films, Loos sent several story ideas to the Biograph Company, whose films she judged superior to those produced by other companies, and on October 1, 1912, she received a check for $25 in payment for her story "The New York Hat." It was the first of more than fifty scenarios that she would sell to the production companies during the next two years from her San Diego home. Those stories quickly captured the attention of D. W. Griffith, one of the most innovative directors in film history, and within a year of that first sale, Loos had become one of his favorite writers.

In January 1914, when the head of Biograph's story department invited her to meet him in Los Angeles, Loos's mother reluctantly accompanied her daughter to the interview, but convinced that a movie set was no place for a respectable young woman, she insisted they return home. A disappointed but determined Loos was soon plotting her escape. A year later, she married Frank Palloma, a poor, but fun-loving musician. Six weeks later, she left him. With that marriage, however, she had secured the freedom to move to Los Angeles (with her mother as chaperone) to accept Griffith's offer of $75 a week to write for Fine Arts-Triangle productions. For the next three years, Loos wrote stories that helped make filmmaking the major industry in Los Angeles and created stars of Douglas Fairbanks and Constance Talmadge. In fact, in a Hollywood career that spanned nearly three decades and included stints writing for Metro-Goldwyn-Mayer (MGM), United Artists, and Twentieth-Century Fox as well as for stars of the silent screen, including Marion Davies and Billie Burke, and the "talkies," including Jean Harlow, Clark Gable, and Spencer Tracy, Rosalind Russell, Myrna Loy, Joan Crawford, and Greer Garson, Anita earned a reputation for writing hits.

Professional success, however, did not bring Loos the rewards of a happy home life, for like her mother, she loved unwisely, marrying a man who, rather ironically, was every bit the gold digger that Lorelei Lee would be. She met that man, John Emerson, a Broadway actor who had moved to Hollywood to direct films, in 1916, after returning from the New York premier of Griffith's film *Intolerance*, on which she had assisted. They were soon collaborating on film projects and then Broadway productions. The tenor of their relationship, however, was perhaps established with their first joint effort, a production of *Macbeth*, the alleged credit line of which, "directed by John Emerson and written by William Shakespeare and Anita Loos," was a source of embarrassment throughout the writer's life. Emerson, fourteen years older than Loos, lacked his wife's talent but not her ambition. He was soon adding his name as cowriter of Loos's scripts and then taking top billing, to which the successful author did not object. As Loos's reputation grew, however, Emerson assumed increasing control of her life, losing his voice for a year, which required a staged operation to cure the condition and prompted Loos to retire from writing at the height of her success to care for him, putting all of her earnings, most of which he lost in bad investments, in his name, from which he gave her an allowance, and finally attempting to strangle her, which led to his institutionalization for schizophrenia in an exclusive sanatorium. Unable, perhaps because she was unwilling, to divorce him, Loos worked constantly to support the man who betrayed her love and lived alone much of her life. Her sadness she hid beneath the veneer of sophistication and in the comic satire of her best creations.

Those creations were not reserved for the silver screen. In 1924, on a train traveling West from New York, where her first successful Broadway production had been mounted, Loos began writing the novel that would both delight and scandalize her Jazz Age audience, *Gentlemen Prefer Blondes*. Serialized in *Harper's Bazarre* and published in 1925, the novel was a huge best seller, going into nine editions in less than six months. In 1926, a Broadway adaptation of the novel achieved moderate success and prepared the way for the novel's sequel, *But Gentlemen Marry Brunettes* (1928), which was also adapted for the stage, under the title *The Social Register*. In 1948, a year after settling permanently in New York, Loos began work on a musical adaptation of *Gentlemen Prefer Blondes*, starring an unknown actress, Carol Channing, that reignited the writer's popularity (and made a star of its lead). Broadway adaptations of two novels by the French author Colette, *Gigi* and *Chéri*, as well as publication of a third, less successful, novel, *A Mouse Is Born* (1950), occupied Loos's talents during the 1950s. Then the writer, now in her seventies, who continued her habit of writing daily, turned her attention to her memoirs, publishing three well-received volumes, *A Girl Like I* (1966), *Kiss Hollywood Good-by* (1969), and *A Cast of Thousands* (1977), that brought Hollywood and Broadway to life for fans of stage and screen. Their publication also put Loos back in the spotlight, leading to retrospectives of her films and invitations to fashionable parties.

When Loos died of a heart attack on August 18, 1981, those who eulogized her at a memorial service a week later, including the actresses Helen Hayes, Lillian Gish, and Ruth Gordon and producers Josh Logan, Leo Lerman, and Morton Gottlieb, recalled the fun-loving, extraordinarily chic writer whose interest in gossip helped her track the pulse of her times. Indeed, as Lerman reminded the mourners, "She just loved gold diggers. . . . We all know that Anita was really the Dorothy [rather than the Lorelei] kind, always thinking of a good time. She knew the argot of these people, she knew how they talked in the twenties, she knew how they talked in the thirties, she followed their progress and she roared with laughter" (Loos, *Rediscovered* 270). She was, as Gottlieb observed, "one of the great philosophers of the mores" (Loos, *Rediscovered* 266), and *Gentlemen Prefer Blondes*, her stellar achievement, encapsulated not only a time but also life.

WHY WE READ *GENTLEMEN PREFER BLONDES*

Since 1925, when Anita Loos unleashed her gold-digging heroine into the public sphere, Lorelei Lee has captured the popular imagination. Interpreted and reinterpreted for stage and screen by actresses as varied as Ruth Taylor, in the now-lost 1928 silent film; Carol Channing, in the 1929 stage musical; and Marilyn Monroe, in the 1953 film version of the stage hit, Lorelei continues to captivate audiences and even to spawn tributes by pop singers such as Madonna and Kylie Minogue to Monroe's iconic performance of the show-stopping musical number "Diamonds Are a Girl's Best Friend." Perhaps it is her curious combination of guileless cunning and sheer exuberance that makes her so appealing. Perhaps it is her spunk, her spirited independence and bold determination to meet the world on her terms. In the early twentieth century, she would have been a revolutionary, challenging traditional notions of femininity and the role and place of women in society. In the twenty-first century, she may still be a subversive figure, joyously disrupting a world of patriarchal power and privilege

Testament to the long-lived appeal of *Gentlemen Prefer Blondes*, the actress Marilyn Monroe played Lorelei Lee in the 1953 film adaptation of Loos's novel. (Sunset Boulevard/Corbis)

that three waves of the feminist movement as well as legislative reforms and generational shifts in attitudes and practices have yet to dislodge. While *Gentlemen Prefer Blondes*, in other words, may open a door into the gender politics of the Jazz Age, it speaks still to the subject in a post-feminist age.

As a bold and audacious flapper, Lorelei Lee is at the forefront of social and cultural change during the Jazz Age, but everywhere she faces formidable challenges from men—and women—whose security she threatens to disrupt. The men in her world, even the most lowly, such as Gus Eisman, the button salesman, wield a power and privilege of which she can only dream, and all of them seem to know what is best for her. Judge Hibbard, for instance, who purchases her ticket to Hollywood following her acquittal for shooting Mr. Jennings, names her Lorelei, as if bringing her into being, and Mr. Jennings, like Mr. Eisman, is merely the first in a series of men who wish to "educate" the young woman. This trope implies that she is ignorant and incapable of thinking for herself when in fact their efforts are focused on controlling their pupil and their lessons on benefiting themselves, not on improving Lorelei. Even Mr. Eisman's generous gift of a grand tour of Europe (one of the most humorous and subversive episodes in the novel) is primarily intended to keep Lorelei from being seduced by another man during his summer business trip to Paris, no matter how often he reminds her that nothing is "so educational as traveling" (11).

In this patriarchal world of power and privilege, Lorelei (and indeed all women, the reason for their resistance to her) is dependent on men for her economic survival, a fact that this "dumb blonde" fully understands. Lorelei, in other words, is not in need of any tutorials on life. Indeed, she understands men far better than they understand women. She knows, for instance, that even an intellectual such as the writer Gerald Lamson, who sends Lorelei a set of books by the English author Joseph Conrad for a birthday present, "does not like a girl to be nothing else but a doll, but he likes her to bring in her husband's slippers every evening and make him forget what he has gone through" (10). She knows as well techniques for getting a proper diamond from Mr. Eisman after he disappoints her on her birthday with a gem "you could hardly see" (7) and for securing first a dozen orchids a day and then a diamond tiara from an English lord notorious for not opening his wallet (46). Lorelei knows that women are marginalized and exploited by patriarchal power, that, as she puts it, "a gentleman never pays for those things [his indiscretions] but a girl always pays" (32). So in a reversal of tactics, she exploits men, wielding the power that comes of her helplessness, her submissiveness, her beauty, of all the traditional characteristics of femininity, to achieve her goals. Lorelei, in other words, is exactly what men have made her, what patriarchal culture has asked her to be.

Loos's tactic for exposing the truth about gender during the Jazz Age is humor. Her irreverent heroine, for example, simply scoffs at the inequities and the expectations that should define and confine her life and uses them to her advantage, and because nothing about her is mean spirited and her worldview seems so guileless, readers applaud her success when they might just as easily condemn her actions. Loos also subverts some traditional conventions to subvert her Jazz Age world. In previous centuries, for example, Lorelei would represent the fallen woman, and her transgressions would, indeed must, end in punishment, usually death. Lorelei, however, manages to redeem her reputation to marry a wealthy man devoted to censuring behavior such as hers, and by the novel's end, she is breathing life into the staid (and nearly moribund) Spoffords of Philadelphia, effectively engineering a generational shift from the nineteenth century to the twentieth century. Loos similarly subverts the traditional Grand Tour of Europe during which upper-class Englishmen put the finish on their education in the eighteenth and nineteenth centuries when she sends Lorelei to tour the great European capitals. Unimpressed by London and Munich, Vienna and Budapest, Lorelei finds only Paris, the European city synonymous with Modernism and to which America's Lost Generation had decamped, worthy of real delight. It is, after all, home to Coty and Cartier. Indeed, she rhapsodizes to Dorothy, if they turn their backs on a monument standing in the middle of the "Place Vandome," they can see "none other than Coty's sign." "Does it not really give you a thrill," she asks her companion, "to realize that that is the historical spot where Mr. Coty makes all the perfume?" (52–53). To Lorelei, the Old World is different from the New only in the matter of degree, and from her perspective, American gentlemen are far more worthy of the name than European. They certainly do not require as much educating.

Through the narrative strategies of *Gentlemen Prefer Blondes*, Anita Loos slyly reveals fundamental truths about gender in her Jazz Age world, truths that resonate still for a twenty-first-century audience. Despite the opportunities open to them, opportunities denied to Lorelei, contemporary women still contend with the power and privileges of a patriarchal system. They encounter inequities and barriers rooted in chauvinistic attitudes and practices. They earn less than men for equal or comparable work and shoulder more than their share of homemaking and childcare. Like Lorelei, they learn early to conform to unrealistic standards of beauty and hypocritical codes of behavior. Ninety years after the publication of *Gentlemen Prefer Blondes*, so much has changed, but so much remains the same. Therein lies one of the reasons for its enduring appeal—that and Lorelei Lee.

HISTORICAL EXPLORATIONS OF *GENTLEMEN PREFER BLONDES*

When Lorelei Lee, the irreverent and subversive heroine of Anita Loos's classic *Gentlemen Prefer Blondes*, captured the public's attention in 1925, the Jazz Age was in full swing. Prohibition, the noble experiment, was in process of failure as bootleggers and rumrunners, bathtub gin and moonshine, speakeasies and "drug stores," indeed a whole new industry devoted to the manufacture, distribution, and enjoyment of intoxicating liquors, developed in response to the public's demand for illegal alcohol. Hot jazz and even hotter clubs and cabarets where patrons could cut loose to the latest dance crazes, such as the Charleston and the Shimmy, were all the rage, and motion pictures and radio were redefining entertainment. Flappers were bobbing their hair and shortening their skirts as if to proclaim in outrageous style their liberation from stifling traditions. Indeed, everyone, everything, everywhere seemed to be on the move, including Lorelei Lee, whose ambition leads her from the cultural desert of Little Rock, Arkansas, to Hollywood, New York, the great cities of Europe (where she realizes that "the most delightful thing about traveling is to always be running into Americans and to always feel at home" [33]), and finally to marriage in Philadelphia. Lorelei's exuberant excess captured the spirit of the Roaring Twenties just as Loos's novel captured its cultural realities, and thus *Gentlemen Prefer Blondes*, a novel that could only have been written during the 1920s, delivered its satiric punch.

At the heart of *Gentlemen Prefer Blondes* is Lorelei Lee, the embodiment of the era's new woman, a flapper, and, as such, a cultural icon. With her close-fitting felt cloche pulled down over her short, blonde hair and her boyish silhouette, she certainly looked the part Loos intended her to play, and the novel's illustrations, by Ralph Barton, reinforced the image. Lorelei, her mouth a perfect bow, her wide eyes most probably outlined in kohl, a long rope of pearls swinging from her neck and sometimes even down her back, is every bit the stylish young flapper. Equally important, however, was her approach to life, for the flapper, according to Kathleen Drowne, "adopted the attitude that life was primarily for having fun, and that few limits should be imposed on the all-important quest for a good time" (247). Lorelei had attitude and more.

The flapper may have symbolized the Jazz Age woman, but, according to Drowne, she had in fact "replaced an older ideal of American femininity from the late nineteenth and early twentieth centuries: the so-called Gibson girl" (246). Popularized by the artist Charles Dana Gibson's pen-and-ink magazine illustrations, the Gibson girl projected an elegance and a sophistication that the pre–World War I American woman sought to emulate. Her "wasp waist," a consequence of the tight corsets she wore beneath her full skirts and prim blouses accentuated with mutton-chop sleeves, created a shapely hour-glass figure that was voluptuous but never vulgar, at least in part because her hair, arranged stylishly on her head in a soft bouffant or chignon, stray tendrils framing her serene face, gave her a classic refinement. The Gibson girl rarely engaged in activities unbecoming her femininity, and she was no suffragette, and while she often seemed to wield a certain amount of power over men in Gibson's satiric illustrations, the source of her power was clearly her beauty rather than her intellect. Frequently pictured cycling in the park, frolicking on the beach, or attending college classes, the Gibson girl combined traditional female beauty with the youth and energy associated with America, thereby representing the modern American woman of her era. By the mid-1910s, however, she seemed as old-fashioned as her mother to the new generation of women who replaced her.

These new women, like Loos herself, may have been born in the late nineteenth century, but they were thoroughly modern products of the twentieth century, a period of social and cultural upheaval that had largely transformed the roles of and expectations for women. Many of those Gibson girls, for example, had attended college and were securing professional office jobs, thereby opening doors for women to opportunities outside the home, but because they did not involve themselves in politics and always presented themselves as ideals of femininity, they seemed not to be fixed on change. The New Woman of the twentieth century, however, embodied change. She championed the right to equal educational and work opportunities as well as other progressive reforms, including suffrage. She sought sexual and reproductive freedom by supporting the birth control movement. She was at the forefront of labor laws to protect the health and welfare of women and children, the motive behind her long and ultimately successful campaign for prohibition as well. Pushing the limits of her male-dominated society, the New Woman was a far more disruptive female ideal than the Gibson girl, for she insisted on her independence and her agency, her right to exercise personal, social, and economic control of her life. Following World War I, however, the flapper displaced the New Woman in the popular imagination, for she exercised a social and sexual liberation that was truly audacious.

A good-time girl who wanted nothing more than fun, the flapper was the perfect antidote to a war-weary world. Causes did not interest her any more than outmoded traditions of respectability and propriety. In addition to her fashion style, for example, which prompted civic leaders and school boards to impose dress codes to ensure her modesty, she engaged in dancing, drinking, and smoking. She drove automobiles, used profanity, and, as F. Scott Fitzgerald observed in one of the first novels to popularize the flapper, 1920's *This Side of Paradise*, "None of the Victorian mothers . . . had any idea how casually their daughters were accustomed to being kissed" (65). Kissing, however, was tame behavior for the sexually liberated flapper, for whom "petting" with young men (often in automobiles) was also common.

In the late 1910s and early 1920s the flapper blazed a trail through society, according to Zelda Fitzgerald, the wife of the era's celebrated author and the epitome of the early flapper, bent on doing "the things she had always wanted to do" (391). She had not yet become a fad, nor had she intended to be one. She had only ever insisted on the freedom to be herself. By the mid-1920s, however, when even middle-aged women were bobbing their hair and raising their hemlines in imitation of the younger generation and Lorelei Lee complained however disingenuously to her future mother-in-law Mrs. Spofford that she "did not seem to like all of the flappers we seem to have nowadays" (94), the flapper had become a fad. In fact, in 1922 Zelda Fitzgerald announced, "The Flapper is deceased," a victim of her own popularity. "Flapperdom," she observed in her essay "Eulogy on the Flapper," "has become a game; it is no longer a philosophy" (392). This second generation of flappers, in other words, was more intent on being a flapper than expressing herself or defying social norms because the flapper had become the era's fashion.

Indeed, throughout the decade the flapper was the pervasive cultural icon. F. Scott Fitzgerald had chronicled her lifestyle and adventures not only in his novels, including *This Side of Paradise* and *The Great Gatsby*, but also in his short stories, which were frequently published in the *Saturday Evening Post*, one of the most popular magazines of the decade. She was also, of course, the subject of *Gentlemen Prefer Blondes*, as well as a popular genre of "flapper novels" by writers such as Beatrice Burton (*The Flapper Wife*, 1925; *The Petter*, 1927). The American cartoonist and illustrator John Held, Jr., created the archetypal image of the flapper through his *Life* magazine covers, which captured her style, her activities, and the general exuberance of the age. Perhaps most appropriately, however, motion pictures, the era's revolutionary entertainment, seized upon the flapper, its radical new woman, as the heroine of so many of its films. In films such as *The Flapper* (1920), *Flaming Youth* (1923), *The Perfect Flapper* (1924), *It* (1927), starring Clara Bow, and *Our Dancing Daughters* (1928), audiences witnessed the flapper's lifestyle and her fashion sense, popularizing both for the country's youth (and many of their youth-obsessed elders) but worrying the majority of those elders, for whom her ubiquity signified anything but her death, no matter what Zelda Fitzgerald proclaimed.

In reaching iconic status, the flapper, according to Drowne, "lost most of the radical associations that had defined her earlier incarnations" (248), except in the popular imagination. So much about the modern American society that was emerging in the early twentieth century was in flux. New inventions, new entertainments, new opportunities were changing old attitudes and challenging old values. The flapper, as the face of these changes, as well as the youth culture of which she was a part and also the representative, scandalized her elders and confirmed their fears of a society in decline. As Zelda Fitzgerald noted in "Eulogy on the Flapper," a recent editorial had "fixed the blame for all divorces, crime waves, high prices, unjust taxes, violations of the Volstead Act and crimes in Hollywood upon the head of the Flapper. The paper wanted back the dear old fireside of long ago, wanted to resuscitate 'Hearts and Flowers' and have it instituted as the sole tune played at dances from now on and forever, wanted prayers before breakfast on Sunday morning—and to bring things back to this superb state it advocated restraining the Flapper" (392). The flapper, however, as her popularity also indicated, would not be restrained, nor would the changes she embodied.

Indeed, the "revolution in manners and morals," as it was commonly called, that occurred during the 1920s and that the flapper symbolized was one of the most significant developments of the Jazz Age. Idolized by a young generation ready for the modern era and vilified by their elders, the flapper was always only ever an extreme embodiment of change, and she would eventually marry and become a good wife and mother. Even Zelda Fitzgerald, in a 1925 essay titled "What Became of the Flappers?" acknowledged this fate. But for a time, Zelda wistfully observed, they had "lent a while a splendor and courageousness and brightness to life, as all good flappers should" (399).

With her unconventional attitudes about sex, her determination to enjoy life, her defiance of traditional values, Lorelei Lee, Loos's spirited young heroine, proved everything a flapper should have been, so it is not surprising that Hollywood and the motion picture industry held a constant allure for this representative of modernity. After all, by the 1920s motion pictures had transformed the entertainment business, and Anita Loos was one of its most successful writers. In making her way west to Hollywood following her acquittal for attempted murder in Arkansas, Lorelei was, therefore, like so many others before and after her, following a dream of success and, as her new name makes clear, reinventing herself to achieve it, and although Mr. Eisman, the "Button King," will lure her away for a time from her job as an actress and she will marry into a conventional Philadelphia dynasty, Lorelei cannot get the magic of Hollywood from her mind. Having played "one of the girls that fainted at the battle when all of the gentlemen fell off the tower" in D. W. Griffith's 1916 film *Intolerance*, for instance, she is convinced that the director who "handled all of those mobs" could just as easily handle the "bolshevicks" who were threatening to "make nothing but trouble" for the country (8), an allusion to the Red Scare of 1919–1920 that had set on edge the nation's citizens. Hollywood made anything seem possible, everything seem real, and because it lies always in the background of Lorelei's life and in the forefront of her dreams, *Gentlemen Prefer Blondes* invites readers to consider the role and place of this new industry that was in process of not only transforming but also reflecting American society.

In 1915, when Anita Loos, following the end of her brief marriage to Frank Palloma, settled, with her mother, in Los Angeles to write for D. W. Griffith's Fine Arts-Triangle film company, motion pictures were on the verge of becoming the dominant entertainment industry of the 1920s, indeed, of the twentieth century. Although the production of the first movie shorts, 15–30-second scenarios created by the Lumiere brothers in France in the 1890s, had captured nothing but movement, no sound, no plot, they quickly resulted in movie "shows," a collection of short scenes of 5–8 minutes each that delighted audiences on both sides of the Atlantic. From the late 1890s into the 1900s, audiences could watch men playing cards, water cascading over Niagara Falls, a train pulling into a station, a whole panoply of action and motion. For many, these shows offered them their first view of places and people and phenomena far outside their experience of the world, fueling a demand for additional shows as well as encouraging advancements in film technology and form. Soon, filmmakers were telling stories, such as Edwin Porter's *The Great Train Robbery* (1903), on film and developing techniques and strategies, such as crosscutting and close-ups, to add variety to their presentations.

In the United States, these early films, running 5–8 minutes and called "one reelers" because they were recorded on one reel of film, were produced by a small group of companies located just outside New York City that effectively controlled their production and distribution. Stifled by this monopoly of the industry, David Wark Griffith, one of the most innovative of directors during this era of silent films, and other dissident filmmakers abandoned their East Coast backers and followed Al Christie, who created the first Hollywood studio, Nestor Studios, in a derelict roadhouse in 1911, and Cecil B. DeMille, who two years later created another in an empty barn, in a rural area near Los Angeles, Beverly Hills, California. There the weather was perfect for outside shooting, and acres of farmland provided plenty of barns that could be transformed into hotel lobbies, family drawing rooms, dance halls, or any sort of interior space that a story demanded. In Hollywood, these filmmakers were soon experimenting with multiple-reel films and reinventing the industry. When Griffith released his first successful feature-length film, *Birth of a Nation*, in 1915, Hollywood was officially on the map, and the modern motion picture industry began its dominance of popular entertainment.

Moving pictures were initially projected during the intermissions of vaudeville shows and other types of live entertainments, but throughout the 1910s they gained in popularity and gradually replaced these amusements, which now seemed tired and outmoded. On main streets in small towns and cities throughout the nation, movie palaces, as they were called, sprang up, giving this new medium a glamor and allure that it had previously lacked. In fact, filmmaking was not initially a respectable profession, one of the reasons, according to Cari Beauchamp, "that women and immigrants flourished in the movies" (Loos, *Rediscovered* 40). Along a still unpaved Hollywood Boulevard signs reading "No dogs or actors" hung from boarding house fences, and the man whose vast property holdings would eventually become Bel-Air, Alphonzo Bell, held tight to his resolve "not to sell one acre of my land to actors or Jews"—at least for another decade (Loos, *Rediscovered* 40). Women and immigrants, however, who were already on the periphery of society, cared little that Hollywood was outlaw territory. Anita Loos, for instance, was simply too thrilled to be writing scenarios and witty title cards for the silent films that these immigrant producers and directors were making to worry about her reputation. By the end of the 1920s, moreover, Hollywood had created its own social hierarchy, complete with stars who embodied the dreams of the ordinary people who filled the nation's movie palaces.

Shining brightest among that panoply of stars were Douglas Fairbanks, Mary Pickford, and Charlie Chaplin, as well as Greta Garbo and Rudolph Valentino, to whose popularity Lorelei attests when she observes, "The French use the word 'shiek' for everything, while we only seem to use it for gentlemen when they seem to resemble Rudolf Valentino" (69). Loos's scripts for Fairbanks, an actor of great energy and charisma, helped establish his film persona and Hollywood success, and they were equally important to the careers of other Hollywood stars, including Marion Davies, Billie Burke, and Norma and Constance Talmadge. In fact, it was *The Virtuous Vamp*, based on one of Loos's stories, that launched Constance's star, and she continued to develop scripts for the actress that helped her remain a box-office favorite.

During these early years of Hollywood, when an industry was being launched and stars were being born, moving pictures were not only revolutionizing entertainment but also reflecting the lives of their audiences. It is not surprising, therefore, that Hollywood in the mid- to late-1920s produced a genre of flapper films, nor that Anita Loos, as one of filmdom's most successful writers, helped develop her screen image. (Equally important to the development of this image were the stories of F. Scott Fitzgerald, but he had less success than Loos in writing for the screen. In fact, in 1931 Loos managed to turn *Red-Headed Woman*, a popular novel by Katherine Brush, into a hit after Fitzgerald was released from his contract to adapt it for the screen.) "As often as not," notes Molly Haskell, women were the authors and adapters of [Hollywood] screenplays and thus helped fashion the image of the flapper and woman of the world" (78).

In films such as *The Offshore Pirate* (1921), adapted from a Fitzgerald short story; *Flaming Youth* (1923); *Dancing Mothers* (1926); *Our Dancing Daughters* (1928); *Our Modern Maidens* (1929); and, perhaps most famously, *It* (1927), stars such as Colleen Moore, Joan Crawford, and Clara Bow embodied the era's female icon—independent, spontaneous, and decidedly sexual, combining, as Ruth Prigozy asserts, "the traits of the vamp and the good girl" to "[emerge] as the sparkling heroine whose pursuit of fun entranced audiences" (148). To this extent, she captured the essence of the true flapper. The overt sexual allure and flirtatiousness of these new women, however, simultaneously evoked the public's deep fears and anxieties about the flapper, and thus, according to Prigozy, their daring and desire were "embedded in morality tales" (140). The fun-loving "It" girl simply used her spirit, Prigozy notes, "in the service of securing the most desirable middle-class goals: money, husband, home" (148). This conventional Hollywood ending thereby reassured audiences that however outrageous her behavior, however radical her outlook, she was never promiscuous and always moral.

In *It*, based on a novel of that name by Elinor Glyn, the most famous and perhaps most important of these flapper films because it added entirely new connotations to a common word, Clara Bow enacted "it" for the nation. "It," as Glyn, who made a cameo appearance in the film, explained, was "a self-confidence and indifference to whether you are pleasing or not, and something in you that gives the impression that you are not all cold." That something was the word that could not be pronounced, sexuality. As Betty Lou Spence, a lingerie salesclerk who uses her wiles to capture the heart of Cyrus Waltham, the owner of the department store where she works, Bow joyfully cavorts through a series of sexually suggestive scenes. At the Coney Island amusement park beach and funhouse, for example, she advises Cyrus, "Hold me tight, Mr. Waltham" as they take a ride on a sliding board, all the while clutching half-heartedly at her skirt to protect her modesty, and in the film's final sequence, set on a yacht, Bow clings to the vessel, every curve of her drenched body accentuated by her clinging garments. Without doubt, Bow was a vamp. She used her charm and sex appeal to seduce or exploit the men on whom she had set her sights. She was willing, moreover, to do what she must—to crash parties and intimidate his girlfriend—to claim her prize. But her vitality and love of life were infectious, and her unself-conscious self-confidence made her sexual allure seem completely natural. Despite their misgivings about the flapper, Jazz Age audiences could not get enough of the era's Jazz Baby, and the "It" girl became, and remains, an indelible image of the period.

Flapper films, like the flapper herself, did not survive the Jazz Age. After all, the Crash of 1929 and the Great Depression of the 1930s were hardly conducive to the carefree lifestyle of this liberated, irreverent woman. The moving picture industry, however, would continue evolving and strengthening its grip on the popular imagination. Indeed, during the Great Depression, when audiences sought escape from the cruel realities of daily existence and a double-bill at the local movie theater cost a dime, Hollywood developed its studio system and entered its "Golden Age." Yet that "Golden Age" had had its birth in the 1920s, when moving pictures seemed the perfect entertainment for a nation on the move. The American people, prosperous, eager for change, embracing the modern, delighted in this new art form, and the movies were here to stay. Any doubt of this truth Loos puts to rest at the end of *Gentlemen Prefer Blondes*, when the newlywed Lorelei has convinced her husband, who has devoted his energies to "senshuring" movies, "to go into the film profession" (120); her father-in-law spends every day at the studio; and her mother-in-law is "having her hair bobbed" and preparing to play Carmen (122). When Philadelphia's elite participates in a popular entertainment, it is without doubt establishment.

With its gold-digging flapper heroines Lorelei and Dorothy, *Gentlemen Prefer Blondes* was, like the novel that defined the era and to which it is a worthy companion, F. Scott Fitzgerald's *This Side of Paradise*, utterly of its time. It is filled with topical references to Bolsheviks (8) and bootleggers (28); to the African American cabaret singer, dancer, and comedian "Florence Mills in Harlem" (13); the Dolly sisters, Hungarian-born identical twins who became famous as vaudeville performers and were known as "The Million Dollar Dollies" for dating wealthy men; Pearl White, a stage and film actress who starred in *The Perils of Pauline* and was known as the "Queen of the Serials;" Maybelle Gilman Corey, an American stage actress who married into wealth (52); and the quintessential gold-digger Peggy Hopkins Joyce, whose six marriages and numerous engagements to wealthy men may have made her the inspiration for Lorelei Lee (77); to American jazz in Paris bars (55) and prohibition (97); and above all to the moving picture industry that would capture its images and reflect them back to eager audiences. It captures as well its mood, its irreverent exuberance, its easy hypocrisies, its outrageous excesses, its discomforting anxieties, indeed all the contradictory reactions to the Jazz Age, with a satiric bite that never breaks the skin. In fact, had Fitzgerald not written *This Side of Paradise*, *Gentlemen Prefer Blondes* could have been *the* Jazz Age novel, for it is certainly a masterpiece.

DOCUMENTING *GENTLEMEN PREFER BLONDES*
The Flapper

The flapper was the embodiment of the Jazz Age woman. With her bobbed hair, her short skirts, and her outrageous behavior—from smoking in public to dancing the Charleston and the Shimmy to abandoning her corsets—she flouted conventions and shocked polite society, expressing the era's revolution in manners and morals. The following documents provide a portrait of the flapper and capture the different perspectives, from enthusiasm to bewilderment, on this new woman.

With their bobbed hair, short skirts, cloche hats, and boyish silhouettes, this group of flappers makes visible in their unconventional style the revolution in manners and mores of the Jazz Age. (Kirn Vintage Stock/Corbis)

Document: From *The Flapper*, 1922

THE NEW FASHIONED GIRL

Let them sing of the girls of the long, long ago,
Who were shocked if their elbow or stockings did show
But I'll chant of the maidens whose ankles are free
To show their half-socks, and the shape of their knees.
Let them praise those back numbers who turned in their toes
And panted and fainted when MEN would propose;
Compared to the short-skirted, bob-headed fry
Who meet all proposals with right to the eye.
Let them shed all their tears in a crocodile pour

For the simple simp sister who flourished of yore
But I'll cast my vote in the way that I feel—
For the girl self-reliant, bright, snappy and REAL.

Source: The Flapper, June 1922.

Document: From "Flappers Flaunt Fads in Footwear," *The New York Times*, 1922

Unbuckled Galoshes Flop Around Their Legs and Winter Sport Shoes Emphasize Their Feet. Stockings Scare Dogs. Artic Leg and Foot Equipment Has Been Adopted for Street Wear

If you are observant you will have noticed within the last few weeks that there has apparently been an increase of forgetfulness on the part of that portion of the feminine pedestrians in Broadway and Fifth Avenue which is classified as flapper. You will have noticed that they apparently had forgotten to buckle their overshoes and you will have noticed that they had taken to wearing overshoes without sufficient provocation on the part of the weather. If you are the parent of a flapper you will wonder at the sudden change of heart on her part which has led her to go to extremes in avoiding wet or even damp feet. Hitherto you have had little success in inducing her even to wear rubbers in a pouring rain and she insisted on wearing satin or suede slippers if the sidewalks were slushy or covered with snow. Now she dons her galoshes the first thing in the morning if the weather prediction is "unsettled." She comes home from school or from a shopping tour with the buckles unfastened and the long tops flapping against each other.

"Well, you are getting absent-minded," you say, "forgot to buckle your galoshes."

"Oh, no," she retorts, with the look of mingled pity, tolerance, scorn and resentment with which the true flapper receives any suggestion from her elders, "all the girls are wearing them that way now."

"Wherefore the reason?" you ask.

"Of course, "she explains, "you couldn't be expected to know. You're still living in at least last year. But you have perhaps heard that there is a movie play, "The Three Musketeers," in which Douglas Fairbanks is the D'Artagnan. You may remember having seen, in the long ago, illustrated editions of Mr. Dumas's novel showing D'Artagnan in his musketeer costume. And you may possibly remember that he wore boots, with turned down tops, which flopped as he walked. It is merely that we girls are following the style set by D'Artagnan. You feel so sort of swashbuckly when you walk along with your overshoe tops flopping round your legs. And then it does attract attention to you."

The Winter sport shoe now affected by the flapper was designed and built originally for men golfers. It is constructed of horsehide and leather strips and has a gray green hue. Its general appearance is that of a racing mud scow. Last Summer it became the prevailing mode for "smart" men at the seashore and mountain and country resorts, being worn largely by those who still believe that "fore" is a mathematical term. With this footwear the proper apparel was knickerbockers and ribbed woolen stockings. If there ever was a shoe which increased the width, thickness, unshapeliness and general homeliness of the human foot and gave it a semi-clubby effect it was this particular Oxford. But the flapper has taken it to her heart and it has become her favorite walking boot.

You remark as you take daughter to lunch at the club that what was once considered inseparable from trimness and grace in feminine footwear has disappeared beneath the lines and bulk of a longshoreman's brogan.

"Yes," she replies, "the only thing that doesn't change in these piping times of peace is the consistency of parents. It used to be 'no wonder you women have corns, the way you pinch your feet with those narrow shoes, two sizes too small for you. Why don't you wear sensible shoes, shoes that give the blood in your feet some chance to circulate and room for your feet to hold their natural position like Miss Jones,' naming the old maid office stenographer. Now when we are doing that very thing, wearing these sport shoes that are the most comfortable thing we ever have worn, the most sensible, you switch around and tell us we have destroyed our 'dainty feet.'"

With the sport shoes the flapper wears heavy woolen stockings of the gaudiest hues and designs. The nearer to exciting a riot, the more dogs they scarce [*sic*], the oftener necks are craned backward to view them, the more desirable these stockings become. The colors and designs most favored are those associated in the past with racetrack touts and jockeys, sporting gents of African ancestry and A. M. E. Zion Church picnics.

Source: "Flappers Flaunt Fads in Footwear," *The New York Times*, January 20, 1922.

Document: From "The Flapper—A New Type," Alfredo Panzini, 1921
Always on the Watch, Eager, Unafraid, Insatiable, and Ready to Spring

"Where are they all going?"

That is the question a fellow is tempted to ask, when he sees so many girls—so many flappers—going around these days.

"Where are they going? Why, they are going . . . around!"

"Why aren't they at home?"

"Home! Excuse me, that word is out of date. Now we say—apartment, boarding-house, moving picture theatre or hotel. . . . "

However, everywhere you look you see flappers going around. That is not the worst of it; you hear them talking . . . around; facing the most profound problems of life with an imperturbability that reminds you of Columbus on the quarter-deck of the *Santa Maria*, of Magellan breaking into unknown seas, of Vasco da Gama doubling the Cape of Good Hope!

Our moralists have applied their wits to the question of our flappers; and they blame our novels, our movies, the Russian ballet, the shimmy, the newspaper, the war, the tea room, the . . . what not!

Our young men, for their part our young intellectuals, who look out unafraid upon the rising flood of proletarian civilization—seem surprised, I might even say worried, at sight of our "present-day" flapper. When she has left them, they really think, down in their hearts: "She's braver, pluckier, than we are!" though, aloud, they content themselves with saying: "Our young girls are . . . rotten!"

I have used the word flapper deliberately, as meaning something more than a "girl". Flapper is a limitless, a widely embracive term, to such a point that serious men have observed—from superficial phenomena only of course—that all women between the ages of fourteen and fifty—make it sixty, if you wish—may be called "girls". Doubtless the short skirt that matrons wear, and the new manner of deportment they have adopted, tend to facilitate such purely visual impressions. At any rate, people consider it witty to remark nowadays that it's hard to distinguish a mother from her daughter.

A Portent!

In this year of our Lord, 1921, a very singular happening occurred in a cathedral not far from my home. A venerable image, a Madonna, was lost in a fire.

The official explanation given for the catastrophe was that a thief, with little respect for religion—one of those lost souls whom Dante represents as tormented in Hell by serpents—started the blaze to cover his theft of the sacred gold and jewels.

That explanation I do not, as a Pagan, accept. I adhere to the ancient myth which said that "The city will stand so long as the Palladium remains unravished!" My mind centers on the fact that our times, precisely, have seen the disappearance of that Woman who is the symbol of Grace and of Redemption from evil Virgin and Mother in one!

Why not? In our civilization no place is left for her. The home is no more! Neither is maternity! For four walls do not make a home, nor does the bearing of children constitute motherhood!

Our flappers all seem to wear masks, masks of one general make, but varying in workmanship from the vulgar mask of the factory girl to the sophisticated mask of the society lady.

In this mask the two elements, or "places," as Dante says, "where the soul most potently worketh," are strangely disfigured. The lips have a dash of red, and the eyes a cold mischievous brightness—not because the soul, but because the pencil, or the drug, "worketh"!

Combined with a filmy, vaporous costume, this facial mask makes the flapper look like a ship cleared for action. At the critical moment will come the deadly salvo, or the destroying torpedo: thunder, flame and storm! . . .

The Flapper Expectant

. . . The lady is on the watch. That firm pose, that firm poise, tells you she is about to spring.

At what? Toward what? Toward the joy of living, a boundless, limitless joy!

There is no shame, no expiation, in this flapper of mine! What does she care for home or husband? Old iron, as we say, rubbish, chips from the bone-yard, in her eyes such things are! She is the strong, the self-reliant girl of our time. She is the fighter—the flapper, in short, raising her proud expectant face in the eyes of the world and demanding her "place in the sun"!

But our flapper, otherwise so entirely self-sufficient, nevertheless lacks one thing she cannot provide from her own resources: she needs love.

A man, to be sure, also needs love, and more insistently than a woman. . . .

A man, however, needs many other things. He needs law and order, for instance; legislatures to wrangle in; courts to quarrel in; academies to flatter his vanity and cover his coat-front with medals. When he is at home he needs a pair of warm soft slippers. Peace and quiet are as essential to a man as love.

Now a flapper can pretend she needs all these things, too. She may take part in politics; she can enter the professions; she can even preside over a congress of feminists or a convention of school teachers. But, unless she be very ugly, she cannot take such things seriously; for the simple reason that the only serious thing in her world is herself—plus the man she needs, to be herself!

The Implacable Aphrodite

... In ancient times, men, in self-defense, made cruel laws against women. She was absurdly veiled. She was imprisoned in the harem, in the convent, in the home. She was condemned to a life of chastity at the spinning wheel. She was burned alive on her husband's funeral pyre. All this, especially, if she was pretty!

These laws have all been repealed
The male has recognized the equality of the sexes

The woman will go on working, of course. She will go to school. She will talk philosophy, physiology and art with you. She will be a stenographer, a school teacher, a movie actress.

But she will not cook for you.

She will not do our washing.

She will not knit her own stockings.

"Don't expect us," she says to you, disconsolate male, "don't expect us to be like the old-fashioned girls who went to church, and did the laundry, and looked up to their husbands as to their God.

"You men are always quoting your values on exchange. Allow us to do the same with one of our values, our single priceless possession—our beauty".

Source: Alfredo Panzini, "The Flapper—A New Type," *Vanity Fair*, September 1921.

Document: From "Her Eternal Youth," *New York Times*, 1922

Spirit That Created Flapper Will Not Surrender to Elders, Though Skirts Are Lengthened—How a Sub-Deb. Puts It

Knees may be covered, but the young spirit is here to stay. Youthful insurgents are busily refuting the assertions from Paris that the flapper is passing out with the abbreviated skirt. Dictators of fashions and of morals appear, in fact, to know very little about the habits, ideals and aspirations of the young person between eighteen and twenty-four. That these dictators should think that with the passing of the short skirt and bobbed hair this eager young army of self-determination which has been gradually throwing off the hampering mantle of dependence and parental dominance will be content to be relegated to the ranks of the negligible female of thirty years ago is proof, it is said, of their limited knowledge of the situation.

"Never," cry in unison the emancipated army. That the weapons of this twentieth century legion are in large part youth and determination adds strength to the cause. The joyous members argue that their detractors are handicapped by years and compromise. With eyes fixed on the sun, the onrushing host gives small credence to prophesies of failure.

From the flippant young thing to the more serious-minded young person who eagerly builds herself a career after she has finished her college course there seems to be a spirit of independence and of fearlessness that has nothing whatever to do with a new fashion in hair arrangement or an increased length of skirt. Both her admirers and her maligners admit that she has given the exponents of self-expression a tremendous boost. There is nothing secretive about the modern girl. The planks in her platform are frankness, common sense and comfort. She refuses to wear uncomfortable clothes because her grandmother considers them ladylike. When conventions interfere with comfort, conventions must go, asserts the flapper. Her teachers and professors give her credit for sense and decision. They tell you she is neither bad, nor is she different from the young of other years.

Her Struggle for "Freedom"

One of the emancipated ones, with a Knickerbocker grandmother and much family opposition behind her "adventure into the open," in telling of her struggle for freedom, said:

"I worked during the war, of course—every one did. And I decided then that never again would I be content to sit at home and do nothing but go to parties. It was hard work at first to get my people to understand how I felt about it. But I finally succeeded. I've been here two years. Now I want a better job. I want more money and I think I'm worth it. Jobs are awfully hard to get, though. I do not want my friends to help me if I can manage to get a better position without their assistance.

"Several of my friends have gone to work because they were so bored at home. One of them is a saleswoman in a smart costume shop. She's been having lots of fun with some of the snobbish friends of her rich family connections. These snobbish ones haven't got used to the 'working girl' idea yet.

"No. I don't think I shall give up working when I marry. It seems to me that you understand the 'tired business man' much better when you have been a 'tired business woman.' It's not very easy being at a desk all day. I certainly wouldn't expect my husband to take me to late parties every night, which seems to be what wives who have never worked do expect." ...

Spirit of Younger Generation

... "There have always been girls who were just a step ahead of the times—girls who were loud, a little over-dressed and a good bit over-mannered. You find those girls today. But I think they are very much in the minority. Most of the girls as they leave college and come to this club have some idea what they want to do. They all want to work. If they find they can't get a job unless they know stenography, they buckle down and learn it. Stenography is one thing they hate. But nine jobs out of ten offered to girls just starting out in the business world today require stenography. And of course some professions are still practically closed to women. I wanted to study engineering but I found that none of the college courses in that subject were open to women." ...

"Just a Magazine Word"

"We think of it as just a magazine word," said this modern exponent of emancipated thought. "We never call each other flappers. In fact, the girls I know resent being put in that class. And they aren't prudes either. They are just as eager for a good time and a free life as any set of girls. Some of them are planning to work when they finish college, but I don't think 50 per cent of the girls who enter college have any definite plans for a career. That comes later. Many of them go to work when they graduate because they live in small towns and do not want to go home and settle down.

"No, I don't think the girls today think less about getting married than they ever did. They are shy in expressing their views some times, or indifferent, but most of them have it in the back of their minds just the same."

But whether the young girl today just entering her teens, is a flapper or not, hers is the inquiring mind which is not to be satisfied with ready-made formulas, either in fashions or morals. What has been good enough for her parents is not always good enough for her. At least she must decide whether it is. That the arbiters of fashion would wipe her aggressive silhouette entirely off the canvas is of small interest to her. After all, she tells you, skirts may go down and morals may go up in the minds of the public, but she will continue to arrange both her skirts and her morals so that they will neither interfere with her comfort nor outrage her common sense. The young mind appears to be canny and the young spirit above the contemplation of bare knees. This young spirit is busy building its future; it is leaving less important matters to the older generation.

Source: "Her Eternal Youth," *The New York Times*, July 2, 1922.

Hollywood and the Motion Picture Revolution

The Jazz Age was an era in motion, and moving pictures offered the perfect entertainment. They made real the dreams of a nation and created a galaxy of stars. They added glamour and excitement to ordinary lives. In the following documents, a pioneering director, D.W. Griffith, and one of the era's stars, Colleen Moore, reflect upon the appeal of the moving picture. Then two visitors from New York, including the stage director Robert Sherwood, seek to understand Hollywood's appeal and provide some insight into contemporary views of the city.

Document: From "Youth, the Spirit of the Movies," David Wark Griffith, 1921

It is youth that wins war. And it is youth that wins audiences. Often, people inquire why movie stars are small in stature and youthful in appearance. Not all of those that are successful are so little—Constance Talmadge, for instance, is not—yet most of the movie heroines are.

Usually, they are little, and they are young. But why?

The answer is that just as all the world loves a lover, so all the world loves youth—youth with its dreams, youth with its eagerness for romance and adventure!

We all love youth. And, after all, few of us, even after we have passed forty, like plays merely as plays. One cannot easily like a play unless in some way it interprets our own lives for us. We have our families, our business, our professions, and we need diversion from our daily problems—that is why nearly twenty millions of us go to a movie every day. Still, we are always interested in youth. If we are past forty, we look back on our youth and think perhaps of things that might have been. And if we are not quite forty, we like to dream with youth of things that still may be. So, either way, we feel the spell of youth. . . .

We need youth because the most successful screen stars are not harassed by the technique of the older stage and the requirements of the newer art are very largely different. So a new kind of actor has come to be—the screen actor—just as a new kind of writer is coming to be—the screen-writer. But that isn't all!

It was Victor Hugo, I think, who said you could count on it—a third of your audience will be women, who want beauty and romance and emotion. Nearer two-thirds of all movie audiences, these days, are women. And women are not jealous of little women!

They are, we are told, less jealous of screen heroines than of heroines on the older stage. But they are not at all jealous of little women on the screen! So one producer told a visitor on the lot who inquired why screen heroines are usually so small.

But the real reason is youth!

We pick the little women because the world loves youth, with all its wistful sweetness. . . .

An audience loves a sweet and kindly face on the screen as in life. The surest guide in the world to lead us out of our daily troubles is a little star who is sweet and gentle and kind, like youth with all its yearnings and simplicity. . . .

Source: David Wark Griffith, "Youth, the Spirit of the Movies," *Illustrated World*, 1921

Document: From "Flappers Here to Stay, Says Colleen Moore," Gladys Hall, 1922

One day, not so very long ago, Colleen Moore and I had luncheon together. I don't suppose I ever met anybody so enthusiastic as Colleen. Even about the subway, upon which—or rather, within which—she had been spending most of her New York visit, frequently getting lost, but gallantly persisting, none the less.

Flappers came up—in conversation, I mean—and I found Colleen as enthusiastic for the maligned misses as most doleful individuals are against them!

"Why," said Colleen, with her head slightly to one side, an alert little manner, sort of characteristic of a humming bird, "Why, I'm a flapper myself!" Colleen is twenty-one, correct flapper age, at any rate—but somehow, until she mentioned it, I really hadn't catalogued her as precisely that. Flappers don't generally do as much as Colleen, and they are more blase—about the subway.

"A flapper," Colleen went on, with wisdom, "is just a little girl trying to grow up—in the process of growing up.

"She wears flapper clothes out of a sense of mischief—because she thinks them rather 'smart' and naughty. And what everyday healthy normal little girl doesn't sort of like to be smart and naughty?

"Little Lady Flapper is really old-fashioned; but in her efforts not to let anyone discover that her true ideal is love-in-a-cottage, she 'flaps' in the most desperately modern manner.

"Left to her own devices she would probably dance and flirt just as girls have always done—but honest, I don't think she'd wear her skirts so short!

"She likes her freedom, and she likes to be a bit daring and snap her cunning little manicured fingers in the face of the world; but fundamentally she is the same sort of girl as grandmamma was when she was young.

"The chief difference is that she has more ambition, and there are more things for her to wish for, and a greater chance of getting them.

"She demands more of men because she knows more about their work.

"She uses lipstick and powder and rouge because like every small girl, she apes her elders.

"She knows more of life than her mother did at the same age because she sees more of it.

"She knows what she wants and what she is doing, all of the time—and she meets life with a small and an eager, ardent hope. She's a trim little craft and brave!

"The flapper has charm, good looks, good clothes, intellect and a healthy point of view. I'm proud to 'flap'—I am!"

Source: Gladys Hall, "Flappers Here to Stay, Says Colleen Moore," *The Flapper*, November 1922.

Document: From "The Monstrous Movies," Charles Hanson Towne, 1921

Hollywood Is Like Nothing So Much as Old Home-Week in Bedlam

... Nothing can be small in California. Everything is magnified ten-fold or more; but the motion-picture industry has gone Nature one better; and the overwhelming scale on which it is run is something that the imagination cannot grasp at once.

The New El Dorado

As the old Forty-niners rushed to the gold fields in search of El Dorado, so now actors, actresses and managers, cameramen and directors, writers, artists and continuity folk, flock to that same section of the country; and they have built cities overnight, just as the gold-seekers did, and camped on the Coast. But with this definite difference: they have gone there to stay. They may rear a Spanish town this afternoon and demolish it next week; but something else will take its place within another twenty-four hours. A pavilion which is an exact replica of one in Italy, let us say, may be erected for one scene in a play, and be absolutely valueless tomorrow. Money is thrown away as chaff before the wind. Almost it would seem that it would be more sensible to send a whole company to Italy than thus to toss gold into the Pacific. But no—all the paraphernalia is here—including the light that Nature has so thoughtfully and lavishly bestowed. Instead of actors being transported to Italy, there, Italy is brought to America—for a week or two; and nothing is thought of the miracle. Next to it, rubbing elbows with it, a Greek village may be in process of construction.

"The world is too much with us," one might say of Hollywood; and indeed the whole world seems literally to be here, concentrated in one tiny corner of the earth. So many assortments are here that it reminds one of those ingenious prisoners who, with nothing else to do, crowd the words of the Lord's Prayer on a pin-head. Hollywood is a contracted dance floor, on which everyone in the world is dancing; and the jazz goes on incessantly. There seems no rhyme or reason here, no method, no system, no direction; it appears a roadhouse—as it is and isn't; and a visitor finds it difficult to adjust himself at first, to fall into step on the crowded, nervous floor.

Is it any wonder? For hodge-podge is Hollywood's first, middle and last name. Confusion is the god that in some mysterious way runs this crazy universe.

What shall be said of a judgment that exploits the so-called "personalities" of little girls with weak chins but big black eyes that "film" well, in stories dashed off like penny-dreadfuls, with ungrammatical captions and incoherent "continuity?" Of actors who care only for the money that they earn, and wouldn't give tuppence for the studios unless their pay-envelope bulged at the end of the week and they could ride back and forth in a ten-thousand-dollar car? Of the young group of perfect cameo-like profiles who leave shops and offices to go into the films, with no knowledge of the technique of acting, and who, when they have a priceless opportunity to watch a really great artist before the cameras (for there are such), sit behind clumps of scenery and smoke innumerable cigarettes? ...

A Critical Close-up

... Yet I repeat that this phenomenon of the movies must be taken seriously. When one goes, as I did recently, to a city like Chicago and finds on the

South Side, a district equivalent to New York's Harlem, a two-million-dollar building of magnificence housing nothing but photoplays, and sees over four thousand people packed in, watching and listening and obviously amused and thrilled, he asks what all this means, and admits, unless he is a *Dumbkopf*, the coming in of a new order. Particularly is he amazed and bewildered when, in the same city, he witnesses a brilliant spoken farce-comedy, deftly played by distinguished actors, given before half-empty benches—yet in the very heart of the town. What is one to say in the light of such overwhelming evidence? Simply that something has entered the world, suddenly, which grips the people, appeals to them, rivets their attention, and drives them out of the old established theatres. The galleries went long ago. Perhaps the balconies and orchestras will leave next. Then what?

One explanation comes, of course, instantly to the observer's rescue. That farce-comedy cost $3.30 to see; the movie house asked only fifty-five cents for the best seat in a gorgeous auditorium. And not only was a good picture revealed, but operatic music was charmingly sung, and an orchestra of over sixty pieces led by a trained director, rendered excellent music. The seats, I may add, were the last word in comfort, better than those in the "legitimate" house, and the sense of charm and barbaric glory was all about—too much of the latter to suit my quiet taste, but there, nevertheless, for the multitude that drinks in such surroundings and takes home the memory of a palace hitherto undreamed of. . . .

Source: Charles Hanson Towne, "The Monstrous Movies," *Vanity Fair*, September 1921.

Document: From "Through Hollywood with Gun and Camera," Robert E. Sherwood, 1922

After all, Hollywood is a vastly overrated place. Although I have been observing it for as much as ten days, I have attended no orgies (and as heaven is my witness I have spared no effort in trying to locate them). I have seen no murders and I have been offered no cocaine, hashish or bhang. Someone told me that he knew a man who made fairly good beer in his kitchen, but that is the only sign of lawlessness that I have observed. . . .

Superficially, Hollywood has somewhat the appearance of a quiet college town. The studios take the place of the university buildings and the picture people take the place of the students. All the stores are catering to this one group and display their wares accordingly.

Behind the town is Mount Hollywood, with a tremendous "H" engraved near its summit. This, too, carries out the collegiate atmosphere, as though the letter had been carved there to commemorate some notable football victory, like "Hollywood 28—Culver City 3."

The movie people themselves—the actors, directors, camera men, stage hands, et al—are in no way extraordinary. They do not seem to take themselves or their work very seriously. They are perfectly willing to admit that many of their pictures contain a certain amount of hokum. One particularly attractive young star informed me that she is hungry for New York because she wants "the chance to see a regular show."

They all work hard when they are on duty in the studios (and it seems to be peculiarly dull, tiresome work), but out of office hours they are for the most part casual and easy-going, and no one seems to worry very much whether school keeps or not.

Of the various studios, Universal City is unquestionably the largest, but at the time of my visit there was little actively there and I saw nothing much except some left-over sets and properties from Von Stroheim's "Foolish Wives."

In the Ince Studio I saw a scene of the interior of Westminster Abbey being converted into a Bowery cabaret. This studio, by the way, is the most beautiful of all, resembling from the front a stately Southern mansion, with an imposing green-liveried Negro butler at the door. There were no mint juleps, however....

At the Paramount Studio I saw four companies at work, two of which were filming what appeared to be death-bed scenes. It was horribly realistic. The patients may have recovered after I left but it seemed to me at the time that there was little hope.

Douglas Fairbanks showed me the settings of his huge new picture—in which he is to be Robin Hood—and gave a remarkable exhibition of archery. He also persuaded me to sit down on his trick sofa, which is electrically wired and gives one a terrific shock. We all had a hearty laugh at this....

And by the way, I attended a ball given by the inhabitants of this notorious community themselves. In all the vast crowd, which included everyone of any note in Hollywood, I observed only two people who were degraded enough to carry flasks.

The other one was Mr. Arthur James, who is also in the magazine business in New York.

Source: Robert E. Sherwood, "Through Hollywood with Gun and Camera," *Life,* April 6, 1922.

Suggested Readings

Addison, Heather. " 'Must the Players Keep Young?': Early Hollywood's Cult of Youth." *Cinema Journal* 45.4(Summer 2006): 3–25.

Burton, Beatrice. *The Flapper Wife*. New York: Grosset & Dunlop, 1925.

Burton, Beatrice. *The Petter*. New York: Grosset & Dunlop, 1927.

Carey, Gary. *Anita Loos: A Biography*. New York: Alfred A. Knopf, 1988.

Cella, Laurie J. C. "Narrative 'Confidence Games': Framing the Blonde Spectacle in *Gentlemen Prefer Blondes* (1925) and *Nights at the Circus* (1984)." *Frontiers* 25.3(2004): 47–62.

Drowne, Kathleen. "Postwar Flappers." In *F. Scott Fitzgerald in Context*. Ed. Bryant Mangum. Cambridge: Cambridge University Press, 2013: 245–253.

Fitzgerald, F. Scott. *This Side of Paradise*. New York: Charles Scribner's Sons, 1920; Scribner's Paperback Fiction, 1995.

Fitzgerald, Zelda. "Eulogy on the Flapper." In *The Collected Writings of Zelda Fitzgerald*. Ed. Matthew J. Bruccoli. Tuscaloosa: University of Alabama Press, 1991: 391–393.

Fitzgerald, Zelda. "What Became of the Flappers?" In *The Collected Writings of Zelda Fitzgerald*. Ed. Matthew J. Bruccoli. Tuscaloosa: University of Alabama Press, 1991: 397–399.

Frost, Laura. "Blondes Have More Fun: Anita Loos and the Language of Silent Cinema." *Modernism/modernity* 17.2(April 2010): 291–311.

Hammill, Faye. " 'One of the Few Books That Doesn't Stink': The Intellectuals, the Masses and *Gentlemen Prefer Blondes*." *Critical Survey* 17.3(2005): 27–48.

Haskell, Molly. *From Reverence to Rape: The Treatment of Women in the Movies*. 2nd ed. Chicago: University of Chicago Press, 1987.

Hefner, Brooks E. " 'Any Chance to Be Unrefined': Film Narrative Modes in Anita Loos's Fiction." *PMLA* 125.1(January 2010): 107–120.

Hegeman, Susan. "Taking Blondes Seriously." *American Literary History* 7.3(Autumn 1995): 525–554.

Horak, Laura. " 'Would You Like to Sin with Elinor Glyn?': Film as a Vehicle of Sensual Education." *Camera Obscura* 25(May 2010): 74–117.

Latham, Angela J. *Posing a Threat: Flappers, Chorus Girls, and Other Brazen Performers of the American 1920s*. Hanover, NH: Wesleyan University Press, 2000.

Loos, Anita. *Anita Loos Rediscovered. Film Treatments and Fiction*. Eds. Cari Beauchamp and Mary Anita Loos. Berkeley: University of California Press, 2003.

Loos, Anita. "The Biography of a Book." In *Gentlemen Prefer Blondes and But Gentlemen Marry Brunettes*. Anita Loos. Ed. Regina Barreca. New York: Penguin Books, 1998: xxxvii–xlii.

Loos, Anita. *Gentlemen Prefer Blondes* and *But Gentlemen Marry Brunettes*. 1925; 1926. Ed. Regina Barreca. New York: Penguin Books, 1998.

Patterson, Martha H. *Beyond the Gibson Girl: Reimagining the American New Woman, 1895–1915*. Champaign: University of Illinois Press, 2005.

Prigozy, Ruth. "Fitzgerald's Flapper and Flapper Films of the Jazz Age." In *A Historical Guide to F. Scott Fitzgerald*. Ed. Kirk Curnutt. New York: Oxford University Press, 2004: 129–161.

Sharot, Stephen. "The 'New Woman,' Star Personas, and Criss-Cross Romance Films in 1920s America." *Journal of Gender Studies* 19.1(March 2010): 73–86.

Sklar, Robert. *Movie-Made America: A Social History of American Movies*. New York: Random House, 1975.

Starr, Kevin. "Lotus land—Los Angeles in the Twenties." *History Today* 40(March 1990): 30–38.

Stevenson, Elizabeth. *Babbitts and Bohemians: From the Great War to the Great Depression*. 1967. New York: Macmillan, 1998.

Tracy, Daniel. "From Vernacular Humor to Middlebrow Modernism: *Gentlemen PreferBlondes* and the Creation of Literary Value." *Arizona Quarterly* 66.1(Spring 2010): 115–43.

Walker, Nancy A. *A Very Serious Thing: Women's Humor and American Culture*. Minneapolis: University of Minnesota Press, 1988.

Zeitz, Joshua. *Flapper: A Madcap Story of Sex, Style, Celebrity, and the Women Who Made America Modern*. Rpt. New York: Broadway Books, 2007.

4

The Sun Also Rises
(Ernest Hemingway, 1926)

SYNOPSIS OF *THE SUN ALSO RISES*

The three-part structure of *The Sun Also Rises* is linked in part to the novel's symbolic geography: the virulent decadence and insidious cacophony of the modern city in opposition to the natural rhythms and pristine landscapes of the countryside. Book One, set in café society among a group of expatriates who have settled in post–World War I Paris, introduces the narrator and protagonist, Jake Barnes, who works as a journalist in the city. Jake, a veteran who had been seriously wounded in that war, struggles to achieve some sense of normalcy in his life, filing his stories by day and drinking to forget at night. In Paris, he befriends Robert Cohn, a rich Jewish writer who lives with a domineering woman, Frances Clyne, and occasionally spends time with the woman he loves, Lady Brett Ashley, a divorced socialite who nursed him through his wartime recovery. Brett, a beautiful but self-centered woman who has also been wounded by war, loves Jake, but his injury, which has left him impotent, makes a relationship impossible for her. When Cohn, restless and dissatisfied with his life, meets Brett, he becomes obsessed with her and grows angry when Jake informs

The first edition cover of Ernest Hemingway's 1926 novel *The Sun Also Rises*, which chronicled the lives of the Lost Generation who survived, but not unscathed, the horrors of World War I. (Herbert Orth/The LIFE Images Collection/Getty Images)

him that she is engaged to a heavy-drinking Scottish war veteran, Mike Campbell. Late that night, after Brett has failed as promised to meet Jake, she arrives unexpectedly at his apartment with Count Mippipopolous, a rich Greek expatriate who, like them, has been wounded by war. They drink, the Count displays his war wounds, proving that he is "one of us," and then Brett, in an anguished conversation with Jake, tells him that she is going to San Sebastian, in Spain. Her departure will make life easier for both of them.

Several weeks later, as Book Two begins with both Brett and Cohn traveling outside of Paris, Jake has been joined by Bill Gorton, a fellow American war veteran recently arrived from New York, with whom he plans a fishing trip to Spain and then to attend the fiesta of San Fermín at Pamplona. Before their departure, Jake has also made plans to meet Cohn on the journey to Pamplona and, running into Brett and Mike Campbell in Paris, agreed to include them among the party. Brett also confides in Jake that she and Cohn had been together in San Sebastian.

Jake, Bill, and Cohn arrive in Pamplona as planned, but when Brett and Mike fail to appear, Jake and Bill depart for the small town of Burguete to fish. Cohn, who believes that Brett loves him and feels possessive of her, determines to wait for her in Pamplona. For five days, at the heart of the novel, in the hills above the city, beyond the fray of complicated human relationships and the disappointments of personal failures, Jake and Bill fish the streams of the Burguete by day and drink and play cards by night, recovering a sense of themselves and restoring a connection with the natural world that feels "good" to the men. Their sojourn ends with a letter from Brett and Mike announcing their arrival in Pamplona the next day, and Jake and Bill leave by bus to meet them.

Arriving in Pamplona, Jake and Bill check into a hotel owned by Montoya, a Spanish bullfighting expert who likes Jake because he possesses a genuine *aficion* for, or love of, the sport. Soon the festivities, including the running of the bulls, begin, and the city is filled with dancing, drinking, and general debauchery that mirror Parisian decadence. Its frenzied rhythms capture as well the tension between the members of Jake's party. Moreover, the introduction into the group of the bullfighter Pedro Romero exacerbates that tension. Romero, a nineteen-year-old prodigy, captures the attention of Brett during the party's first day at the bullfight, when she cannot take her eyes off him. After persuading Jake to introduce them, she and Romero begin an affair that arouses the jealousy of all the men who love Brett—Jake, Cohn, Campbell, and Romero—and ends in a series of violent fights. Cohn, who had been a champion boxer in college, beats up all his competitors but fails to win Brett. Romero, despite the savagery of the beating he sustained from Cohn, fights brilliantly in the ring the next day, killing a bull that had gored a man to death in the streets and presenting the trophy of its ear to Brett, who has watched his performance from the stands. She and Romero then leave for Madrid together.

Book Three records the aftermath of the fiesta. Jake, Bill, and Mike rent a car and drive out of Spain to Bayonne—Cohn has previously departed on his own. Bill returns to Paris, Mike decides to stay in Bayonne, and Jake heads back to San Sebastian for several quiet days of relaxation. A telegram from Brett, however, pleading for his help, sends him to Madrid, where he finds her alone and broke in a cheap hotel. She bravely tells him that she has ended her affair with Romero because she feared she would ruin him and that she has decided to return to Mike. Jake purchases train tickets for their journey from Madrid, and the novel ends with the couple riding in a taxi to the station. Brett talks of what might have been between them, and Jake responds, "Yes, isn't it pretty to think so?" punctuating this sad tale of love with an even sadder truth.

HISTORICAL BACKGROUND: HEMINGWAY, PARIS, AND THE MODERN MOMENT

In 1925, following a third excursion to Pamplona, Spain, to observe the Festival of San Fermín and the running of the bulls through the city's narrow and twisted cobbled streets, this time with some American and

The author Ernest Hemingway (1899–1961) in 1933, five years after his novel *The Sun Also Rises* had captured the distrust and disillusionment of the Lost Generation shaped by World War I. (AP Photo)

British expatriate friends, Ernest Hemingway drafted the novel that defined a generation, *The Sun Also Rises*. Like other expatriates, he was living in Paris, the city, his early mentor Sherwood Anderson had advised him, where the *avant-garde* reigned. If he wanted to be among the vanguard of artists who were redefining art, architecture, music, dance, and, most importantly for Hemingway, literature, then he needed to get to the French capital as soon as possible. So the newly married foreign correspondent of the *Toronto Star*, accompanied by his wife Hadley, set sail for the Continent in late 1921. Arriving in Paris, the city that would be their primary home for most of the decade that was the Jazz Age, they settled into a small flat with neither hot water nor an indoor toilet on the left bank of the River Seine, and Hemingway set about establishing his place in the movement that was Modernism. *The Sun Also Rises* was his finest contribution to it.

Modernism was a response to World War I. Begun in 1914, when the transformative changes of the twentieth century were barely in process, the Great War, as it was called in Europe, plunged the Continent into turmoil and social and economic upheaval, sweeping away the old order. A war that began with cavalry charges ended with tanks and aerial bombardments. Brutal beyond words, it relied on mustard gas, barbed wire, trench warfare, and futile charges across "No Man's Land" as each side sought to claw its way to victory. When it concluded with an Allied victory against Germany and the Central Powers in 1918, a generation of young men lay dead at Ypres and the Somme, Verdun and Passchendaele, and as far as

Gallipoli. Indeed, more than nine million combatants were killed before the armistice that ended the conflict on November 11, 1918.

While the changes associated with the twentieth century had been in motion before the conflict, World War I accelerated them. The slaughter on the Western Front had demolished fundamental truths, for instance, the ideal of heroism, as well as the progressive view that humans were making steady moral progress and notions of culture as a body of established beliefs and values, but left nothing with which to replace them. A new economic, social, and political environment, moreover, was emerging in the urban centers of a fully industrialized world that was itself creating doubt and uncertainty. The new prosperity that had accompanied that industrialization, for instance, had created a consumer culture based on mass-produced, rather than handcrafted, items, what came to be known as "kitsch," cheap, cheerful, but ephemeral, lacking the quality of individual workmanship and thereby devaluing in some essential way human endeavor. That prosperity, nevertheless, was exciting. It promised change and whispered possibility, on both sides of the Atlantic Ocean. In America, it ushered in the Jazz Age, the Roaring Twenties; in France, *les Années folles*, the Crazy Years.

Like its American counterparts, Paris roared in the 1920s. The French, too, vibrated to the syncopated rhythms of jazz, its energy new and modern. Eager patrons crowded its revues, just as they filled Harlem's Cotton Club. Yet perhaps because the French had lived with war, the joie de vivre was visceral and intense, more authentic than the roar in America, which was at least in part a reaction to Prohibition. Perhaps because the French were unencumbered by the provincial moral standards of Americans, they were far less judgmental of the new sexual freedoms. The gyrations of the exotic African American dancer Josephine Baker, after all, pushed boundaries that would have been unthinkable in New York. Moreover, no prohibitions against alcohol dampened the spirits of the Parisians. The *belle vie* of Paris, with its bon vivant café culture and lively, even decadent nightlife, was the European center of cosmopolitanism and beckoned to a new generation of American writers and artists and intellectuals who were seeking escape from insularity and provincialism at home. It helped as well that they could live cheaply in the French capital.

When Hemingway arrived in Paris in 1922, Gertrude Stein had already established herself as the doyenne of Modernism. Not only had her own experimentation with repetition in her novel *Three Lives* (1909) placed her firmly within the literary avant-garde, but her salon at 27 rue de Fleurus, its walls mounted with paintings by Pablo Picasso, Paul Cézanne, and Henri

Matisse, also fostered a community of writers and artists in all mediums who were revolutionizing modern culture. There, for instance, Hemingway met Ezra Pound, whose Imagist poetry was challenging previous notions of poetic form and function. That introduction led to an introduction to the exiled Irish writer James Joyce, whose experiments with stream-of-consciousness were redefining narrative form and with whom Hemingway spent many a drunken evening in the city's bars. Such experimentation and innovation were the defining characteristics of Modernism in all its forms. Indeed, Ezra Pound had admonished its poets to "Make It New." Paris seemed just the place to make that happen.

Consequently, a steady stream of American expatriate writers, including Sherwood Anderson, Djuna Barnes, Kay Boyle, John Dos Passos, Hilda Doolittle (H. D.), and F. Scott Fitzgerald, passed through or settled in Paris during the 1920s. Like Hemingway, they eventually made their way to Shakespeare and Company, a bookstore and lending library near the Jardin du Luxembourg operated by another American expatriate, Sylvia Beach. The petite woman stocked English-language books and championed the writers who patronized her shop. In fact, Shakespeare and Company published Joyce's Modernist masterpiece *Ulysses* (1922) when every other publisher rejected the manuscript as too controversial.

In his memoir of the period, *A Moveable Feast*, published posthumously in 1964, Hemingway captured the ebb and flow of life among this expatriate community. He strolls from one Montparnasse café to another, from the Dôme to the Select to the Rotonde to the Closerie de Lilas, his favorite, where he could generally write undisturbed. He drops by Stein's apartment to discuss literature and discovers a host of new writers among the books at Shakespeare and Company, where a generous Sylvia Beach lets the penniless writer, who was often hungry, borrow without purchasing a subscription. He describes his friendships and feuds and rivalries with contemporaries, and while his portraits are not always flattering and he is probably unfair to several, including Stein, with whom he eventually quarrels, and Fitzgerald, who will feel betrayed when his friend criticizes him in his story "The Snows of Kilimanjaro," his portrait of the artist as a (sometimes callow) young man makes the time and place endlessly fascinating. Indeed, he asserts on the book's title page, "If you are lucky enough to have lived in Paris as a young man, then wherever you go for the rest of your life, it stays with you, for Paris is a moveable feast." Paris during this modern moment was clearly the only place that could have been and was indeed the backdrop to Hemingway's novel of the postwar generation, *The Sun Also Rises*.

ABOUT ERNEST HEMINGWAY: THE MAN WHO WROTE THE LOST GENERATION

In 1922, shortly after the forty-eight-year-old American expatriate writer Gertrude Stein met twenty-two-year-old Ernest Hemingway in Paris, she famously pronounced, "You are all a lost generation." In Hemingway and others like him, including the Americans John Dos Passos, Kay Boyle, Ezra Pound, Hart Crane, and F. Scott Fitzgerald, the Irishman James Joyce, and the Englishman Ford Madox Ford, she had recognized some quality of aimlessness, of disillusionment, of *ennui* and disaffection that differentiated this generation of young men and women who had come of age during World War I from her generation. Four years later, in *The Sun Also Rises* (1926), Ernest Hemingway would publish the novel that defined his generation. A *roman à clef*, based, in other words, on the lives of people who had been among his circle of friends and acquaintances, as well as his own experience, the novel established Hemingway's literary reputation and remains his finest achievement. The young man from Oak Park, Illinois, who had already experienced war and was now in process of establishing himself as a writer, would eventually win a Nobel Prize in Literature and leave a body of work, the best of which examines the effects of war and concepts of masculinity. In his depiction of the Lost Generation, however, Hemingway left his most indelible legacy of the Jazz Age.

The American expatriate writer Gertrude Stein (1874–1946) sits in her Paris studio in 1930 flanked by a portrait of her by Pablo Picasso as well as other modern paintings by avant-garde artists of the period. Stein's salon was a center of artistic and intellectual life during the Jazz Age, and Ernest Hemingway credited the writer with coining the phrase "the Lost Generation." (Library of Congress)

Ernest Miller Hemingway was born on July 21,

1899, in Oak Park, Illinois, a conservative Chicago suburb. The first son and second of six children born to his physician-father and musician-mother, Ernest, who disliked his name because it reminded him of the playwright Oscar Wilde's naïve and self-absorbed hero in *The Importance of Being Earnest*, developed into a young man of considerable physical prowess and intellectual ability. As a four-year-old child he learned from his father to hunt, fish, and camp in the woods at the family's summer home near Petoskey, Michigan, experiences that instilled a passion for adventure and a love of the natural world that he reflected in his fiction, including *The Sun Also Rises*. At Oak Park and River Forest High School, a teenage Ernest participated in boxing, water polo, track and field, and football. Sports were not, however, his only interest. He excelled in English and had a talent for writing that he put to use as not only a writer but also the editor of the school's newspaper and yearbook, effectively serving an early apprenticeship for his career.

Hemingway put that apprenticeship to use at his first job, working as a journalist for six months at the *Kansas City Star*, where he reported on local stories, including military recruitment during the early days of World War I, and was expected to follow its style guide, which included among its rules "Use short sentences. Use short first paragraphs. Use vigorous English." Hemingway later claimed that his experience at the *Star* helped him develop the style for which he became famous, short declarative sentences stripped of qualifiers, of unnecessary adjectives and adverbs and subordinators. Reporting the news in Kansas City was not sufficient enticement, however, to keep the young man from enlisting in 1918 as a Red Cross ambulance driver in a war-ravaged Europe, and he set sail for the Continent in May 1918.

Arriving in Paris as the city was under bombardment from German artillery, Hemingway made his way to the Italian front, where, on July 8, he was seriously injured by mortar fire. Despite the severity of shrapnel wounds to both his legs, Hemingway assisted the rescue of Italian soldiers with injuries more critical than his, gallantry for which he was awarded the Italian Silver Medal of Bravery. Following an operation to repair the damage to his legs, Hemingway was transferred from a field hospital to a Red Cross facility in Milan, where he spent the next six months recuperating. There love and war became intertwined. He fell in love with Agnes von Kurowsky, a Red Cross nurse seven years his senior. By the time he was released and had returned to the United States in January 1919, the lovers had promised to marry. Two months later, however, Agnes wrote that she had become engaged to an Italian officer, and Hemingway spent the remainder of the year recovering from his war wounds.

Restless and uncertain about his future, Hemingway accepted a position as a staff writer and foreign correspondent for the *Toronto Star*, but still unsatisfied, he returned to Chicago. There he met a beautiful young redhead eight years his senior, Hadley Richardson, with whom he fell in love. The couple married on September 3, 1921; in November, eager for adventure, they set sail for Paris, with letters of introduction from Sherwood Anderson, who advised Hemingway that the French capital was the center of the modern movement. In Paris, Hemingway worked as foreign correspondent for the *Toronto Star*, writing travel stories and reporting on the Greco-Turkish war as well as Europe's most avant-garde city. For the twenty months in which the Hemingways resided in Paris's Latin Quarter, they went frequently to Gertrude Stein's salon on the Rue de Fleurus, where they met Pablo Picasso, Joan Miró, and other revolutionary artists as well as the other young writers of the period, including Ezra Pound and James Joyce, who were in process of redefining literature for the modern age. Hemingway's memoir *A Moveable Feast*, published posthumously in 1964, brings the period vividly to life and provides a singular view of the Lost Generation's expatriate community.

In January 1924, following a brief return to Toronto, where their son John was born in September 1923, the couple returned to Paris, and Hemingway, intent now on pursuing a literary career, entered one of his most productive creative periods. He published *In Our Time* (1925), a collection of short stories that focused on Nick Adams and contained one of his finest efforts, "Big Two-Hearted River," as well as *The Torrents of Spring* (1926), in which he lampooned former mentor Sherwood Anderson. Following a third trip to the Festival of San Fermín in Pamplona, Spain, in June 1925, this time accompanied by a group of British and American expatriate friends, he wrote *The Sun Also Rises* in eight weeks and then spent the winter revising it for publication in 1926. He concluded the decade by publishing his 1929 novel *A Farewell to Arms*, in which he drew on his war experience, including the heartbreak of his first love.

One of the casualties of Hemingway's literary success was his marriage to Hadley, who divorced the writer in 1927 after he began an affair with her friend Pauline Pfeiffer, who worked in Paris for *Vogue* magazine. Hemingway converted to Roman Catholicism to marry the wealthy woman, who grew up in St. Louis, in 1927, and the couple had two sons, Patrick, born in 1928, and Gregory, born in 1931, before divorcing in 1940. Hemingway would marry two additional times: from 1940 to 1945, to the American journalist Martha Gellhorn, who he met when they were reporting on the Spanish Civil War in the late 1930s and with whom he traveled to report on China during World War II; and from 1946 until his death in 1961, to the British journalist Mary Welsh. Each of his marriages prompted the ever-restless Hemingway to move home: with Pauline, he settled primarily in Key West, Florida; the Finca Vigia, or Lookout Farm, in Cuba, was the primary residence of Hemingway and Gellhorn; and he and Mary Welsh spent the majority of their time in Ketchum, Idaho.

No matter where he established home, however, Hemingway could not resist the call of adventure. An avid outdoorsman who admired the skill of the bullfighter, becoming an *aficionado* of the sport; the deep-sea fisherman, and the big game hunter, he traveled frequently to Spain, especially during the 1920s, and purchased a boat, named the *Pilar*, from which he fished the Caribbean and patrolled for German submarines during World War II. He also refused to be sidelined from reporting on world conflicts. Ever a journalist, he reported on the Spanish Civil War (1937–1938) and observed the D-Day landings on Normandy and was present at the liberation of Paris and the heavy fighting in the Battle of Hürtgen Forest in 1944. At one point in 1944, in breach of Geneva Convention rules, Hemingway even became the de facto leader of a resistance group, for which he was formally charged but acquitted. In 1947, he was awarded a Bronze Star for bravery during World War II.

In 1940, at the end of a decade during which he had published only one novel, *To Have and Have Not* (1937), Hemingway published the novel that revitalized his career, *For Whom the Bell Tolls*, set during the Spanish Civil War. Twelve years later, he published *The Old Man and the Sea* (1952), a novel that he considered "the best I can write ever for all my life" (Desnoyers 12). Others must have agreed with that assessment, for in 1954 Hemingway was awarded the Nobel Prize in Literature "for his mastery of the art of narrative, most recently demonstrated in *The Old Man and the Sea*, and for the influence that he has exerted on contemporary style." The recognition effectively marked the end of a distinguished career. Although in late 1956 the writer would retrieve a forgotten trunk filled with notebooks and journals that he had stored in the Ritz Hotel in Paris in 1928 and begin work on his memoir *A Moveable Feast* as well as several other novels that would be published after his death, he did not publish another major work during his lifetime.

Hemingway lived hard. In addition to the wounds he sustained in World War I, he suffered a severe break to his writing arm in an automobile accident in 1930; contracted amoebic dysentery that caused life-threatening intestinal complications on safari in 1933 and had to be evacuated by plane for treatment in Nairobi, an experience that he used in his short story "The

Snows of Kilimanjaro;" and was nearly killed in two successive plane crashes in Africa in 1954. Indeed, newspapers erroneously printed his obituary. In truth, however, Hemingway spent much of his life in chronic pain. He also drank heavily. In the years following World War II, moreover, he battled health problems, including headaches, high blood pressure, and diabetes, and was diagnosed with hemochromatosis, a genetic condition that inhibits the body's ability to metabolize iron and causes mental and physical deterioration. He fell increasingly into depression as his literary contemporaries died and his talent waned. He also became convinced that the government had him under surveillance. On July 2, 1961, Hemingway committed suicide, shooting himself like his father had before him.

Hemingway's best work, including *The Sun Also Rises*, has never been out of print, testament to the writer's importance to the American literary tradition. His prose style, which looks deceptively easy to imitate, remains much admired and, since 1977, is the subject of an annual International Imitation Hemingway Competition, the object of which is to submit one "really good page of really bad Hemingway." Winners are flown to Italy to Harry's Bar, where, according to founder Giuseppe Cipriani, during the winter of 1949–1950 the writer had his own corner table. Perhaps his greatest legacy, however, is his depiction of a generation, the Lost Generation, as they sought meaning and purpose in a world cut loose from its moorings by war. In their brave attempts to prevail, Hemingway found hope.

WHY WE READ *THE SUN ALSO RISES*

The lyrics of a popular song posed a lighthearted but worrisome question in 1919: "How you gonna keep 'em down on the farm after they've seen Paree?" As America's fighting men returned from the front at the end of World War I, family and friends awaiting their arrival in small towns and rural communities, the lyrics suggested, feared that their soldiers, having seen the wide world—or at least Paris—would be reluctant to settle again for an ordinary life. Seduced by the City of Light's decadent charms and amoral liberalities, young men who had departed as unsophisticated farm boys, earnest shopkeepers, and gauche laborers would have been transformed, the song implied, into debonair men about town who preferred glamor and excitement to dull routine. While the fears expressed in the song's lyrics were largely unfounded, and the vast majority of America's soldiers simply picked up their lives where they had abandoned them in 1917, when the United States entered the war, Hemingway's *The Sun Also Rises* testifies to the Lost Generation that war did indeed create. It provides as well an international context for the decade known as the Jazz Age in the United States and *Les Folles Années* in France. Unhinged by war, the world on both sides of the Atlantic Ocean was in process of unsettling change.

The Sun Also Rises is above all else the novel of the Lost Generation. Indeed, its most famous epigraph, Gertrude Stein's pronouncement "You are all a lost generation," established that point, and Hemingway's depiction of aimless, dissolute, utterly damaged survivors of war documents it. This is a generation that has lost its bearings. After all, everything in which it had believed had died on the battlefields where more than sixteen million young men had been slaughtered. Nothing could be the same for them again. So they nurse their wounds, the psychic ones, the physical having long since healed, generally in private, seldom speaking of their pain (others might tell their stories, but never will they do so), and seek in alcohol and sensation escape from their haunted past. Jake and Brett and Mike could not return to their previous lives, for they no longer existed. So they become expatriates, the word itself signifying their tentative and tenuous status in the world—without a country, eternal wanderers—and settle temporarily (nothing is permanent) in Paris, the modern Babylon.

Granted, the United States was roaring in the 1920s, but moral censure accompanied the festivities. Prohibition, after all, was the law of the land, and the hijinks of the nation's flaming youth were the subject of concern in newspaper editorials and church sermons. Indeed, the crusades of the popular evangelists Billy Sunday and Aimee Semple McPherson, who saw the potential of radio to increase the reach of her conservative message, and the 1925 Scopes "Monkey" Trial provide evidence of the clash between fundamentalism and modernism that divided American opinion throughout the decade. Life in Paris, however, was unencumbered by such moral quandaries. In its cafés and cabarets on Montmartre and in Montparnasse, a cosmopolitan and bohemian culture flourished. After five long years of war and deprivation, the French were eager to enjoy life again, to restore the beautiful ease of the Belle Époque that war had interrupted. Unlike Americans, who were fearful and suspicious of immigrants from other cultures, the French even embraced cultural practices from abroad. War had, in fact, increased the nation's experience of new cultures, and Paris quickly became the center of a creative and experimental international movement to redefine society and the arts. The city was primed, in other words, for the Lost Generation. There, as Hemingway discovered, they could participate in and perhaps even create the modern world. They could at the very least live in the moment, enjoying the city's liberal attitudes toward alcohol, sex and sexuality, and even sexual identity without risk of judgment and free from the hypocrisy and prejudice and rampant materialism that even the roar of the decade could not conceal.

The Sun Also Rises subtly evokes the differences between the United States and France that prompted so many to become expatriates: the beer, the Pernod, the champagne that flow freely; the *poules* who walk openly on the streets; the homosexual men attracted to Brett's ambiguous gender signals; the unconventional relationships between men and women, Cohn and his partner Frances, for instance, and all of Brett's many sexual conquests; the *bal musettes* where music and dancing are part of the fabric of daily life; the Ku Klux Klan in the midwestern states. The only real drawback to the City of Lights is the presence of so many Americans.

Hemingway's novel also makes clear that the Lost Generation will prevail. Although it delineates the decadence and despair of the central characters, Jake Barnes, its protagonist, however morally compromised by the love for Brett that leads him to betray his promise to Montoya to protect Romero, still manages to live productively. He values his work as a journalist and takes pride in posting his stories on deadline (31–32). He also pays his bills as well as others' who could afford to pay but do not. Jake, in other words, strives to live decently and responsibly even if such behavior seems outmoded and ineffectual. By the end of the novel, moreover, when he looks honestly at his relationship with Brett, he acknowledges the false illusions on which it has been based, responding, "Isn't it pretty to think so?" to her wistful assertion that they "could have had such a damned good time together" (216). As much as he might wish to believe it, as hard as it must be to say it (he has, after all, been drinking all day), Jake is capable of accepting the truth, and that is a beginning.

Hemingway prefaces *The Sun Also Rises* with two epigraphs. The first is the assertion that this is a novel of the Lost Generation. The second, however, a passage from Ecclesiastes that includes the novel's title, is an equally important assertion of the natural order, of the cycles of ends and beginnings that are the continuum of all existence and phenomena. However broken by war, however disillusioned about life, however despairing of the future, this Lost Generation too shall pass, the epigraph reminds readers with a promise of hope; another generation will succeed it. Hemingway's novel is thus a chronicle of survivors and survival that, one hundred years after the first shots of World War I rang out on the European continent, continues to testify to the nature and effects of that conflict.

HISTORICAL EXPLORATIONS OF *THE SUN ALSO RISES*

The Sun Also Rises, Ernest Hemingway's novel of the Lost Generation, explores the sad but brave lives of young men and women who live without illusions. Set amid the decadent excess of post–World War I Paris and the fiesta of San Fermín in Pamplona, Spain, the novel focuses on Jake Barnes, cruelly wounded in the fighting, and a group of American and British expatriates who, like him, the war has set free from the past. Searching now for meaning and purpose, this lost generation also struggles to forget, so it takes solace in alcohol or brief respite in good places far removed from the chaos of the modern world. Yet as the novel's final paragraphs make clear, they must inevitably live with the truth, which is both their tragedy and their salvation. In *The Sun Also Rises*, his greatest achievement, Hemingway thus defines a generation made by war and records the turmoil of the modern moment.

World War I had created the Lost Generation, as the writers of the period made patently clear. British poets such as Rupert Brooke, Siegfried Sassoon, and Wilfred Owen, writing from the trenches of the Western Front (where Owen would be fatally wounded just days before the armistice), exposed the war's brutality and senselessness. In his most famous poem, "Dulce et Decorum Est," Owen described a gas attack on retreating troops "drunk with fatigue" (l. 7), their "blood-shod" (l. 6) feet barely capable of motion. When one unfortunate soldier fails to secure his gas mask, Owen's speaker can only look on in horror as his comrade-in-arms writhes in pain until he dies and then help fling his body onto the back of a wagon as they proceed to camp. The experience will haunt his dreams, he knows, and has taught him the lesson he seeks to impart to his audience: that it is neither sweet nor honorable to die for one's country.

Just as Owen condemned the "old Lie" (l. 27) that sent a generation to war, the American poet Ezra Pound faulted a "botched civilization" for the conflict. In his poem "Hugh Selwyn Mauberley" (1920), he railed against the dishonesty and corruption for which so many had been sacrificed and captured the disillusionment and distrust that were the legacies of World War I: "believing in old men's lies, then unbelieving came home, home to a lie,/ home to many deceits, home to old lies and new infamy" (IV, ll. 5–6). In 1914 the young men of Europe had marched off to war to protect their homelands. Four years later, when the United States finally entered the conflict, American soldiers began a moral crusade, following the call of President Woodrow Wilson to "make the world safe for democracy" and to fight "the war to end all wars." In the trenches, however, such idealism had been revealed as a lie. The "myriad" who had died, "and of the best, among them," had fought to preserve the privileges of an hereditary nobility, for a corrupt and outmoded way of life, "For an old bitch gone in the teeth,/ For a botched civilization" (V, ll. 3–4), Pound wrote.

There had been no glory in their deaths, no good purpose either. What the war had done instead was strip young men and women of illusions, leave them bereft of ideals. They had been raised to believe in the progress of the industrial age, that it would transform the world for the good of all, and, just as important, that the good of all included goodness. They had been encouraged to put their faith, in other words, in humankind's steady moral progress. World War I had disabused them of such ideals and left nothing with which to replace them. As F. Scott Fitzgerald would observe of the postwar protagonists of his first novel *This Side of Paradise* (1920), "Here was a new generation, shouting the old cries, learning the old creeds, through a revery of long days and nights; destined finally to go out into that dirty gray turmoil to follow love and pride; a new generation dedicated more than the last to the fear of poverty and the worship of success; grown up to find all Gods dead, all wars fought, all faiths in man shaken" (284). Here was Gertrude Stein's Lost Generation and the subject of *The Sun Also Rises*.

The central figures in Hemingway's novel have all been wounded by war. Jake Barnes's experience of World War I has left him impotent, a sexual dysfunction that operates metaphorically in the novel to convey both the physical and psychic wounds of the postwar generation, and Lady Brett Ashley, who had served with a Voluntary Aid Detachment (VAD) during the war, had lost her true love to war-time dysentery (34) and now awaits her divorce from the British aristocrat whose service on the high seas left him a dangerous paranoid (176). Engaged to Mike Campbell, a Scots veteran whose bankrupt status functions as a metaphor for his inability to cope with his war experience, she has effected a masculine toughness that manifests as sexual freedom to mask her pain. This group of war-damaged expatriates has lost faith in love, duty, honor, fidelity, in all high ideals, as well as the institutions that uphold civilizations. Mike, for instance, cares nothing for the medals he was awarded for his service and has not even bothered to collect them (118–119). Indeed, he tells a humorous story that mocks any notion that medals are somehow a reflection of heroism, as if to say "what heroism lay in war." Jake, a Roman Catholic, no longer practices his faith. When they meet someone like Count Mippipopolous, veteran of "seven wars and four revolutions" who gamely displays the scars of two arrow wounds on his torso, they know instinctively that he is "one of us" (53). War is the ritual that initiates the members of this club.

Those who have not experienced the horrors of war continue to live with civilization's illusions. To them, war was a temporary inconvenience, a detour from their life's path, and at its end they resumed their course into the future. Robert Cohn, the Jewish American novelist and former boxer, represents this group. He may be the father of three young children and living in Paris with a woman who is not his wife, but Cohn is effectively an innocent. He believes in love and honor and even chivalry. Infatuated with Brett, he believes that they are in love after they spend a week together in San Sebastian, Spain, and determined to marry her and thereby defend her reputation, he spends much of the novel seeking desperately to win her. He even knocks Jake unconscious for insulting her and beats up Pedro Romero, the young Spanish bullfighter with whom Brett has begun an affair. Only someone like Cohn, who believes in outmoded romantic ideals, could fail to understand that he had never been more than a diversion to her, someone with whom to escape briefly her painful reality. Cohn hovers on the periphery of the Lost Generation, a perpetual outsider and even a figure of ridicule, barely tolerated because he lacks knowledge of the code of stoicism by which they live, his idealism mere sentimentality.

Hemingway's Lost Generation are expatriates by choice. Patriotism and nationalism were among the casualties of World War I, so this generation lives now where life best suits them. Paris is ideal. Its cosmopolitanism, its café culture, its tolerance of difference, its respect for the creative mind and arts, its joie de vivre were a stark contrast and quite preferable to life in the United States and Great Britain. Some expatriates, however, have no real appreciation for and no real desire to integrate into the Parisian way of life. They have come merely to live cheaply. Paris holds no appeal to them beyond its bars and cafés and *bal musettes* where they can lose themselves in drink, and many complain of life there, even as more of them continue to arrive, their money transforming the city. Jake, for instance, who works in the city, understands its rhythms and appreciates its differences, but rarely eats at Madame Lecomte's restaurant on the Ile Saint Louis anymore because, he tells her, "too many compatriots" (67) crowd it, seeking an authentic experience that their numbers ironically make impossible.

Hemingway's depiction of the Lost Generation makes clear that it was not a homogenous group. Some, in fact, were little more than grounded tourists, while others, especially those with money or privilege, were dangerously decadent. In the novel, Jake becomes the generation's moral center. His work keeps him grounded and gives him a reason to be. He is responsible, submitting his stories on deadline and paying his bills (as well as the bills of others). Lonely and unhappy, his impossible love for Brett a constant ache, he cries at night, in the privacy of his room, rather than make a public fool of himself like Cohn does. Indeed, his stoicism is a key element of his inner strength. He has accepted an important life lesson, one that he shares with Cohn: "You can't get away from yourself by moving from one place to another" (10). Yet his love for Brett makes him vulnerable to her self-absorption, and in Spain, he betrays his principles for her. Aimlessness, disillusionment, and a world-weary cynicism were the conditions of life for the generation who came of age during World War I, and *The Sun Also Rises* brilliantly captures its follies and failures and brave resolve to prevail.

The novel also reveals much about attitudes toward gender and race and ethnicity during the 1920s in both the United States and Europe. Lady Brett Ashley, for instance, is the embodiment of the era's new woman. Independent, unconventional, and sexually liberated, Brett is as assertive as any man. Indeed, she adopts a masculine toughness that sees her through the challenges of living in the aftermath of war. Like the period's flappers, she wears short skirts and has cut her hair, or bobbed it, short and styles it "like a boy's" (19). She also flouts the feminine fashion in hats, choosing a masculine felt hat in Paris rather than the typical cloche (70) and wearing a Basque beret like Mike's in Spain (116). She drinks and swears and smokes in public and refers to everyone as "chaps." Awaiting a divorce so that she can marry Mike Campbell (although she loves Jake), she engages in a brief and meaningless affair with Robert Cohn and seduces the bullfighter Pedro Romero. A "man's woman" (indeed she has no women friends), Brett does not swoon at the carnage in the bullring and graciously accepts Romero's gift of a bull's ear when most women (and even some men) would have been revolted by it.

Everything about Brett Ashley typifies the way in which expectations of women changed in the Jazz Age. Since the late nineteenth century, women's horizons had been expanding. Women were increasingly emancipated from the home as they were admitted to study at colleges and universities, secured employment in the administrative and financial sectors, and gained control of their own finances and even their choice of marriage partner. World War I accelerated the pace of this change. Brett, for instance, had served in a VAD, assisting medical personnel in military field hospitals during World War I, work that would have been deemed unsuitable for a genteel woman of a previous era, but the slaughter occurring in Europe demolished gender barriers as well. Indeed, writers such as Vera

Brittain, Enid Bagnold, and Naomi Mitchison performed admirable service in VADs during the war and in some cases, in Brittain's *Testament of Youth* (1933), for instance, provided reports from the front that were every bit as important as those recorded by the men who fought. Because a generation of men had died in the war, marriage was no longer an expectation for women, nor was motherhood. Increasing numbers of women also engaged in premarital sex and used birth control. They were, in other words, taking control of their sexual identity. By 1920, when American women gained the vote, a privilege that British women over the age of thirty had enjoyed since 1918, women like Brett Ashley would not have been uncommon. They would not, however, have been entirely accepted, a fact that Hemingway also conveys in his novel.

Brett is a disruptive force in *The Sun Also Rises*. No man seems capable of resisting her sexual allure, and desire to possess her pits one man against another. Jealous of Cohn's affair with Brett, for instance, Jake verbally abuses him, and he fights with Mike about the woman they both love. Cohn, too, fights with both Jake and Mike and badly beats Romero to prove his love for and devotion to the woman he calls "Circe" (125). Brett, it seems, would not be bothered by the comparison. After all, when Jake encounters her at a *bal musette*, accompanied by a crowd of homosexuals, she wears a "slipover jersey sweater" that accentuates her shapely figure, its "curves like the hull of a racing yacht" (19), and later, in Spain, when the revelers at the fiesta dance around the striking woman, she relishes the attention (135). Like the mythological figure in Homer's tale *The Odyssey*, Brett is indeed capable of bewitching men and transforming them into beasts.

The ambivalent nature of Hemingway's characterization of Brett suggests an equally ambivalent response to the era's new woman. In Brett, the novel's male characters have a competitor rather than a companion, someone who can match them drink for drink, who faces unpleasant realities without flinching, who asserts her sexual self with masculine prerogative. Her independence and self-confidence, which would have been unusual and unacceptable in previous generations of women, who were taught to depend on and defer to men, to conceal their thoughts and feelings, to be modest about their talents and chaste about their body, are as much the reason for her attractiveness as her physical charms. Yet the very qualities that make her men's equal also make her fearsome, a witch, a bitch, to use the term that Hemingway scholars have long attached to her, an unruly woman who does not know her proper role and place within the sphere of gender. This Jazz Age woman threatens to overturn the traditional social order and to displace men from their position of power and privilege. Romero, in fact, asks her to grow her hair long, as if to tame this representative of the new woman. As attractive as that woman may have been, Hemingway's depiction of Lady Brett Ashley suggests, society was not entirely ready to embrace her.

If people were ambivalent about the Jazz Age woman, they were less so about Jews and people of color. Despite the democratization that was occurring during the 1920s, racism and anti-Semitism remained firmly entrenched in Western society. Discrimination against Jews was and is an historic problem. Relegated to living beyond the pale, in ghettos that restricted their freedom of movement and limited their opportunities, vilified as moneylenders or usurers, victimized by successive waves of ethnic cleansing and pogroms, Jews had long been a persecuted minority. Indeed, Shakespeare's Jew of Venice, the moneylender Shylock in his play *The Merchant of Venice*, gives some indication of these historic prejudices against Jews. Modernist writers reveal similar attitudes. In "Hugh Selwyn Mauberley," for instance, Ezra Pound rails against "usury age-old and age-thick" (IV, l. 7), an oblique allusion to the Jews, many of whom were connected to the banking and manufacturing industries and thus, some believed, had profited from World War I. F. Scott Fitzgerald's *The Great Gatsby* also reflected the era's anti-Semitism in its treatment of the Jewish gangster Meyer Wolfsheim, Gatsby's criminal associate in his bootlegging business. Wearing cufflinks mounted with human molars, Wolfsheim, the man who fixed the 1919 World Series, is predatory and corrupt, the very stereotype of the Jewish businessman.

Hemingway's treatment of Robert Cohn, the Jewish American novelist in *The Sun Also Rises*, provides further evidence of anti-Semitism during the 1920s. Born into New York's elite Jewish society and educated at military school, where he distinguished himself on the playing field, Cohn had never experienced race consciousness until he entered Princeton University, an Ivy League institution where America's white Anglo-Saxon Protestant elite established the rules and asserted their superiority. At Princeton he was quickly made to feel his difference. To compensate for his sense of inferiority, he became a boxer. Indeed, he was a middleweight boxing champion, but as Jake reports in the novel's first paragraph, "I never met anyone of his class who remembered him" (3). Neither intellect nor athletic prowess is sufficient to win acceptance in WASP America.

Because he did not see action in World War I and intensely dislikes expatriate Parisian life, Cohn also can never hope to be accepted as "one of us" among Jake's circle of friends, but his Jewish heritage further alienates him from the group. Jake's friend Bill Gorton, for instance, who joins the group for a fishing trip that precedes the fiesta of San Fermín, never tires of complaining of Cohn's Jewishness. "Haven't you got some more Jewish friends you could bring along?" (89), he chides Jake, and Mike's contempt for the man who has cuckolded him goes beyond sexual jealousy. He repeatedly derides him for his race, using the word "Jew" as if it were profanity. (Bill actually uses a racial slur at one point [142].) Even Jake, who rather likes Cohn, gets exasperated early in the novel by his "hard, Jewish, stubborn, streak" (9) and eventually pities him for his innocence and hates him for his inability to be gracious in defeat. Like the Jews of old, Cohn becomes the group's scapegoat. The perpetual outsider, he becomes the focus of their unhappiness and disappointments. The successful novelist unscathed by war must be made to suffer, and he does. So much about Cohn's personality is irritating: his romantic idealism in an age when ideals have been dashed, his arrogance, his bravado, his foolishness, his defensiveness. His Jewishness, however, defines him for all the novel's characters, just as it would have defined him for the larger community of his time, and thus *The Sun Also Rises* reveals the era's anti-Semitism.

Book Two opens with a curious discussion between Jake and Bill, who has just arrived from Vienna to join his friend for a fishing trip in Spain, that extends the novel's depiction of racial prejudice against people of color. In Vienna, Bill has been spectator at a prizefight between a "local white boy" and a massive black man whom Bill compares to Tiger Flowers, who would become the first African American middleweight boxing champion in 1926. When the black boxer knocks down the local talent, a riot ensues, and Bill helps rescue the black man from the irate crowd. Later he takes him round to the promoter to collect both his clothes, which he had had to abandon in the melee, and his winnings. The promoter, however, claims that the boxer owes him money for the damages to the venue. Moreover, he claims that the boxer had "violated [his] contract." He was supposed to throw the fight and let the local boy emerge the victor. The incredulous boxer, who claims that he never hit the boy, tells Bill, "I didn't do nothing in there for forty minutes but try and let him stay. That white boy musta ruptured himself swinging at me" (63). Needless to say, the boxer leaves only with his clothes, his watch having been stolen, and Bill advances him money for his fare home.

Bill's travel story seems little more than a digression in the novel. It is unrelated to the major characters and fails to advance the plot. It does, however, provide evidence of racial discrimination during the era and may even anticipate the rise of European fascism that would culminate in World

War II. During World War I, shortages of men of fighting age eventually caused both Britain and France to recruit Africans and men of African descent from their Caribbean colonies into their forces. The move was controversial, stirring long-held fears about arming blacks, many of whom would have been the descendants of slaves, and, compounding the problem, asking them to shoot at white men. African Americans also enlisted for service in World War I, and many distinguished themselves in the fighting, but under French rather than American commanders. Prejudice against African Americans, who were thought to be inferior to whites, relegated them primarily to support roles until French officers agreed to lead them into battle, where they were every bit as good at combat as their white counterparts.

Promised French citizenship for their service to the mother country, France's black colonial troops were deeply betrayed when they were deported to their homelands after World War I. African Americans, however, fared a bit better. It was the age of jazz, and the French were as wild about the music as Americans. They were captivated as well by Josephine Baker's provocative dance moves. African American musicians and performers consequently found themselves welcomed into Paris's cabarets and revues, but not fully into its society. Indeed, their exoticism marked them as "other," and it was as "others" that they functioned in society, enacting rather than challenging traditional beliefs about and views of race. One of France's most popular performers of the 1920s, Chocolat the clown, for instance, who was humiliated and abused in his comic routines by white performers, reinforced the view that blacks were inferior to whites, and even Josephine Baker's famous banana dance emphasized her primitive roots.

While Bill has nothing but admiration for the black boxer, calling him "splendid" (63) and "wonderful" (62), and is appalled by the "injustice everywhere" (63), after all, the local boy had hit his opponent when he had his arm raised to speak to the crowd (62) and then is cheated of his earnings, his treatment makes clear the reality of race prejudice in Europe during the Jazz Age. A black man simply cannot beat a white man; he must always demonstrate his inferiority to the white man. In fact, Theodore "Tiger" Flowers faced just the sort of discrimination in his career that Hemingway's black boxer experienced. On his climb to the championship, Flowers lost several controversial rulings that denied him what seemed certain victory for what were probably reasons of race.

En route to their fishing trip in Spain, Jake and Bill become irritated and even a bit testy when they learn that the train on which they are travelling is filled with Roman Catholic pilgrims who have booked every seat for the four luncheon services, forcing other passengers to wait until late afternoon for a meal. Confronting a priest returning from the dining car, Bill pointedly challenges him, asking, "When do us Protestants get a chance to eat, Father?" (76) and then asserts, "It's enough to make a man join the Klan" (77). The exchange, like Bill's travel story about the black boxer, seems once again out of context and unnecessary to the novel, but in fact it reinforces the point of Bill's tale as well as Hemingway's depiction of Robert Cohn. Despite the general loosening of social and moral restrictions and the democratizing effect of consumer culture during the 1920s, race consciousness in all its many forms remained a barrier to full equality. In the Midwest of the United States, from which Bill, a Chicagoan, has just arrived, a resurgent Ku Klux Klan was protecting "true Americans" from immigrants, Catholics, Jews, and, of course, African Americans. In Europe, where increasing numbers of people of color were settling (Bill's black boxer, in fact, has a wife and children in Cologne, Germany.), the National Socialist German Workers' Party, under the leadership of Adolf Hitler, was on the rise. Hemingway was clearly aware of these tensions and recognized that their inclusion in *The Sun Also Rises* was necessary to an understanding of the era. In fact, rather than out of context, they are entirely within the context that defined their world.

One of the qualities that also distinguishes Jake from the novel's other central characters is his appreciation for the bullfight. Indeed, he is an *aficionado*. Bullfighting is an art to him, not blood sport. He understands and respects both the matador and the bull as worthy adversaries who engage in a well-choreographed dance of death. His reverence for the sport's rituals, moreover, has earned him the respect of Spaniards such as Montoya and admitted him to the community's inner circle. When *The Sun Also Rises*'s expatriates travel to Spain to experience the country's traditional spectacle, Jake thus becomes their guide, providing Hemingway the opportunity to offer a primer on the subject and thereby make bullfighting central to the novel's thematic interests, especially its exploration of masculinity, and its treatment of postwar ennui.

In *Death in the Afternoon*, his 1932 study of the bullfight, Hemingway asserted, "Bullfighting is the only art in which the artist is in danger of death and in which the degree of brilliance in the performance is left to the fighter's honor" (77). Bullfighting, in other words, is a demonstration of style, technique, and courage. It is an art heightened by the presence of death. In each of its three distinct stages or *tercios*, the matador and the bull test their mettle, and while the matador may initially be supported by the *picadors* and the *banderilleros*, who help weaken the animal, he must ultimately face the bull alone, with only his *muleta*, or red cape, and sword to demonstrate with his death-defying maneuvers domination of his opponent. If his performance has been well executed, the matador earns not only the crowd's spirited applause but also, if they wave their white handkerchiefs, the bull's ear, tribute to his courage and skill. After all, with each twirl of the *muleta*, he has dared the bull to gore him, taunted his adversary to kill or be killed, and he has triumphed.

For Hemingway, the matador, as exemplified by Pedro Romero, represents an ideal of masculinity. Bold and brave, he exhibits the kind of grace under pressure that makes clear his ability to master fear. Firm and resolute, he refuses to back down from a fight, whether his opponent is in the ring or a hotel room. Indeed, Romero's refusal to submit to Cohn's beating as well as Cohn's efforts to end their fight with a handshake foreshadows his triumph over the bull the next day. Romero may be bruised and battered, his body may ache with every move, but his spirit is undaunted. He may only be capable of hitting Cohn from his sitting position on the floor, but he continues to punch him and thereby vanquish him, and when the bull charges one last time, Romero stands firm, becoming "one with the bull" (191) as he kills it. In the face of a challenge, a man can do nothing more.

The bullfight also functions as an antidote to the horrors of World War I. Its rituals and structures impose order on a beautiful struggle between determined opponents who face each other honorably, one on one, to the death. World War I, in contrast, had defied all the rules of war. Trench warfare and mustard gas, barbed wire, machine guns, and armored tanks, indeed all the mechanized butchery of modern warfare, had stripped the conflict of any shred of honor and dignity and made a mockery of its conventions. Hemingway's Lost Generation had been left with the chaos and disorder, with the emptiness and meaninglessness. In the *corrida de toros*, combat, and, by extension, their experience, could be metaphorically redeemed. As Hemingway wrote of the spectacle, "It's just like having a ringside seat at the war with nothing going to happen to you" (*Selected Letters* 88). In the bullring, men could face death with dignity. They were not, like Jake had been in his war, emasculated by meaningless conflict.

War is messy business Hemingway's Lost Generation discovered. Not only had it led to a massive slaughter of the brave, but it had also erased the hopes and dreams of those who survived and stripped them of their ideals. As a metaphor for war, however, the bullfight contained the violence; its rituals ordered the chaos. Its elemental conflict between two valiant opponents restored honor and dignity. In the bullring a man could master his fear and display his courage. After the appalling brutality of World War I, Hemingway had discovered a traditional spectacle that could restore belief and placed it at his novel's center to emphasize the qualities it rendered visible year in and year out. In that spectacle, he could be certain that his generation, too, would prevail.

DOCUMENTING *THE SUN ALSO RISES*
The Lost Generation

World War I left the young men and women who came of age during that conflict disillusioned, distrustful, disheartened, severed from the old truths but without the certainty of new ones. They were, as the American expatriate writer Gertrude Stein told a new arrival to Paris, Ernest Hemingway, "a lost generation." The following excerpts from writers and literary men and women of the period who, like Hemingway, settled in Paris following World War I document the expatriate experience and the intellectual and cultural life that attracted this generation to Europe.

Document: From *Exile's Return: A Literary Odyssey of the 1920s*, Malcolm Cowley, 1934

But there was one idea that was held in common by the older and the younger inhabitants of the Village—the idea of salvation by exile. "They do things better in Europe: let's go there." This was not only the undertone of discussions at Luke O'Connor's saloon; it was also the recurrent melody of an ambitious work, a real symposium, then being prepared for the printer. (p. 74)

 . . . One after another they come forward to tell us that American civilization itself is responsible for the tragedy of American talent. (p. 76)

Life in this country is joyless and colorless, universally standardized, tawdry, uncreative, given over to the worship of wealth and machinery. . . . And what is the remedy? (p. 77)

Early in July 1921, just after finishing his preface and delivering the complete manuscript to the publisher, Mr. Stearns left this country, perhaps forever. His was no ordinary departure: he was Alexander marching into Persia and Byron shaking the dust of England from his feet. Reporters came to the gangplank to jot down his last words. Everywhere young men were preparing to follow his example. Among the contributors to *Civilization in the United States*, not many could go: most of them were moderately successful men who had achieved security without achieving freedom. But the younger and footloose intellectuals went streaming up the longest gangplank in the world; they were preparing a great migration eastward into new prairies of the mind.

"I'm going to Paris," they said at first, and then, "I'm going to the South of France. . . . I'm sailing Wednesday—next month—as soon as I can scrape together money enough to buy a ticket." Money wasn't impossible to scrape together; some of it could be saved from one's salary or borrowed from one's parents or one's friends. Newspapers and magazines were interested in reports from Europe, two or three foundations had fellowships for study abroad, and publishers sometimes made advances against the future royalties of an unwritten book. In those days publishers were looking for future authors, and the authors insisted that their books would have to be finished in France, where one could live for next to nothing. "Good-by, so long," they said, "I'll meet you on the Left Bank. I'll drink your health in good red Burgundy, I'll kiss all the girls for you. I'm sick of this country. I'm going abroad to write one good novel." (p. 79)

Source: Malcolm Cowley, *Exile's Return: A Literary Odyssey of the 1920s.* New York: Penguin, 1934, 1951, 1994. Reprinted with permission.

Document: From "American Bohemians in Paris," Ernest Hemingway, 1922

The scum of Greenwich Village, New York, has been skimmed off and deposited in large ladlesful on that section of Paris adjacent to the Café Rotonde. New scum, of course, has risen to take the place of the old, but the oldest scum, the thickest scum and the scummiest scum has come across the ocean, somehow, and with its afternoon and evening levees has made the Rotonde the leading Latin Quarter show place for tourists in search of atmosphere.

It is a strange-acting and strange-looking breed that crowd the tables of the Café Rotonde. They have all striven so hard for a careless individuality of clothing that they have achieved a sort of uniformity of eccentricity. A first look into the smoky, high-ceilinged, table-crammed interior of the Rotonde gives the same feeling that hits you as you step into the bird house at the zoo. There seems to be a tremendous, raucous, many-pitched squawking going on broken up by many waiters who fly around through the smoke like so many black and white magpies. The tables are full—they are always full—someone is moved down and crowded together, something is knocked over, more people come in at the swinging door, another black and white waiter pivots between tables toward the door and, having shouted your order at his disappearing back, you look around you at individual people. (p. 23)

... You can find anything you are looking for at the Rotonde—except serious artists. The trouble is that people who go on a tour of the Latin Quarter look in at the Rotonde and think they are seeing an assembly of the real artists of Paris. I want to correct that in a very public manner, for the artists of Paris who are turning out creditable work resent and loathe the Rotonde crowd.

The fact that there are twelve francs for a dollar brought over the Rotonders, along with a good many other people, and if the exchange ever gets back to normal they will have to go back to America. They are nearly all loafers expending the energy that an artist puts into his creative work in talking about what they are going to do and condemning the work of all artists who have gained any degree of recognition. By talking about art they obtain the same satisfaction that the real artist does in his work. That is very pleasant, of course, but they insist upon posing as artists. (pp. 24–25)

... But the gang that congregates at the corner of the Boulevard Montparnasse and the Boulevard Raspail have no time to work at anything else; they put in a full day at the Rotonde. (p. 25)

Source: Ernest Hemingway, "American Bohemians in Paris," *The Toronto Star Weekly*, March 25, 1922.

Document: From *Being Geniuses Together 1920–1930*, Robert McAlmon and Rev. Kay Boyle, 1968

The influx of people who came to be called "expatriates" had begun before this, but now they hung out in Montparnasse at the Dôme and the Rotonde. At the time I was doing Lipps, the Deux Magots, various bistros, all around St. Germain or the Boulevard St. Michel. I was hardly aware of Montparnasse, even as a legend, and Sylvia Beach informed me it was ghastly. . . . In the daytime I was busy writing the short stories which went into *A Hasty Bunch*, a title which [James] Joyce suggested because he found my American use of language racy. I was at that six weeks, and just as it was finished a flock of "expatriates" descended upon the Rue Jacob, Sts. Pères, St. Germain section. . . . They all stayed in the same hotel, and Vicki Baum's *Grand Hotel* couldn't touch the drama and intrigue which occurred in that hotel, but as I didn't stay there, that is somebody else's story, but I fear the rest will be silence. . . . How that little group of pilgrim expatriates loved each other! (pp. 33–34)

By 1922 or 1923 there were quantities of Americans who had settled in France, to stay indefinitely either in Paris or in small towns nearby. The American bars had not yet come into being, and there was a great deal more entertaining in the home than was later to occur. . . . (pp. 37–38)

The summer of 1923, France as a whole celebrated the three-day fourteenth of July period as usual, but in Montparnasse there were a number of people of various nationalities who extended the gala days to a three months' period. . . . (pp. 38)

The fourteenth of July celebration started with an impetus which made its gaiety continue for weeks. Enough of afterwar recklessness and enough of dawning hopefulness were about for dissipations to have a mass velocity. This momentum, like great periods in art or history, occurs seldom, and not even in everyone's lifetime. In the [Latin] Quarter, foreigners of many nationalities collected daily about the Rotonde, then in bad favor with Americans, for its *patron* was a bastard. He asked ladies not to smoke or to appear hatless on the terrace of the Rotonde, and the English-American quarterites moved at once across the street to the Dôme, which then became their favorite hangout. The Rotonde has since belonged to the French bourgeois, or to the foreigner who sits for hours over one coffee or one beer. On the thirteenth I came in from the forests of Rambouillet where I had been for two months writing on a two-decker novel. I felt entitled to a letdown for a few days before getting back to work. . . . (pp. 38–39)

Migration season struck the Quarter as the first wintry chill began to drive habitués into the smoky and thick interiors of the customary hangouts. I went to Berlin. . . . No one knew from one day to the next what the dollar would bring in marks, but everybody knew that, whatever happened, the dollar bought in Berlin as much as ten or twenty dollars would buy elsewhere. It made for wildness. In spite of the poverty-stricken situation of the people there were several smart cabarets and one futuristic dance place for tea dancing as well as for night encounters. Otherwise there were joints and dives of every order, and there was no telling whom one might encounter, anywhere. From Russia, Poland, the Balkan States, from Scandinavia, England, France, and South and North America, visitors flocked into Berlin, and even hardened Berlin night-lifers could not tell with certainty how the tone or quality of any night club might change from week to week. (pp. 106–107)

Now, after a month of Paris, I felt I must get away. I had no love, merely an infatuation for the place. Upon arriving there after an absence, I was always in a fever of excitement, and couldn't do quickly enough the bars of Montparnasse and the cabarets of Montmartre, and the Champs Elysées district. Like Fanny Hill, however, my fever for curiosities abated as the blood stream flowed more coolly and the arteries hardened. Crossing the Seine into the Place de le Concorde on a misty spring morning, or seeing Notre Dame des Champs from river level at dawn, when well on with drink, still brought a foaming ecstasy into me, a stroke of lightning to the heart or mind about the wonder of it. But I knew all too well that Paris is a bitch, and that one shouldn't become infatuated with bitches, particularly when they have wit, imagination, experience, and tradition behind their ruthlessness. (pp. 124–125)

> Source: Robert McAlmon and Rev. Kay Boyle, *Being Geniuses Together 1920–1930*, Garden City, NY: Doubleday & Company, 1968. Reprinted with permission from Ian von Franckenstein.

Document: From *Paris Was Yesterday. 1925–1939*, Janet Flanner, 1972

1925

Josephine Baker has arrived at the Théâtre des Champs-Élysées in *La Revue Nègre* and the result has been unanimous. Paris has never drawn a color line. Covarrubias did the sets, pink drops with cornucopias of hams and watermelons, and the Civil War did the rest, aided by Miss Baker. The music is tuneless and stunningly orchestrated, and the end of the show is dull, but never Miss Baker's part. It was even less dull the first night, when she did what used to be, what indeed still should be called, a stomach dance (later deleted).

1926

The appearance here of Ernest Hemingway's *roman à clef*, *The Sun Also Rises*, has stirred Montparnasse, where, it is asserted, all of the four leading characters are local and easily identifiable. The titled British declassee and her Scottish friend, the American Frances and her unlucky *Robert Cohn* with his art magazine which, like a new broom, was to sweep aesthetics clean—all these personages are, it is maintained, to be seen just where Hemingway so often placed them at the Select. . . . (p. 12)

1927

The night (May 21, 1927) a young tourist named Captain Charles Lindbergh landed his plane *The Spirit of St. Louis* at Le Bourget, concluding his historic flight across the Atlantic Ocean, the Paris news vendors screamed through the streets, "*Bonnes nouvelles!* The American has arrived."

At their Montmartre night clubs Zelli and Florence stood champagne to the Americans, as did excited patrons in humble bars, gallantly offering bad brandy to their Yankee clients. The prettiness of French journalism the next morning must also be noted. Of Lindbergh, *L'Intransigeant* wrote, "He has a heart of steel in the body of a bird. He is a carrier pigeon. . . . The Ministry of Foreign Affairs flew the Stars and Stripes, as did most of the tramcars. (p. 22)

For five decades, journalist Janet Flanner (1892–1978), writing as Genet, served as Paris correspondent to *The New Yorker* magazine. Her "Letters from Paris" chronicled life in the "City of Light" from 1925 to 1975, including the Jazz Age, when she frequented Gertrude Stein's salon and attended Josephine Baker's first performance in *La Revue Negre*. (Corbis)

1929

The Wall Street crash has had its effect here. In the Rue de la Paix the jewelers are reported to be losing fortunes in sudden cancellations of orders, and at the Ritz bar the gritty ladies are having to pay for their cocktails themselves. In the Quartier de l'Europe, little firms that live exclusively on the American trade have not sold one faked Chanel copy in a fortnight. A wholesale *antiquaire* in the Boulevard Raspail has a cellar bulging with guaranteed Louis XIV candlesticks which are not moving. In the Rue La Boëtie a thrifty young Frenchwoman, who as a Christmas gift bought herself a majority of stock in the art gallery where she works, finds that all the forty-nine blue Dufys are still hanging on the wall and that it is not likely her stock will pay a dividend. In real-estate circles certain advertisements have been illuminating: "For Sale, Cheap, Nice Old Château, 1 Hr. frm Paris; Original Boiserie, 6 New Baths; Owner Forced Return New York Wednesday; Must Have IMMEDIATE CASH; will Sacrifice."

Generally the French people's sympathy in our disaster has been polite and astonishingly sincere, considering that for the past ten years they have seen us through one of the worst phases of our prosperity—which consisted of thousands of our tourists informing them that we were the richest country in the world, that they should pay their debts, that we had made the world safe for democracy, that we were the most generous people in the world, that they should pay their debts, and that we were the richest country in the world. Only in a few malicious French quarters has it been suggested that now certain small American investors can afford to paste Wall Street stocks on their suitcases or toss them to the crowd, as they pasted and tossed five-franc notes here that marvelous summer when the franc fell to fifty. (pp. 61–62)

Source: Janet Flanner, *Paris Was Yesterday: 1925–1939.* Ed. Irving Drutman. San Diego and New York: Harcourt Brace Jovanovich, 1972, 1988.

The Art of the Bullfight

The bullfight has a long tradition in Spain, where matadors are heroic figures who face death with "grace under pressure," as Ernest Hemingway would have said. Indeed, for Hemingway, bullfighting was less a sport and more an art, and it fascinated him, providing an example and confirming his view of a hard, stoic masculinity. The following excerpts provide several perspectives, including Hemingway's own reports, on the spectacle.

Document: From *Being Geniuses Together 1920–1930*, Robert McAlmon and Rev. Kay Boyle, 1968

A year or so later the lot of us were in Paris at the same time, and after a trip to London I talked of going to Spain, Hemingway wanted much to see a bullfight, and after a week of talking about it we headed toward Spain.... (p. 178)

The day that we were to see our first bullfight we agreed that the horse part of it might bother us, so we had a few drinks before taking our seats. We took a bottle of whisky with us, with the understanding that, if shocked, we would gulp down a quantity to calm ourselves. My reactions to the bullfight were not at all what I had anticipated. At first it seemed totally unreal, like something happening on the screen. The first bull charged into the ring with tremendous violence. When the horses were brought in, it charged head on and lifted the first horse over its head. But the horns did not penetrate.

Instead of a shock of disgust, I rose in my seat and let out a yell. Things were happening too quickly for my mind to consider the horse's suffering. Later, however, when one of the horses was galloping in hysteria around the ring, treading on its own entrails, I decidedly didn't like it. I have since discovered that many hardened Spanish *aficionados*, and in one case I knew of, the brother of a bullfighter, had to look the other way on such occasions. Hemingway became at once an *aficionado*, that is, a passionate bullfight fan or enthusiast, intent upon learning all about the art. If I suspect that his need to love the art of bullfighting came from Gertrude Stein's praise of it, as well as from his belief in the value of "self-hardening," it is only because his bullfight book (*Death in the Afternoon*) adopts such a belligerent attitude in the defense of bullfighting. There are countless English and Americans who were bullfight enthusiasts many years before that summer of 1924 when Hemingway and I both saw our first, but he made it into a literary or artistic experience.

By the end of that day my temper about everything connected with the bullfight was much what it is now. I resented the crowd's brutality and the way people threw mats and articles of clothing into the ring at moments in which the matadors were in danger. The crowd itself was taking no chances. The bull was—when he was—a magnificent animal, a snorting engine of black velocity and force. The matadors did their dance well, moved beautifully, and played seriously with death. The role of the horses I decided to overlook as confirmation of Spanish brutality which was probably no worse than many French and Anglo Saxon cruelties. (pp. 179–180)

The days and nights were hot with a heat that sweated through one's flesh and bones. However, the fiesta spirit was rampant, and everybody was willing to drink plenty of pernod and forget the heat. The town during the first two days before the bullfights came on was quiet till noon, when the café terraces were crowded. After lunch the streets were empty again, but at six o'clock the fiesta gaieties began. Throngs of peasants from the mountains roamed through the city, their necks encircled with necklaces of garlic, and various-shaped goatskin bags of wine thrown over their shoulders. Some of these bags were made in the form of ships, and some in the shape of dolls or animals. To drink, one held the goatskin high with one hand and squeezed it with the other, and a small stream of goaty-tasting wine spurted into one's open mouth. This took some learning, but the natives were adept. Little crowds of natives continually came and went, blowing whistles or playing more or less primitive instruments. Groups formed and danced solos in circles....

The first two nights, all of the American-English gathered there proceeded to lose one another. But each one eventually tagged onto or got picked up by some wandering group of musicians or boys from the mountains, and the dancing and drinking continued till early morning. The town slept till well past noon, and then we all went to inspect the bulls that were to be used in the corridas.

The third morning, the day of the first bullfight, everyone was up by six o'clock, and out in the boarded street down which the bulls for the day were to be driven. Hundreds of boys and young men stood along the sides of the street and ran ahead of the bulls that were being driven to the bull ring. A few got butted or knocked against the walls by an excited and bewildered bull, but no one was badly injured or killed, as is sometimes the case. Later, when the fierce bulls had been driven into their corrals to wait for the afternoon corridas, the amateur fun began. A heifer, light-bodied steer, or yearling bull—but seldom—would be released into the ring. Hundreds of aspiring bullfighters were in the ring, and the panic-stricken heifer, steer, or young bull would dash here and there, sometimes charging, but as often merely looking for a means of escape.

Hemingway had been talking a great deal about courage, and how a man needs to test himself to prove to himself that he can take it. I dunno. But Hemingway was persuaded that he must prove himself. With his coat he tried to attract the charge and the repeated charge of a steer, but the two-hundred-odd others in the ring were also trying to capture that mystified animal's attention. Finally Hemingway took a charge straight on face, and then, catching the steer's horns, attempted to throw it. He did break its strength, and got cheered by the crowd, but when the steer was released it ran away bellowing a bewildered moo, its tail wagging pathetically, and an expression on its face indicating that it was having no fun at all. (pp. 274–275)

Source: Robert McAlmon and Rev. Kay Boyle, *Being Geniuses Together 1920–1930*, Garden City, NY: Doubleday & Company, 1968. Reprinted with permission from Ian von Franckenstein.

Document: From "Bull Fighting a Tragedy," Ernest Hemingway, 1923

... It was the first bull fight I ever saw, but it was not the best. The best was in the little town of Pamplona high up in the hills of Navarre, and came weeks later. Up in Pamplona, where they have held six days of bull fighting each year since 1126 A.D., and where the bulls race through the streets of the town each morning at six o'clock with half the town running ahead of them. Pamplona, where every man and boy in town is an amateur bull fighter and where there is an amateur fight each morning that is attended by 20,000 people in which the amateur fighters are all unarmed and there is a casualty list at least equal to a Dublin election. But Pamplona, with the best bull fight and the wild tale of the amateur fights, comes in the second chapter.

I am not going to apologize for bull fighting. It is a survival of the days of the Roman Coliseum. But it does need some explanation. Bull fighting is not a sport. It was never supposed to be. It is a tragedy. A very great tragedy. The tragedy is the death of the bull. It is played in three definite acts. (p. 95)

. . . It is a tragedy, and it symbolizes the struggle between man and the beasts.

NO one at any time in the fight can approach the bull at any time except directly from the front. That is where the danger comes. There are also all sorts of complicated passes that must be done with the cape, each requiring as much technique as a champion billiard player. And underneath it all is the necessity for playing the old tragedy in the absolutely custom bound, law-laid-down way. It must all be done gracefully, seemingly effortlessly and always with dignity. The worst criticism the Spaniards ever make of a bull fighter is that his work is "vulgar." (p. 96)

Source: Ernest Hemingway, "Bull Fighting a Tragedy," *The Toronto Star Weekly*, October 20, 1923.

Document: From "Pamplona in July," Ernest Hemingway, 1923

. . . Maera is Herself's favorite bull fighter. And if you want to keep any conception of yourself as a brave, hard, perfectly balanced, thoroughly competent man in your wife's mind never take her to a real bull fight. I used to go into the amateur fights in the morning to try and win back a small amount of her esteem but the more I discovered that bull fighting required a very great quantity of a certain type of courage of which I had an almost complete lack the more it became apparent that any admiration she might ever redevelop for me would have to be simply an antidote to the real admiration for Maera and Villalta. You cannot compete with bull fighters on their own ground. If anywhere. The only way most husbands are able to keep any drag with their wives at all is that, first there are only a limited number of bull fighters, second there are only a limited number of wives who have ever seen bull fights. (p. 106)

Source: Ernest Hemingway, "Pamplona in July," *The Toronto Star Weekly*, October 27, 1923.

Race, Ethnicity, and the Ku Klux Klan

Despite its European setting, The Sun Also Rises *captures in its background the shadows of ethnic and racial strife that was characteristic during the Jazz Age, not only in the United States but also, perhaps to a lesser degree, in Europe. The following documents provide evidence of that strife, which was most visible in the resurgence of the Ku Klux Klan during the 1920s. The first two articles report on efforts to ease anti-Semitism in the United States, including one which focuses on "The New Hyphenism" in postwar America. The next three documents focus on the rise of the Klan during the 1920s in regions of the country where it had previously not been prominent and for reasons that included racism but also expressed fears about an undermining of the Protestant foundations of the nation.*

Document: From "For Christian-Jewish Friendship HP," *The Literary Digest*, 1922

Christian blood for the Passover was once believed by non-Jews to be an essential of the ancient Judaic rite and in numerous instances, history recorded, this carefully fed tradition has been responsible for the ordered slaying of Jews. But ancient superstitions and grudges are being dissipated in the light of knowledge, and here in the Western World, we are assured, the Jew and non-Jew are gradually arriving at a mutual understanding and respect which are clean of religious prejudice. However, there is still much blind antagonism between Jew and Gentile, the responsibility for which, tho not altogether one-sided, rests heavily upon the younger faith. Yet Christianity is the daughter-religion of "Mother Israel," a circumstance alone which imparts "an abiding and inevasible obligation upon the Christian Church in its relation to a people directly descended from those who were the founders and disciples of Israel." Thus writes Dr. Stephen S. Wise, a prominent New York rabbi, in *The American Hebrew* (New York), which devotes its Passover number to a symposium on a means to a better understanding between the two faiths. Jew and non-Jew were invited to a frank discussion, and the result affords a brighter outlook for the settlement of the ancient grudge. . . .

[According to Wise,] "Whatever Christians may have taught or believed touching [the death of Jesus at the hands of the Jews] in the past, their duty in the present is clear as are the heavens in the noon hour—the duty of affirming that incalculable and eternal is the debt of Christians to Israel, of whose gifts Jesus is treasured as the chiefest.

"And a third reason, perhaps most binding of all, to more Christian churches consciously to do battle against existent prejudice respecting the Jew ought to be found in that consciousness of reparation owing to the Jew for nearly nineteen centuries of Christlessness, which have been suffered by Christ's people. . . .

"Nothing, in a word, could have been more unmessianic than the attitude of Christendom toward Israel, the people of Jesus—tho I do not forget that there have been in every generation Christian men and women who have borne themselves as the new brothers and sisters of Jesus toward his older brothers and sisters." . . .

The basic cause of the gulf between Christians and Jews—whatever other causes, economic, racial, or what not, may be added thereto—is a religious one, says Dr. Edward N. Calisch, President of the Central Conference of American Rabbis, and he maintains that the Jews did not reject Jesus of Nazareth; but the Christ of a Pauline Christianity that "was formulated more than a century and a half after his death." Happily, he considers, this theology is "losing its ascendency, and real religion is coming into its own among the children of men. The throne of dogmatism, like many other thrones, has been toppled over, and a spirit of religious democracy is making its way into the heart of mankind. Creeds, and catechisms may be useful things in their way, but character and conduct are more important." There are, the writer holds, beautiful ideals common to all religions, "and a recognition of this fact leads to a sympathy and appreciation in whose presence polemics and more theological hair-splitting are a futile waste of time." It appears to Dr. Calisch, then, that the synagog could profitably undertake a campaign of education along these lines. . . .

What the American Jew needs to develop, writes Walter Lippmann, formerly associate editor of *The New Republic*, is the habit of self-criticism. If the spokesmen of the Jewish people would devote one-half the energy they now expend in answering attacks to attacking the evils that stare every one in the face, he says, "they would make a real contribution to the unity of American life. . . ."

"Start by believing that the non-Jews are human beings and not too much beneath you—or above you! So many of our Jews eulogize the history of the race and assume superiority of the Jew, yet are fearful before the non-Jew.

"Our Jews must clear their minds of their own hate, their own fear, their own belief, that there is a terrible misunderstanding between Jew and non-Jews. I would say to one who was crying about the prejudice he had found everywhere, clean out your mind of that belief. Get it out. Believe that most people don't care what you are or where you go to church or where you were born or what your name might be. What have you for sale, what talent is yours, what have you to offer in friendship? Don't go hangdogging about when there is a crowd of assorted folks, feeling in your heart that something's between you and the rest."

"Didn't President Wilson, the Presbyterian, and ex-President Taft, the Unitarian, and Cardinal O'Connell, the Roman Catholic, and Bishop Rhinelander, the Episcopalian, and Bishop Berry, the Methodist, and Russell Conwell, the Baptist, in the name of Christian sentiment, and representing millions of Christian church folk, issue an appeal for fair play?" asks Samuel Purvis, D. D., a Methodist minister and author of "The Romance of the Jew." With gentle sarcasm Dr. Purvis ridicules the much-heralded story that the Jews are attempting to gain control of the world, and mentions that he has heard similar stories concerning the Masons, Catholics, and Methodists, who are just now "accused of being up to the neck in politics and of taking away the little brown jug from their neighbor's parched and thirsty lips and trying to control these United States." And from one who is familiar with prejudice, but himself prepossessed with the Jews, comes this note of cheer and warning:

"You are not only Jews, you are American Jews, part of the great American Commonwealth. And, believe me, as a Christian preacher and a man of affairs, you have the good-will of every good American. I'd stake all on that. There would have been race and religious riots and pogroms long since if that were not true. . . .

"If I were a Jew I would minimize my class consciousness and emphasize my religion. It's a great one! Worry less about anti-Semitism and more about the crying indifference of the Jews to Judaism as a religion. Set your spiritual house in order. If you serve faithfully the God of your fathers, no weapon that is formed against you shall prosper. You have the Bible and thousands of years of history back of you to prove that!

"To your tents—and to your knees—O Israel!"

Source: "For Christian-Jewish Friendship HP," *The Literary Digest,* May 20, 1922.

Document: From "New York and the Real Jew," Rollin Lynde Hartt, 1921

For the thousandth time, Lucille Rogers sang "Eli! Eli!"—"My God! My God!"—before a Ghetto audience on New York's East Side. As usual, there was a frenzy of applause, but not a Jew among her hearers recognized that anything exceptionally dramatic had occurred.

It had. "Eli! Eli!" is the wail of a Jewess crucified by Anti-Semites, and on the day when the East Side prima donna sang "Eli! Eli!" for the thousandth time, Henry Ford's Dearborn *Independent* made Anti-Semitism a reality in America by accusing the Jews not only of having caused the unrest that has followed the war, but of plotting to overthrow this and every other government and rule the world—a monstrous charge, very nearly as shocking to Jewish-American sensibilities as a pogrom in East Broadway.

During the past few weeks Jews have talked of little else. In Orchard Street the pushcart mercants [*sic*] gasp "Eli! Eli!" Persecuted—here—in 'free' America! Oi, oi, oi, what a country!" Half way up the Metropolitan Tower, in the offices of the American Jewish Congress, Mr. Bernard Richards said to me one morning, "Isn't this a shame? Thruout [*sic*] the war we all pulled together. Now we are pulling apart." The Jewish newspaper row fringing Seward Square seethes with wrath, and there are evidences of distressed apprehension. Jew-baiting has begun. Where will it end?

Meanwhile *Facts*, a Jewish brochure, cries, "Henry Ford, you are a liar, a self-confessed traitor, and lower than an anarchist!"—apparently with the intention of goading him into suing for damages, as then a court of justice would announce its decision regarding the forged "Protocols of the Learned Elders in Zion," upon which his wholesale accusations against the "formidable sect" are chiefly based.

Happily there are Jews who can laugh. Over their pot cheese and sour cream at Strunsky's, the intellectuals of the Ghetto exclaim, "Who would have imagined that Gentiles could be so superstitious?" and in East Side bookshops they blurt out, jeeringly, "Rule the world! Could anything be funnier? True, a certain Leon Brauenstein, better known at Trotsky, is war minister in Russia. One Jew. One—count him! But the mass of formerly prosperous Jews in Russia (they belonged to the bourgeoisie) have been stripped of their all if not butchered outright. Formidable, are we? Look at us here in New York. See how harmless we are and on the whole how helpless!"

A point well taken. With its 1,500,000 Jews, New York is the world's greatest Jewish city. Nearly half the Jews in North America live there. Nearly 10 per cent of all the Jews on earth do. From "Cohency" Island to "Kike's Peak" and beyond, they swarm. Every fourth New Yorker is a Jew. There are five times as many Jews in New York as in any other municipality under the sun, and more Jews than were ever before gathered together in a single place. Columbia University is one-third Jewish, the City College 97 per cent Jewish, the Washington Irving High School, with its 6000 pupils, almost wholly Jewish. Jews monopolize the real estate business, the ready-made clothing business, the theatrical business. There are Jewish policemen. There are Jewish firemen. A famous bridge has been rechristened "the Jewish Passover." But are these Jews in New York a formidable sect? Are they a power financially, even? When Zangwill was asked to write on "Why Jews Succeed," he replied, "They don't," and the New York Jews agree with him. Note what happened when the great Zionist drive (slogan, "rebuild the Jewish homeland now") undertook to raise a mere matter of $10,000,000.

Apart from coteries who declare, "We are not a race, but only a religious sect," and from other coteries who assert, "Nationalism is narrow and evil; what the world needs is universal brotherhood," all good Jews are Zionists. Two hundred and fifty Jewish volunteers from New York—the first Jewish military unit in 2000 years—fought under Allenby, with the seven-branched manora [sic] on their caps and the shield of David as their standard. When Palestine became a Zionist state, innumerable New York Jews paraded, cheering. Ghetto shops display maps of Palestine, with the names in Hebrew letters. Zionist calendars appear in Jewish homes—gayly lithographed affairs, showing the Goddess of Liberty draped in the Stars and Stripes, while before her a Jewish maiden waves aloft the blue and white flag of Zion with its six-pointed blue star. . . .

Nothing is more pitifully absurd than the alleged wealth of New York's Jewish population. Here and there some Straus or Schiff or Baruch amasses riches on a grand scale, tho seldom on the grandest. Frequently, because of their oriental instinct for display, Jews appear splendidly prosperous. Thanks to their native generosity, impressive buildings house their Mount Sinai and Beth-Israel hospitals, their Clara de Hirsch Home for Working Girls, their Y.M.H.A., and their Hebrew Benevolent and Orphan Asylum, while a few Jewish centers of worship . . . lead the undiscerning to conclude that in general the New York Jews are rich. Whereas, the bulk of them (witness the throngs that block your way on the clothing district sidewalks at the noon hour) have with incredible suffering barely attained the sweatshop level of existence and shudder lest they drop from that. Formidable? About as formidable financially as they are politically!

Irish Boston has it Irish mayors. Jewish New York has had no Jewish mayors, and just now the president of its board of aldermen is a Mr. La Guardia. A member of that board voted against granting the freedom of the city to Professor Einstein, Jewish savant, and Dr. Weismann, successor to Dr. Hertzl as leader of world-wide Zionism. Police authorities in New York fearlessly enraged every Jew by forbidding the sale of Passover wine. And even when Jews find themselves in a position to become "formidable," they decline to. Of the great New York dailies, two are Jewish. See if in either the *World* or the *Times* you can trace the machinations of a "formidable sect."

Far from scheming to overthrow the established order of things, anywhere, Jews are phenomenally adaptable.... Next to his ambition to learn English, a Jewish immigrant's most earnest desire on reaching New York is to master every paragraph in Cushing's "Manual of Citizenship." He takes a Yiddish newspaper, it is true . . . and very foreign it looks to us, with its Jewish-German text reading from right to left and printed in Hebrew characters with all the vowels left out; but more and more the Yiddish press is conforming to American standards, in spirit as well as in make-up. Then, too, our newly arrived Jew seeks amusement at a Yiddish theater, . . . where serious drama is admirably presented. But more and more the Yiddish players borrow their "script" from Broadway, translating and adapting it, while frequently an English phrase or sentence survives intact. And, despite this supposed conservatism, the Jew is soon tempted to discard his religion. . . .

Ambassador Page, then editor of the *Atlantic*, once remarked to me, "The most interesting fellow in America is the Jew, but don't write about Jews; without intending it, you may precipitate the calamity America should be most anxious to prevent—I mean Jew-baiting."

More than twenty years have since passed. The calamity is here. Jews feel hunted. They tend to become more Jewish at heart, less American at heart. Therefore, write about Jews. It cannot make matters worse. It may make them better—especially if some reader is prompted to stroll the Ghetto and see with his own eyes, hear with his own ears. Try it. Drop in, anywhere, and announce your curiosity. You will be charmingly received. But I warn you. It is hard to get away.

Source: Rollin Lynde Hartt, "New York and the Real Jew," *The Independent*, June 25, 1921.

Document: From "The Klan Walks in Washington," *The Literary Digest*, 1925

"OH, say, not so!" gasped a Maryland newspaper the other day when everybody was "quivering in excited anticipation of 100,000 ghostly apparitions walking through the streets of the national capital to the stirring strains of the "Liberty Stable Blues," and word came from Washington that the mammoth parade of the Ku Klux Klan had been called off. This Maryland paper, the Baltimore *Evening Sun*, cried, "Darn! Thus goes

170 The Jazz Age

a-glimmering the thrill of a lifetime." But the mammoth parade had not been called off, and news that it had not was provocative of new comment the country over. For example, "Go to it, Klan!" said one editor; "let the nineties gleam!" The Baltimore *Sun* in its editorial headed "Have a Heart!" said "Washington languishes, a fit place for hookworms and sleeping sickness. Into that depressing solemnity comes the Ku Klux Klan to kick up a few didoes. Deprive it of its fiery cross! Gosh, No!" The Syracuse *Herald* said: "Ku-Kluxism is least harmful and menacing when the sun shines on it. Only in the dark can it make trouble. For that reason, we say, let them parade." When Thomas L. Avaunt, the former Klan official who is now the head of the Protestant Knights of America, protested to President Coolidge against the proposed demonstration, the Memphis *Communal Appeal* protested, "Avaunt, Mr. Avaunt, and let the Ku Klux parade!" This was the common attitude, except at the Capitol, where a certain apprehension prevailed, and the Washington *News* took pains to declare, "There isn't going to be the slightest disorder," while the Washington *Evening Sun* said, "There is no occasion for alarm," adding:

> "Agitation on the score of possible violence is unwarranted by any of the known factors in the case. Permission for the parade was granted by the District Commissioners on condition that the Klansmen march without masks. The fact that otherwise they wear the costumes of the order is not of any more importance or significance than the marching of uniformed organizations of any description. The Commissioners could not discriminate between applicants for the right to use the streets for parading purposes, and their action in granting the permit was not only justified but required."

Nevertheless, a Universal Service dispatch from Washington to New York *American* informs us, all precautions have been taken to prevent disorder, and Thomas L. Avaunt was arrested and later released. He distributed an anti-Klan circular which read: "All Christian men and women bow their heads in shame when they know that their city will soon be bathed in blood."

It was not "bathed in blood" or at all harmed, tho the numbers of the arriving hosts exceeded expectation. On the day of the demonstration, the Washington *Evening Star* reported:

> "Thousands of these white-robed figures, old and young, who congregated east of the Capitol, flaunting American flags and banners emblazoned with the mystic symbols of the Klan, long before the hour set for the start of the unique parade. There were men in white satin robes; they were the units.

Others wore garments of a cheaper material; they were the rank and file of the 'invisible empire.' Mingling with them in countless numbers were the families of the Klansmen."

The parade itself marshaled "from 60,000 to 80,000 white robed men and women," as the correspondent of the New York *Times* estimates, and H. L. Mencken tells us in the New York *Sun*,

> "The Klan put it all over its enemies. The parade was grander and gaudier, by far, than anything the wizards had prophesied. It was longer, it was thicker, it was higher in tone. I stood in front of the Treasury for two hours watching the legions pass. They marched in lines of eighteen to twenty, shoulder to shoulder. I retired for refreshment and was gone an hour.
>
> "When I got back Pennsylvania Avenue was still a mass of white from the Treasury down to the foot of Capitol Hill—a full mile of Klansmen and their ladies.
>
> "No one seems to know what brought them in. When the gentlemen of the press went to Klan headquarters they were kicked out. It is not even established who commanded the parade. The Imperial Wizard, the Hon. Mr. Evans, was in it, but he profest to be only a guest. One tale has it that the Klansmen of the North organized the show to annoy and dismay their brethren of the South. Another had it that it was planned by local majors of the palace to shame and get rid of the august Evans. But if any such evil purpose lurked under the surface there was certainly no sign of it on top."

Other explanations of the purpose of the Klan parade are offered by various newspapers. According to the Louisville *Post*, "it was the application of a pulmotor to a dying cause." To the Atlanta *Constitution* "the real significance of the gathering" was to be found in "the secret meeting of Klan chiefs." Carlisle Bargeron, of the Washington *Post*, thinks that a desire to outdo the Holy Name Society's demonstration furnished the incentive, while Paul R. Mallon tells the Pittsburgh *Post* that the affair was "a gesture of Northern Klansmen toward wresting control of the organization from the South."

As the Providence *Journal* reminds us, "some months ago the Klan leaders invited Mr. Coolidge to review the forthcoming parade. Of course they did not really expect him to accede to their request. They were merely bent on putting him in a hole because he reviewed the parade of a Catholic society of which the admirable purpose is to discourage the taking of the Lord's name in vain."

Source: "The Klan Walks in Washington," *The Literary Digest*, August 22, 1925.

Document: From "Klan and Church," Lowell Mellett, 1923

The moonlight's fair [no doubt] *tonight along the Wabash. From the fields* [perhaps] *there comes the scent of new-mown hay. Through the sycamores the candle-lights are gleaming—*

No land could be lovelier than Indiana under moonlight. No air could be blessed with sweeter fragrance than that of new-mown hay. The home land of the Hoosiers keeps its hold on our hearts, even though many changes have come since Theodore Dreiser wrote the simple ballad to describe it, and his brother, Paul Dresser, composed the music which we all sang or hummed or whistled a generation ago. The moonlight remains undimmed by the years, but the scent from the fields is of scorching rubber and gasoline. Through the sycamores the blast-furnaces are gleaming.

Indiana is part of the modern world. All that any other state has, Indiana has—all the wonders. The chambers of commerce are quite explicit about this. They point to the dozen or more automobile factories in Indianapolis, to say nothing of those in South Bend, Connersville, Kokomo, Elkhart, and elsewhere. Of course, the state never has stopped producing politics and literature, and it now talks pridefully of its Brown-County art colony, "the largest this side of the Alleghanies."

And yet—can it be that through the sycamores of our Hoosier minds the candle-light is still gleaming: Even the cabins among the cornfields have electric lights, but what is our mental illumination?

So long ago that 'On the Banks of the Wabash' had not yet been written, I was a boy in Indiana. One happy hot afternoon I trailed along the streets of our little town, following a parade of the Knights of St. John. Perhaps this juvenile order no longer exists; I have never seen another of its parades, in any event. The Knights of St. John appeared to be small brothers of the Knights of Columbus. Their uniforms were blue and their little rifles were wooden. They were a bit awkward about the business of parading. Many of them were too small and their legs in unaccustomed long trousers, had to stretch to keep the step.

Catholics were still something of a novelty in us natives. We had profound knowledge of the Protestants churches. We knew the Methodist, the Christians, the Baptists, the Presbyterians, the Campbellites, the Protestant Episcopals; knew which had the least irksome services; which Sunday School had the shortest sessions. But the Catholics happened to be newcomers. They came in on the boom that followed the discovery of natural gas and the building of many glass factories and steel and iron mills. They were strangers to us and consequently feared. It was some time before we realized that one of us were about as good, pound for pound, in battle as one of the funny-talking lads from Pittsburgh. That having been established, in due course the barriers went down. The newcomers were absorbed into the community and soon was as if they always had been there.

Most everybody ceased to feel any strangeness, but a few held out. The few most sensitive to fear continued in a state of alarm. There was Pood Wamsley, for example. Pood, a little older than the rest of us, was our self-ordained oracle. We listened to his opinions concerning affairs. Most of these opinions he obtained in the back room of his father's undertaking establishment where, of an evening, when there was no undertaking afoot, leading citizens often congregated to discuss matters of moment.

The day following the parade of the Knights of St. John, Pood rounded us up and, glancing over his shoulder every now and then to make sure no Roman spies were lurking about, he gave us a whispered harangue to this effect:—

"Didja see them Cath'lic kids p'radin' yestiddy? Lissen! 'Ja know what they're doin'? Ever' one of them is bein' trained to be soldiers when they grows up. That's what them Cath'lics is doin'. Son's they git 'em all trained and they're growed up, they're goin' to seize the whole country and take charge of it an' ever'thing!"

"Howja know?" one of his aghast hearers inquired.

"I know," returned Pood, mysteriously. "There's certain people watch' ever'thing they do, and when the time comes—"

He broke off with a far-away, portentous look.

"How kin they do it?" someone asked.

"How kin they do it? Don't ja know that ever'time a boy baby is born in a Cath'lic fam'ly they take and bury a gun under the church for him to use when he grows up? And they bury enough am'nition for him to kill fifty people with!"

"Well, why's the marshal let 'em, then?"

"Huh! The marshal! Bob Mounts don't know nothin' that's goin' on!"

"Why n't somebody tell him?"

"The time ain't come yet. It's a-comin' though! Trouble is—the govinment. Can't expect to do nothin' while's Cleveland's president. They say that, sekurtly, he's mebbe a Cath'lic himself!"

Up to that point I think Pood had us almost convinced. We were forgetting how funny some of the little fellows had looked the day before, trying to keep a march step that was too long for their legs. What had seemed a delightful show was beginning to take on a sinister aspect. It was occurring to us that we ought to have a smarter town marshal than Bob Mounts. But when Pood brought out that about President Cleveland, some of us rebelled. We were Democrats! We argued the matter lucidly with Pood. "Aw, he is not!"—"How'ja know he ain't?"—"Well, he ain't. I know it. You're crazy!"—

And then we broke up his alarm feast in favor of scrub beaseball.

Thirty years ago this was. And now I've been back home again in Indiana, among the folks I used to know. And two of them have told me—in this enlightened summer of 1923—that every time a Catholic boy baby is born, a rifle is buried beneath the church against the day when the Church proposes to turn these United States over to the Pope!

Hoosiers surely have not been believing this ever since the days when that serious little circle met in the back room of Wamsley's undertaking shop and Pood repeated to us the weighty opinions there expressed. Worry about the Catholics apparently had disappeared under the pressure of more imminent and real problems. To-day it has been revived. It is part of the state of mind that accounts for the amazing growth of the Ku Klux Klan in the old Hoosier commonwealth; that enables Indiana to compete with Ohio for the distinction of having a larger Klan membership than any other State. It helped make possible the remarkable election results of last fall, when practically every candidate opposed by the Klan went down in defeat.

In Indiana, as in other states, the Klan has the usual trilogy of fears. It fears the Jews, the Negroes, and the Catholics. But I heard little concerning the Jews and the Negroes. I heard much concerning the Catholics.

This is true of the Negroes, notwithstanding the immense Negro population of Indianapolis and notwithstanding the fact that this city was the home of the notorious Bungaloos, a hoodlum organization that amused itself with anti-Negro riots in the earlier years of the present century.

It is true as to the Jews, especially in Indianapolis, although there the Jews appear to dominate big retail business as completely as they do in most cities. One intelligent member of the race, who has been studying the situation in a detached sort of way, pointed out to me that in Indianapolis the Jews do not engage in small trade to any extent, and suggested that this accounts for the apathy toward them on the part of the Klan. In the smaller cities, he said, I should find the Jews competing with the smaller business concerns, and should find the Klan actively antagonistic.

This upon investigation seemed to be the case. Here the anti-Jewish sentiment appeared to be the natural antipathy of small tradesmen toward a race that somehow always manages to do well in trade.

Very clearly the crux of the Klan problem in Indiana is the Catholic Church. The Klan is feeding on a revival of anti-Catholic feeling and renewed circulation of Catholic goblin stories. Men actually join the Klan because they believe that a magnificent home (a million-dollar palace, is the term usually used) is being built in Washington, D.C., to house the Pope, and that the Vatican is soon to be moved to the American capital!

This will sound strange to those of you who do not share the Klan's panic on the subject of the Catholic Church. It has been your observation, no doubt, that a good Catholic is just about as devout a church member as a good Protestant—and no more so. But it is customary for many Protestants to assume that the Catholic priest has some strange and complete control over the actions of the men and women of his parish; that he is a great deal more than their spiritual adviser; that all members of the Church walk about with bated breath in fear of incurring the priest's wrath. They forget that the older parishioners probably knew the priest when he was a small and irreverent boy.

Many have believed it is a fixed policy of the Church to keep its members down to a definite level of ignorance. Ku Klux Klan organs now assiduously spread this idea. The truth seems more nearly to be that the effort to spread education—general education, not merely sectarian education—is as great among Catholics as among Protestants.

Indeed, one of the most serious charges against the Church that you hear in Indiana is that they are endeavoring to obtain control of the public schools. Why? To wreck the public-school system, to be sure! The Catholics have had control of the School Board in Indianapolis for years, several excited informants told me, and, they would say, look how the schools have deteriorated!

Investigation revealed that the Catholics had been represented on the School Board by one member. The superintendent of schools in a certain city, I was told in a confidential whisper, is a Catholic. But I had known this man intimately for half a life-time and knew the contrary to be true. Running down other such allegations was like running down atrocity stories in the German-occupied districts of France; the stories nearly always evaporated as one got near their source.

It would be unwise to assert that no case whatever can be made against the Catholics in some corners of Indiana. There are instances in plenty when, forming a majority of the voting population, they have voted themselves into power. There are instances in which shortsighted leadership has led them to abuse their power. There are communities where, while in a minority, they have been as clannish as the Klan, and have made themselves a solid and obstructive political *bloc*. But, recalling Catholic candidates who have failed to get the Church vote and have succeeded, the conclusion is that, as individuals and as a group, no case of undesirable citizenship can be maintained against them.

However, unreasonable as are the allegations on which the Klan's growth is largely based, this growth is the most important fact in Indiana to-day.

One finds a friend who is neither Klan nor anti-Klan, fighting hard to preserve his neutrality. One finds a politician seeking to make each side think he hates the other. One finds a business man engaged in the same precarious undertaking, for now the business boycott has come in to harass further the middle-of-the-road folks.

"If," said a man to me, "you were widely reputed to be a member of the Klan and were not a member, what would you do about it? Would you publicly deny it? Or would you keep quiet? Well, no matter what you would do, I'd just keep quiet."

He is a judge on the bench, a scholar, a man of high standing in the law, an honest, scrupulous jurist. But he is baffled by the religious war he finds raging about him, baffled into complete silence on a subject that touches real principle with him.

When certain Klan leaders had told me all the wild stories about Catholics they could think of, and certain Catholic laymen had told me all the wild stories about the Klan they could think of, I started out to find some of the rank and file, some of the plain Klansmen.

I found a great many, and who do you suppose they were? They were old friends of mine; folks I'd known all my life; just some of the best citizens of Indiana, that was all. The best citizens—save for this one weakness. Not the stuff of which cowardly mobs are supposed to be made, not the sort which drags women out at night to tar-and-feather and lash, naked, against trees. Clean, decent family men. Not even religious fanatics; their average church attendance probably not very high; men who have done more thinking even if misguided thinking, about religion and churches during the present fever than in any ten years of their lives.

How true the stories of Klan outrages in other states may be, they were not committed by such men as I found in the Klan in Indiana. That is, they were not committed by men in the state of mind of the Indiana Klansmen to-day. What state of mind they may get into presently cannot be foretold. They cannot vision themselves running amuck and they do not believe the tales concerning Klansmen who have run amuck in other states.

This feeling concerning themselves is shared by whole communities. Good people who could not conceivably join the Klan themselves have only good-natured curiosity regarding the organization. They amuse themselves by trying to identify the members when the latter turn out for public parade in their hoods and gowns. The shape under the sheet or the familiar shoes of a sturdy marcher often tells a wife for the first time that her husband is a member; but when she allows this information to spread about the block, it seldom excites real surprise—certainly not horror. It is not thought that this respectable neighbor has suddenly become a terrorist, a doer of evil deeds in the dark.

Much effort has been spent in Indiana, as in other states, to convince possible Klansmen that they became victims of a gigantic money-making scheme when they wrote their names in blood on the dotted line. But this has proved only a slight deterrent. That it has been a money-making enterprise for certain men is admitted. But so was—for example—the Loyal Order of the Moose.

The present U.S. Secretary of Labor, James J Davis (a Hoosier, by the way), might be called the Simmons of the Moose, in that respect. Yet the rapid growth of the Moose could not be attributed simply to the fact that Davis had an excellent profit-taking idea. Tens of thousands did not join the Moose just because they wished to make Jim the Puddler a millionaire. No, he had a conception of enjoyable human fellowship that appealed to them.

So it was with the men who originated the Ku Klux Klan. They have made money, no doubt, an immense amount of it, but they did have something that appealed to thousands of other men. Unfortunately, the thing they had was not so wholesome a thing as that which Davis had. The thing they had was fear—fear, based on error, as most fears are; fear, based on superstitious ignorance of the Catholic Church.

This fear is not to be dissolved by the voice of one fellow Hoosier asserting that there is no basis for it. All this assertion is likely to do is to convince some of his friends that he is a paid propagandist for the Catholic Church and to convince other friends that he is a paid propagandist for the Ku Klux Klan.

But here is a suggestion which, if acted upon, may help prevent the Ku Klux Klan in Indiana going the way it has gone in many other states and may help destroy the notion that there is any proper place in Indiana society for such an organization.

The suggestion is Publicity.

You may assume that I mean legislation to compel the publication of every secret order's membership lists, such as New York's recent enactment. My anti-Klan friends will applaud, crying: "That's the ticket! Drag them into the daylight!" My pro-Klan friends will begin digging in their heels and preparing to resist.

But I mean publicity concerning the Catholic Church. And I do not mean the usual sort of newspaper publicity. The newspapers have pretty well indicated the course they may be expected to pursue in the face of this truly grave menace. When the Klan was a far-off matter, not an intimate problem, they printed all the stories of brutal outrages that came over the wires. When it came closer home, they lapsed into silence. Now that they have reason for suspecting that every other reader may be a Klan member or sympathizer, many of the newspapers content themselves with careful avoidance of the issue.

It might have been possible for a newspaper of wide influence in Indiana to head off the Klan's growth at one stage by printing the facts, but no newspaper has influence sufficient to accomplish that now.

By printing what facts? The facts concerning the Catholic Church, to be sure. There is the essence of the whole question. Are the firmly fixed beliefs of tens of thousands of Hoosier Protestants concerning the Catholic Church true or untrue? Find out. And print what is found.

No newspaper, of course, ever has thought of doing this, because the newspapers have feared the Catholic Church. There is one article of the Klan faith that has a real basis. Klansmen will tell you that newspapers fear to print anything they think may offend the Church. And Klansmen are not altogether mistaken on this point. The tradition has grown up in newspaper offices that such news is unsafe to handle, that the Church has some mysterious power to punish those who offend.

There is nothing mysterious about it, of course; it is simply that many readers are Catholics and might cancel their subscriptions. Many editors and sub-editors, however, seem to feel that the authority of the Church would be exercised to compel its members to do this. There is good reason for doubting the existence of any such shortsighted policy.

In my experience, the newspaper men who have seemed most free and unworried in their handling of news concerning the Catholic clergy, including sometimes unpleasant news, have been Catholic newspaper men. They have less fear of their own Church than Protestant newspaper men have. One result of this news-suppression has been the growth of belief in all sorts of weird tales about the Church; mouth-to-mouth stories of pagan immoralities, involving all ranks in the Church organization. It is not conceivable that Catholic churchmen prefer general circulation of malicious or ignorant inventions to a condition in which they would receive from the press exactly the same treatment as the Protestant clergy receive.

But the remedy for the Klan problem. The suggestion toward which I have tried to pave the way is a statewide survey of the Church activities in Indiana. It should be possible to organize a commission of intelligent men and women to collect the facts concerning the churches and what the churches do. It can be shown what proportion of the state offices are and have been held by Catholics, and how this corresponds to the number of Catholics themselves. It can be shown how much the Catholics contribute to the support of the public schools, how many are serving on public-school boards, how many are teaching in the public schools.

Catholic churches could be forced open, if necessary,—which it would not be, of course,—to prove or disprove the tales of buried rifles and ammunition. This suggestion may draw a smile, but I am not certain that it is not the most important I have to make. The tales are preposterous, to be sure, but I would take the only possible course to eradicate them from the minds of those who do not consider them preposterous.

Further, a commission of inquiry might call publicly for the presentation of every charge against the Catholic Church that any responsible person or responsible group of persons might have to make, and then investigate the truth of those charges. They could bring the whole truth out of the darkness of rumor into the daylight of established fact.

What do the people of Indiana receive in the place of the truth, now? Two or three days of each week the down-town streets of the larger Indiana cities resound with the voices of boys selling *The Fiery Cross*, a Ku Klux Klan weekly. These are bought eagerly and in great numbers by persons determined to hear and believe the worst concerning the Catholic Church.

On the same days, on the same corners, other boys are crying just as loudly the sale of *Tolerance*, an anti-Klan weekly, containing every intolerant idea concerning the Klan that the latter's enemies have to offer. They are bought eagerly and in great numbers by persons determined to hear and believe the worst concerning the Klan.

As for the neutral publications, they appear to be waiting warily for the storm to blow over. It may blow over and it may not. It has not blown over in many another state without having first been responsible for shameful incidents which those states will spend years deploring. Witnessing the trend it has taken there, it is hard to believe that Indiana will escape her share of bitter regrets unless some means is found to clear the air before the storm descends.

Source: Lowell Mellett, "Klan and Church," *Atlantic Monthly*, November 1923.

Document: From "A Judicial Spanking for the Klan," *Literary Digest*, 1928

A Daniel has come to judgment, is the opinion of many a newspaper writer, when a Federal judge in a formal opinion read from the bench delivers a denunciation of the Ku Klux Klan in terms as strong as any private enemies of that organization have ever used. When Judge W. H. S. Thomson, in ending the complicated Klan case at Pittsburgh, speaks of the Klan as an "unlawful organization" coming into court "with filthy hands after open and flagrant violation" of the law, he represents, in the opinion of the Cincinnati *Enquirer*, "the fierce sunlight of the forces of law and order and civilized process, before which the terrorism and sinister tendencies of Ku Kluxism must fade and shrivel into nothingness." Now this is the first time, the Birmingham *News* reminds us, "that a United States court has spoken on this particular matter; it has remained for the Pennsylvania judge to give a national character to the indictment of the methods and the interests of the predecessors of the Knights of the Great Forest." Not that our papers accept at face value the mass of testimony given at the Pittsburgh trial, accusing Klan officials of all kinds of chicanery, blackmail, violence, terrorism, and even murder. Far from it. The Buffalo *Courier-Express* is mindful that most of the specific outrages mentioned occurred back in 1923 and 1924, and "events of four or five years ago can not [sic] necessarily be taken as measuring-sticks of what Klansmen or their successors are to-day." Much of the testimony must be taken with a grain of salt, observes the New York *Herald Tribune*, seeing that the witnesses "are former members of the Klan, and therefore credulous romantics to start with, and that in addition they harbor a bitter grudge against the organization, and are seeking deliberately to discredit it." The Boston *Transcript* is aware that "there is a tendency to preposterous exaggeration, to a sort of crazy lying in people who are in any way associated with this fanatical organization." But the Norfolk *Virginian-Pilot* speaks for all of these papers, and many more, in declaring that the significance of the Pittsburgh "revelations" is "something apart from their circumstantial veracity":

> "This particular charge may be untrue, and that particular charge may be exaggerated, but the general picture of the great American Camorra as it functioned prior to its metamorphosis into the Knights of the Great Forest, remains authentic. It checks at too many points with facts generally known, for its veracity to be doubted. The picture is one of a tragic mobilization of simple, unsuspecting people, by unscrupulous exploiters, of the systematic poisoning of their minds by appeals to prejudice and false alarms, and of the

criminal employment of these people by dangerous men to keep alive the delusion that the Klan was engaged in patriotic and valuable work, and that all participants in that work were but discharging their duty to society, to country, and to God. So thoroughly were the poor tools of the organizers and kleagles deluded by this specious gospel of vigilantism, that they organized themselves into 'wrecking crews' and 'battalions of death,' lent themselves to espionage, threatenings and blackmail, joined in kidnappings, tarrings, and floggings and participated in scores of other abominations—altho the simplest of them know what they were doing was mean, infamous, and criminal of decent social behavior, and by the letter and spirit of the law."

"The Ku Klux Klan can not [sic] afford to pooh-pooh charges away at this time," reflects the Brooklyn *Eagle*.

"It should welcome some form of investigation that will thoroughly disclose its proceedings of the past few years. If it has acted lawfully and uprightly it stands under the obligation to have its reputation cleared. If it has done even a part of the things charged against it, the decent element in its membership must want to know the truth."

Such is the general impression made by the Pittsburgh trial. The case was exceedingly complicated, there being both suit and counter-suit. As briefly summed up in a Pittsburgh dispatch to the New York *Herald Tribune*—

> "The Klan sought to enjoin five members of western Pennsylvania Klans from doing business under the name of the organization, at the same time seeking $100,000 damages from each of the defendants, who had been 'banished' for their acts.
>
> "In retaliation, the five 'banished' members filed a counter-suit against the order asking that its charter be revoked and a receiver appointed, and accounting be given of $15,000,000 which the Klan is said to have collected from more than 300,000 members in the State of Pennsylvania."

Additional liveliness was given to the case by the fact that the attorney for the banished members was one of the group. For three days the liveliest sort of testimony was offered, with sharp cross-examinations, spirited sparring of counsel, humorous incidents, and exhibitions of temper and frayed nerves. The anti-Klan testimony as it came from the mouths of witnesses during three days of the trial is well summed up in Judge Thomson's final opinion quoted below. One piece of testimony which aroused much newspaper attention was a deposition made by D.C. Stephenson, now in the Indiana State prison under conviction of murder. Stephenson had been high in the counsels of the Klan, and gave a detailed account of how Hiram Wesley Evans maneuvered six years ago to make himself successor as supreme head or Imperial Wizard of the Klan to its modern founder William J. Simmons. The full story runs to more than 40,000 words and, according to the New York *World*, "is the most astonishing record of the use of criminal means, including debauchery, blasting of reputations, torture and even murder, for the purpose of obtaining and retaining control of a secret organization of intimidation that has been revealed since the exposure of the activities of the Molly McGuires in the Pennsylvania coal-fields, half a century ago." Only a part of this deposition was admitted in evidence, the chief items, according to a New York *World* dispatch, being—

> "His charge that Grand Dragons were instructed by Evans to follow his orders blindly and that if they failed to do would be unseated, punished, and their characters attacked.
> "His allegation that the 'Black Mask Robe Gang' was authorized by Evans, and was the official robe when Klansmen went on killing and whipping parties.
> "His charge that Evans had boasted that a negro had been burned at the stake in Texas; that Klansmen had cut off a negro's ears, and that 'KKK' had been branded on the forehead of another negro.
> "His testimony that after a riot in Perth Amboy, New Jersey, in 1923, Evans had told him 'if the Klan can make it look as if we are being persecuted, it will help increase our membership.'"

Mr. Simmons also made a deposition attacking the present Evans regime as "grossly disgusting," and stating that when he was head of the order there never was a riot involving the Klan. As opposed to the witnesses whose testimony alleging violence so imprest Judge Thomson, the Klan attorneys produced witnesses who stated that Klan demonstrations were always peaceful and law-abiding and that on the particular occasion of the riot at Carnegie, Pennsylvania, the parading Klansmen were unarmed, and the victims of an unprovoked attack, in which a Klansman was killed. The notable witness offered by the Klan was the Imperial Wizard himself. Mr. Evans, as a New York *Times* correspondent sums up his answers to questions and cross-questions, "denied that men were ever burned, flogged or tarred and feathered by the Klan, and declared that the organization would not tolerate such an action."

In bringing the case to an end, Judge Thomson first dismissed the cross-suits against the Klan as being beyond the jurisdiction of his court, the matter being the concern of the State of Pennsylvania. The main suit brought by the Klan against the exiled members was dismissed two days later on Friday, the 13th of April, on the ground that "this unlawful organization, so destructive of the rights and liberties of the people," has come into court "with filthy hands and can get no assistance here." In justifying this decision the Judge declared (as the Pittsburgh *Post-Gazette* prints the opinion) that the Klan originally obtained its charter in the State of Pennsylvania, as a charitable and patriotic organization, but that—

> "In violation of the charter and in violation of its own constitution, it has established and is maintaining a form of despotic rule, which is being operated in secret, under the direct sanction and authority of the plaintiff's chief officers. That in violation of the rights and liberties of the people, it has set up tribunals not known to the law, before which citizens of the commonwealth, not members of the Klan, are brought, subjected to some form of trial, and upon conviction, severe corporal punishments are imposed, painful, humiliating and often brutal in their character, and, in some instances, destructive of life itself. . . .
>
> "That the plaintiff organization, through its actual operations and teachings, has stirred up racial and religious prejudices, fomented disorder and encouraged riots and unlawful assemblies, which have resulted in flagrant breaches of the peace of the law, bloodshed and loss of life, and that such assemblies and riots have, in many instances, been for the avowed purpose on the part of the officers in control of increasing the membership of the organization. . . . "

In particular, Judge Thomson states that the evidence establishes violations of the law in Pennsylvania, including physical punishment of a negro, the kidnaping of a little girl, and the personal responsibility of Hiram W. Evans for the riot and bloodshed at Carnegie, on the ground that he gave the Klansmen the order to march in spite of the refusal of civil authorities to permit such a parade.

That the rank and file of Klan membership was responsible for all the acts of violence charged at Pittsburgh seems impossible to papers like the New York *Sun*, New York *World*, and Indianapolis *News*. What important, says the Indiana paper, is the light shed on the character of the Klan leadership. People were induced to join the Klan, because they were told that in this way they would help in dry-law enforcement and like expressions of forms of vice neglected by various authorities. "Their mistake was in not investigating the character of the leadership." It is the "exposure of the truth about this leadership" which has "practically wrecked the Klan as a force," in the opinion of *The News*. That this is the beginning of the end and that the Klan has evidently spent its force are statements made by the New York *Evening World*, St. Louis *Post-Dispatch*, and St. Louis *Star*. But the Milwaukee *Journal* is not so certain—"one would have thought that the disclosure or rather the partial disclosure, in Florida and Georgia, Texas and Indiana would have broken the Klan. They did not. It only changed its seat and went on doing business at the same old stand." Similarly *The New Republic* ventured a guess that the results of this "terrible indictment" upon the rank and file Klan membership "will probably be negligible":

> "They are emotionalists, who will, no doubt, find little difficulty in persuading themselves that Judge Thomson has some ulterior motive for uttering his burning words. In fairness it should also be noted that the cruelty of the Klan has in nearly every district been the work of only a part of the membership, hundreds of thousands of Klansmen being leading citizens in small towns in the West and South, as earnest and anxious for the welfare of the country as they were ignorant and misguided. The Klan is dying; but it is boredom and reluctance to pay dues which have cut its membership in two, and not any change of heart. The former Klansman will continue to think and vote as tho he were still a member of the order."

Source: "A Judicial Spanking for the Klan," *Literary Digest*, April 20, 1928.

Suggested Readings

Baker, Carlos. *Ernest Hemingway: A Life Story*. New York: Charles Scribner's Sons, 1981.

Baker, Kelly J. *The Gospel According to the Klan: The KKK's Appeal to Protestant America, 1915–1930*. Lawrence: University Press of Kansas, 2011.

Berman, Ron. "Protestant, Catholic, Jew: *The Sun Also Rises*." *Hemingway Review* 18.1(Fall 1998): 33–48.

Blee, Kathleen, and Amy McDowell. "The Duality of Spectacle and Secrecy: A Case Study of Fraternalism in the 1920s Ku Klux Klan." *Ethnic and Racial Studies* 36.2(2013): 249–65.

Broer, Lawrence R. *Hemingway's Spanish Tragedy*. University: The University of Alabama Press, 1973.

Bruccoli, Matthew, ed. *American Expatriate Writers: Paris in the Twenties*. Detroit: Gale, 1997.

Bruccoli, Matthew J. *Scott and Ernest*. Carbondale: Southern Illinois University Press, 1978.

Burgum, Edwin Berry. "Ernest Hemingway and the Psychology of the Lost Generation." In *Ernest Hemingway: The Man and His Work*. Ed. John McCaffery. New York: World Publishing Co., 1950: 277–296.

Chalmers, David M. *Hooded Americanism: The History of the Ku Klux Klan*. New York: New Viewpoints, 1976.

Cowley, Malcolm. *Exile's Return. A Literary Odyssey of the 1920s*. 1934. New York: Penguin Books, 1976.

Desnoyers, Megan Floyd. "Ernest Hemingway: A Storyteller's Legacy." *Prologue: A Quarterly of the National Archives* 24.4(Winter 1992). Ernest Hemingway Collection. John F. Kennedy Presidential Library and Museum. Online. June 24, 2015.

Donaldson, Scott. *By Force of Will: The Life and Art of Ernest Hemingway*. New York: New York Press, 1977.

Field, Allyson Nadia. "Expatriate Lifestyle as Tourist Destination: *The Sun Also Rises* and Experiential Travelogues of the Twenties." *Hemingway Review* 25.2(Spring 2006): 29–43.

Fitch, Noel Riley. *Sylvia Beach and the Lost Generation: A History of Literary Paris in the Twenties and Thirties*. New York: W.W. Norton, 1985.

Fitzgerald, F. Scott. *This Side of Paradise*. New York: Charles Scribner's Sons, 1920; Scribner Paperback Fiction, 1995.

Flanner, Janet. *Paris Was Yesterday. 1925–1939*. 1972. Ed. Irving Drutman. San Diego: Harvest/Harcourt Brace Jovanovich, 1988.

Goldberg, David J. "Unmasking the Ku Klux Klan: The Northern Movement against the KKK, 1920–1925." *Journal of American Ethnic History* 15.4(1996): 32–49.

Gopnik, Adam. *Americans in Paris: A Literary Anthology*. New York: Library of America, 2004.

Griffin, Peter. *Along with Youth*. New York: Oxford University Press, 1985.

Hansen, Arlen J. *Expatriate Paris: A Cultural and Literary Guide to Paris of the 1920s*. New York: Arcade Publishing, 2012.

Hays, Peter L. "Imperial Brett in *The Sun Also Rises*." *ANQ* 23.4(Fall 2010): 238–242.

Hemingway, Ernest. *Death in the Afternoon*. New York: Charles Scribner's Sons, 1932; Scribner's Classics, 1999.

Hemingway, Ernest. *The Sun Also Rises*. 1926. New York: Scribner Paperback Fiction; Simon & Schuster, 2006.

Hemingway, Ernest. *A Moveable Feast*. 1962. New York: Scribner, 2010.

Hemingway, Ernest. *By-Line: Ernest Hemingway. Selected Articles and Dispatches of Four Decades*. Ed. William White. New York: Charles Scribner's Sons, 1967.

Hemingway, Ernest. *Selected Letters 1917–1961*. 1981. Ed. Carlos Baker. New York: Scribner, 2003.

Jackson, Keneth. *The Ku Klux Klan in the City, 1915–1930*. Chicago: Ivan R. Dee, 1992.

Josephs, Allen. "'Toreo': The Moral Axis of *The Sun Also Rises*." *Hemingway Review* 6.1(Fall 1986): 88–99.

Kaye, Jeremy. "The 'Whine' of Jewish Manhood: Re-Reading Hemingway's Anti-Semitism, Reimagining Robert Cohn" *Hemingway Review* 25.2(Spring 2006): 44–60.

Kinnamon, Kenneth. "Hemingway, the Corrida, and Spain." *Texas Studies in Literature and Language* 2(Spring 1959): 44–61.

Lloyd, Greg. *Eugene Bullard: Black Expatriate in Jazz-Age Paris*. Athens: University of Georgia Press, 2006.

Lynn, Kenneth S. *Hemingway*. New York: Simon & Schuster, 1987.

MacLean, Nancy. *Behind the Mask of Chivalry: The Making of the Second Ku Klux Klan*. New York: Oxford University Press, 1994.

McAlmon, Robert. *Being Geniuses Together 1920–1930*. Revised and with supplementary chapters by Kay Boyle. Garden City, NY: Doubleday & Company, 1968.

Mellow, James R. *Charmed Circle: Gertrude Stein & Company*. New York: Praeger Publishers, 1974.

Mellow, James R. *Hemingway: A Life without Consequences*. Boston: Houghton Mifflin, 1992.

Meyers, Jeffrey. *Hemingway: A Biography*. New York: Harper & Row, 1982.

Monk, Craig. *Writing the Lost Generation: Expatriate Autobiography and American Modernism*. Iowa City: University of Iowa Press, 2008.

Munson, Gorham. *The Awakening Twenties*. Baton Rouge: Louisiana State University Press, 1985.

Nagel, James, ed. *Ernest Hemingway: The Writer in Context*. Madison: University of Wisconsin Press, 1978.

Onderdonk, Todd. "'Bitched': Feminization, Identity, and the Hemingwayesque in *The Sun Also Rises*." *Twentieth Century Literature* 52.1(Spring 2006): 61–91.

Pegram, Thomas S. *One Hundred Percent American: The Rebirth and Decline of the Ku Klux Klan in the 1920s*. Chicago: Ivan R. Dee, 2011.

Pizer, Donald. *American Expatriate Writing and the Paris Moment: Modernism and Place*. Baton Rouge: Louisiana State University Press, 1997.

Reynolds, Michael S. *Hemingway: The Paris Years*. Cambridge, MA: Basil Blackwell, 1989.

Rodriguez-Pazos, Gabriel. "Bulls, Bullfights, and Bullfighters in Hemingway's *The Sun Also Rises*." *Hemingway Review* 34.1(Fall 2014): 82–94.

Schwartz, Jeffrey A. " 'The Saloon Must Go, and I Will Take It with Me': American Prohibition, Nationalism, and Expatriation in *The Sun Also Rises*." *Studies in the Novel* 33.2(Summer 2001): 180–202.

Spilka, Mark. "The Death of Love in *The Sun Also Rises*." In *Hemingway and His Critics*. Ed. Carlos Baker. New York: Hill & Wang, 1961: 80–92.

Stanton, Edward F. *Hemingway and Spain*. Seattle: University of Washington Press, 1989.

Traber, Daniel S. "Whiteness and the Rejected Other in *The Sun Also Rises*." *Studies in American Fiction* 28.2(Autumn 2000): 235–254.

Von Cannon, Michael. "Traumatizing Arcadia: Postwar Pastoral in *The Sun Also Rises*." *Hemingway Review* 32.1(Fall 2012): 57–71.

Wade, Wyn Craig. *The Fiery Cross: The Ku Klux Klan in America*. New York: Simon and Schuster, 1987.

Wagner, Linda W. *Ernest Hemingway: Six Decades of Criticism*. East Lansing: Michigan State University Press, 1987.

Wagner-Martin, Linda. "Racial and Sexual Coding in Hemingway's *The Sun Also Rises*." *Hemingway Review* 10.2(Spring 1991): 39–41.

Williams, Wirt. *The Tragic Art of Ernest Hemingway*. Baton Rouge: Louisiana State University Press, 1981.

Wiser, William. *The Great Good Place: American Expatriate Women in Paris*. New York: W.W. Norton, 1991.

Zwerdling, Alex. *Improvised Europeans: American Literary Expatriates in London*. New York: Basic Books, 1998.

5

Passing
(Nella Larsen, 1929)

SYNOPSIS OF *PASSING*

Passing opens with its mixed-race first-person narrator, Irene Redfield, receiving a letter from a former acquaintance (although others considered them friends), Clare Kendry, which prompts her to recall an incident that occurred sometime during a visit to Chicago. On a hot summer day Irene had sought refuge from the heat in the rooftop tearoom of the exclusive Drayton Hotel, where she unexpectedly encountered Clare, a mixed-race woman who, unlike Irene, "passes" as white. It had been years since Irene had last seen Clare, who disappeared when her father died and she went to live with her two paternal white aunts. Now she stood before her again—and had caught her "passing" too. Several days later, and with an equal measure of fascination and misgiving, Irene joined Clare and her mixed-race friend, Gertrude Martin, who also passes as white, once again for tea. As their afternoon was coming to its end, Clare's white husband, John (Jack) Bellew, arrived, and the conversation took a decidedly uncomfortable turn when, unaware of the women's mixed-race heritage, he voiced some offensive racist opinions with all the assurance of superiority that his whiteness gave him and silenced the women. From this uncomfortable remembrance Nella Larsen fashions her equally disturbing narrative of race and identity.

When the novel's contemporary plot resumes, Larsen grounds Irene in her social world. Married to an African American physician, Brian Redfield, and the mother of two young sons, she lives in Harlem, New York, and is an active member of its African American community, including the Negro Welfare League (NWL). One day, Clare appears at Irene's door, concerned that she had not received a reply to her letter. During their conversation, Clare confesses to Irene that she wishes to participate in the black community, and Irene reminds her of what she risks should her husband discover the truth of her identity. Clare, however, will not be deterred from her intention and, after attending the NWL dance, begins spending much of her time at the Redfield apartment. Her frequent presence there eventually arouses Irene's suspicion that Clare and Brian, who is dissatisfied with his comfortable life and dreams of meaningful work in South America, are engaged in an affair.

One day, during a shopping trip with her friend Felise Freeland, who is visibly black, Irene encounters Jack Bellew. Clearly aware now of Irene's race, he also, by implication, realizes that the woman he calls in jest "Nig" is, like Irene, mixed race and that he has been deceived in his marriage. Irene considers whether to warn Clare about the encounter but decides against it. Later, at a party hosted by Felise on the top floor of her apartment building, Bellew crashes the gathering to accuse Clare of being a "damned dirty nigger!" Irene rushes to Clare, who sits at an open window, and the beautiful woman, who has alternately frustrated and fascinated Irene, falls to her death. Was that death an accident? Did Clare commit suicide? Or did Irene murder her? Larsen's ambiguous ending leaves her readers with nothing more than their speculations, rather like the enigma of her racial identity.

HISTORICAL BACKGROUND: *PASSING* AND THE HARLEM RENAISSANCE

Harlem was in vogue during the 1920s. The raucous jazz tunes that escaped from the doors of New York's northern suburb's clubs and cabarets had given birth to an era, the Jazz Age, and helped make fashionable all things African American for a rising black middle class and a white elite in pursuit of the new. A "New Negro Movement," as it was known at the time, taking its name from the title of an influential anthology of

African American literature and thought published in 1925 by the philosopher and writer Alain Locke, was challenging pervading stereotypes of African Americans and fostering the aspirations and achievements of a new generation of writers and thinkers, artists and musicians of color. For nearly two decades, but especially in the 1920s, the Harlem Renaissance, as the cultural movement eventually became known, infused new life into an African American community in process of change. Among its artifacts is Nella Larsen's 1929 novel *Passing*, the tale of two childhood friends, Irene Redfield and Clare Kendry, reunited in adulthood that captures the era's spirit even as it exposes the gender, class, and racial issues that change could never quite erase, for like the decade of which it was part, the Harlem Renaissance was itself filled with contradictions.

The Great Migration of African Americans from the rural South to the major cities of the industrial North during the early twentieth century was in part a catalyst for the Harlem Renaissance. Fleeing the Jim Crow South of segregation, persecution, and limited opportunity, more than five million African Americans settled in Chicago, Philadelphia, Detroit, Cleveland, and New York City and throughout the West and Midwest, hoping to escape discrimination, violence, and hatred; to secure rights that had been denied them in the South, including the right to vote; and to gain access to jobs and educational opportunities that would improve their and their families' lives. Creating communities and establishing churches, schools, newspapers, and small businesses, many African Americans thrived and increasingly enjoyed middle-class prosperity. They also formed organizations, most notably the National Association for the Advancement of Colored People (NAACP) in 1909 and the National Urban League in 1910, to advocate for full political and social integration into the nation's life. By the 1920s, African Americans in New York City, where for more than a decade black entrepreneurs had established their businesses and black churches had been founded on a large block along the 135th Street (where Nella Larsen would work at a branch of the New York Public Library), were primed for the full flowering of their cultural and intellectual life that was the Harlem Renaissance.

For African American writers, the Harlem Renaissance provided an opportunity to develop authentic voices and to enlarge the scope of their subject matter and concerns. Freed from the need to write slave narratives that could be used by abolitionists in support of their cause as well as tales of racial uplift that had provided aspirational models following Reconstruction, a new generation of writers who had never experienced slavery but had known racial discrimination, including Langston Hughes, Zora

Neale Hurston, Jessie Redmon Fauset, Jean Toomer, Claude McKay, and Nella Larsen, began to write about black middle-class experience and the hopes and dreams, doubts and fears, joys and triumphs shared by blacks and whites that spoke to a common humanity. Zora Neale Hurston's 1933 short story "The Gilded-Six Bits," for example, is a tale of marriage tested by infidelity, a color-blind subject, and Jessie Redmon Fauset's 1928's *Plum-Bun*, like Larsen's *Passing*, a novel about racial identity, adopts the traditional form of the *bildungsroman*, or novel of development, to structure the story of its protagonist Angela Murray. Larsen's characters, moreover, like Fauset's, are educated members of the black middle class. Irene's husband, for instance, is a physician, and they mingle comfortably with Harlem's social and intellectual elite. Whatever their subject, whatever their approach, the writers of the Harlem Renaissance focused on race—racial identity, racial consciousness, racial discrimination—in all its many forms and complexity to convey the reality of African American life.

Despite their talent, or perhaps because they were talented (the difference in perspective is telling), many writers of the Harlem Renaissance, as well as many artists and musicians, owed much of their success to white patronage, one of the ironies of the movement. Harlem's jazz musicians, for instance, performed for white audiences in the city's clubs and cabarets. Similarly, African American writers depended at least in part on a white elite for their success. Indeed, in March 1924, the National Urban League sponsored a dinner attended by a group of African American writers and the white publishers, editors, and critics who could give their work the serious consideration that it deserved in an effort to pursue what the historian David Levering Lewis has called "civil rights by copyright" (xvi). Moreover, writers such as Langston Hughes, Zora Neale Hurston, and Nella Larsen accepted the patronage of wealthy white women such as Charlotte Osgood Mason, who were known colloquially as "Miss Annes," and men such as the writer and photographer Carl Van Vechten.

As the term "Miss Anne," with its mixture of respect and submission, implies, the relationship between black artists and white patrons was complicated. Black artists needed and were grateful for the support, both moral but especially financial, that their white patrons provided, but it left them at the same time indebted to a person who evoked the historical slave master. Their white patrons, moreover, no matter how sympathetic to issues of race or appreciative of African American culture, were at some level condescending to people who were perceived as inferior to them. Among the goals of the New Negro Movement were to dismantle stereotypes about African Americans and advocate for equality by demonstrating that they were intelligent and capable people who were not inferior to whites. Attaining those goals, the patronage system suggested, would not be easily achieved. Indeed, the system perpetuated to some extent the stereotypes to which it was a response.

The Harlem Renaissance did not end racial inequality. In fact, racially motivated violence continued throughout the era. Nevertheless, this flourishing of African American arts introduced new voices and new forms and established a pathway to integration into the nation's cultural heritage. It also raised important issues about race and racial identity for both blacks and whites. Many African American writers would explore them in their poetry, fiction, and drama, among them Nella Larsen in her provocative novel *Passing*.

ABOUT NELLA LARSEN: A LIFE ON THE COLOR LINE

When Nella Larsen died on March 30, 1964, at the age of seventy-two, few would have suspected that one of the most significant female voices of the Harlem Renaissance had just been silenced. Many assumed that she had died years before. After publishing two well-received novels, *Quicksand* (1928) and *Passing* (1929), and a few short stories during the Jazz Age, however, the novelist had slipped silently into literary obscurity, working primarily as a nurse in New York City until her death. In the 1970s, however, as a new generation of scholars sought to rescue the literary works of women and writers of color, Larsen's novels were rediscovered and reissued for a new audience interested now in the issues of gender, racial, and class identity that are central to her fiction. They were central to her life as well and perhaps account for her obscurity in death.

Born in Chicago, Illinois, on April 13, 1891, Nellie Walker was the child of mixed-race parents. Her father, Peter Walker, was an Afro-Caribbean immigrant from the Danish West Indies who quickly disappeared from her life; her mother, Marie Hansen, a Danish immigrant, was a seamstress and domestic worker who married a fellow Danish immigrant, Peter Larsen, several years later. Nellie, a mixed-race child, soon had a white half-sister and assumed her stepfather's surname. From her beginnings, in other words, race complicated Larsen's identity. Indeed, she experimented with different versions of her name—Nellye Larson, Nellie Larsen—before settling finally on Nella Larsen.

Educated with her half-sister at a private school in Chicago, Larsen was a sensitive and lonely child who seems to have been aware of her liminal

Nella Larsen (1891–1964) receives a Harmon Foundation Award for her 1928 novel *Quicksand*. The Harmon Awards were created in 1926 to recognize "Distinguished Achievement among Negroes" and testify to the patronage of a white elite in the Harlem Renaissance. (Bettmann/Corbis)

status as neither white nor black and to have experienced racial prejudice in her white immigrant Chicago neighborhood. Her stepfather, according to one biographer, "viewed her as an embarrassment" (Brown-Guillory 696), and she limited her contact with her family, according to another biographer, because, she said, "It might make it awkward for them, particularly my half-sister" (Davis, "Nella Larsen" 183). As a child, she lived for several years with maternal relatives in Denmark, and then in 1907, Larsen's parents enrolled her at Fisk University in Nashville, Tennessee, an historically black institution, where she studied science for a year. She never returned home. Instead, she lived again in Denmark, where she attended classes at the University of Copenhagen. In 1912, Larsen began training as a nurse at Lincoln Hospital Nursing School in New York City. Completing her course, she accepted a position in 1915 as head nurse at the John A. Andrew Memorial Hospital and Nurse Training School of Tuskegee Institute in Alabama, where she experienced Booker T. Washington's model of education as well as the Jim Crow South. Within a year, the disillusioned young woman had returned to New York, where she worked as a nurse first at Lincoln Hospital and then for the city's Bureau of Public Health, serving during the Spanish flu epidemic of 1918. Yet it seemed as if she would never find her place in the world.

Larsen's status and identity changed once again in 1919 when she married a prominent physicist, Elmer Imes, the second African American to earn a doctorate in physics. Moving from Jersey City, New Jersey, to Harlem in the 1920s, the couple quickly established themselves among Harlem's black professional class, counting among their acquaintance W. E. B. Du Bois, the writer James Weldon Johnson, and other leaders of the NAACP. Larsen, nevertheless, never felt entirely comfortable in this world. The circumstances of her birth, her mixed-race heritage, her lack of a college degree, all of which were important to a rising middle-class black culture that valued family and school ties, made Larsen aware of her peripheral status. Here was another world in which she did not quite belong.

Larsen's interest in the arts, however, helped secure her place in the Negro Awakening or the New Negro Movement, which eventually came to be known as the Harlem Renaissance. Volunteering as a librarian in 1921, Larsen helped prepare the first Negro art exhibit at the New York Public Library and then, in 1923, became the first African American woman to earn certification from the New York Public Library School, sponsored by Columbia University. Eager to continue participating in the lively Negro arts culture that was flourishing in the city's northern suburb, Larsen sought and received a transfer to the Harlem branch of the New York Public Library, where she worked as a children's librarian until late 1925, when she took a sabbatical and began to write her first novel.

Shortly after her marriage, Larsen had in fact begun to pursue an interest in writing, publishing her first short stories in 1920 and two articles about Danish games in the *Brownies' Book*, a children's magazine edited by Jessie Redmon Fauset, one of the most influential African American women writers of the era. Encouraged by the support of important figures in Harlem's interracial literary and arts community, including Fauset and the photographer Carl Van Vechten, Larsen found an appreciative audience for her first novel, the largely autobiographical *Quicksand* (1928), which chronicles the unsuccessful efforts of its mixed-race protagonist Helga Crane to find love and fulfillment and a place where she can belong. Her second novel, *Passing* (1929), the tale of two mixed-race friends who follow different paths to identity, received equally strong reviews.

Larsen's literary career ended, however, in 1930, when on the publication of her short story "Sanctuary" the writer was accused of plagiarizing Sheila Kaye-Smith's short story "Mrs. Adis," which had been first published in the United Kingdom in 1919. While the charges were never proved and did not prevent Larsen from becoming the first African American woman writer to be awarded a Guggenheim Fellowship, she never published again. She used her fellowship to travel to Europe for several years, spending time in Mallorca and Paris, where she worked on a third novel, the manuscript of which has never surfaced. Divorced from her husband in 1933, Larsen returned to New York, where, struggling with depression, she lived on alimony until Imes's death in 1942. She then returned to nursing, living quietly in her Brooklyn apartment in the obscurity that would be penetrated only on her death in 1964.

Quicksand and *Passing* are, of course, Larsen's legacy. The issues of race, class, and gender that they examine certainly defined the writer's life and continue to resonate with contemporary readers, thereby guaranteeing that she will not be forgotten. Life on the color line may have been fraught, but Nella Larsen made something worthy and lasting of it.

WHY WE READ *PASSING*

Questions of race and racial identity are without doubt central to Nella Larsen's novel *Passing*. Early in the novel, in fact, Brian and Irene Redfield speculate about the reasons that African Americans who choose to pass as white inevitably and no matter the cost seek to reestablish links with the culture that shaped their identity. Neither can provide an answer, and Brian actually confesses, "If I knew [why], I'd know what race is" (185). Brian's confession echoes the sentiment in the Countée Cullen poem "Heritage" that provides the epigraph to Larsen's novel: "One three centuries removed/ From the scenes his father loved,/ Spicy grove, cinnamon tree,/ What is Africa to me?" In a novel in which the central characters can pass as white, what is it that makes them black? Larsen does not provide an answer to the question. She offers instead a drama of ambiguity that, like its unresolved and unsettling ending, disrupts the certainties on which constructions of race have been based but that also confirms that race matters. It mattered during the Jazz Age, and it matters still in a multicultural, multiracial nation where racial lines are increasingly blurred but the color line persists.

Against the backdrop of the Harlem Renaissance, when all things African American were suddenly fashionable, the world of Larsen's novel is rife with race consciousness, and Clare Kendry and Irene Redfield embody its complexities. Clare, for instance, who is married to a white man unaware of her mixed-race heritage, has passed seamlessly into white society. "What difference would it make if, after all these years," she teases her racist husband, "you were to find out that I was one or two percent coloured?" (171). (Her husband, by the way, asserts absolutely, and ironically, that there "never have been and never will be" [171] a person of color in his family.) Obviously aware of the "one drop" rule on which the biological basis of race had been formulated, Clare chooses to ignore a definition of self imposed by others because it prevents her from achieving her desires. Based on a stock character in African American literature, the tragic mulatta, the mixed-raced daughter of a white slaveholder and his black slave, Clare should struggle with her identity, unable to find her place in either black or white society, and suffer the consequences of self-loathing and rejection, such as alcoholism, depression, and promiscuity, but she does not. Indeed, she seems relatively untroubled by her status, for what she seeks is to pass between both societies, asserting her right to self-definition and effectively subverting racial classifications. Her death clearly calls into question such possibilities.

For her part, Irene Redfield, capable of passing but fully invested in her racial heritage, is firmly entrenched in the black middle class, signified by her membership in the Negro Welfare League and the round of teas and dances that fill her social calendar. Eager to uplift the race, she and her fellow club members work tirelessly to promote the achievements of African Americans and thereby affirm a sense of racial identity and belonging that had been virtually erased by slavery, a laudable goal. Larsen's treatment of the means of achieving it, however, those teas and dances attended by the black bourgeoisie and liberal white intellectuals and philanthropists, satirizes the effort and suggests that Irene's race pride is a self-deception. Deeply anxious about her security, Irene strives to be the perfect lady, aware of the rigid standards to which she must conform if she wishes to maintain her status within her community. Her philanthropy is thus a carefully choreographed performance for the black middle class and, perhaps more to the point, for the white patrons of these events, who are more than a little patronizing in their presumption of superiority. Despite her awareness of Hugh Wentworth's rather "contemptuous" attitude toward "everything and everybody," for instance, Irene is incapable of concealing from Clare her pride in her friendship with the celebrated writer or of leaping quickly to his defense at Clare's criticism of him (198), responses that undermine Irene's philanthropic motives and race pride. By exposing Irene's conventionality, selfishness, and hypocrisy, Larsen acknowledges yet another aspect of race, that blacks have effectively internalized their inferiority in a society where whiteness sets the standard.

Race, as the examples of Irene Redfield and Clare Kendry reveal, is contested ground and nearly impossible to define. Is it biological? Is it based on geographic origin? Is it socially determined, a matter of shared habits and customs and beliefs? The answer remains elusive and fraught with disagreement. Even in the United States, where laws pertaining to race have long implied a definition of the term, the vocabulary by which dark-skinned people have been and continue to be identified by others as well as themselves, from offensive racial slurs to relatively neutral (but often political) words such as "Negro," "colored," "black," and "African American," demonstrates that notions about race and the characteristics on which it is based are subject to historical, cultural, and political change.

Yet however resistant to definition, race has the power to define and confine the self. While Clare and Irene might have been able to pass from one side of the color line to the other, for example, the line still existed, and discovery had consequences. Moreover, they would always have been considered "colored" in a society dominated by whites and would thus have negotiated a diminished world, for their color would have made them inferior. It would have determined their opportunities and set limits on their dreams. In a nation that privileges self-definition and invites self-reinvention, such boundaries and limitations are clearly ironic, as Larsen's use of passing as a metaphor intends. They are also tragic, a source of so much wasted potential and self-hatred (or at least self-deception). To Countée Cullen's query, "What is Africa to me?" Nella Larsen, it seems, would have answered, "Everything." In a multiracial, multicultural nation, where citizens must no longer tick one of three or four boxes on a census form, one of which is "Other," to signify their race and an African American president governs from the White House, such an answer resonates still and may account for *Passing*'s continued relevance in the United States. During the Harlem Renaissance, that first full flowering of African American culture, race mattered. Nearly a hundred years later, in the aftermath of the civil rights movement, of federally mandated interaction between races and equal opportunity for all, race still matters.

HISTORICAL EXPLORATIONS OF *PASSING*

In Chapter Two of Nella Larsen's 1929 novel *Passing*, Irene Redfield transgresses the color line. On a hot, humid summer day in Chicago, the attractive woman, one of the novel's two central characters, seeks relief from the stifling heat in the rooftop tearoom of the city's elite Drayton Hotel. Nobody, of course, stops the fashionably dressed woman from taking a seat and ordering refreshments, but somebody certainly would have done had he known that Irene was African American. Nothing about her appearance or demeanor, however, betrays her racial heritage, the fact that she is a mixed-race woman, and Irene, on this occasion, is grateful that she is able to pass as white and thus enjoy privileges that would be denied her if her skin were darker.

Harlem may have been in vogue during the Jazz Age, but as this scene from as well as the title of Larsen's novel implies, the color line, that invisible barrier that separated (and continues to separate) blacks from whites for centuries, existed still during the 1920s. In the half-century since the Civil War had secured the emancipation of slaves in the nation's Southern states, African Americans remained second-class citizens throughout the country, their status determined by their race. One drop of African blood defined their racial identity, no matter the color of their skin, and that one drop of blood placed each person on one side or the other of the color line, effectively determining the rights and privileges that everyone was expected to accept as his or her own. Individuals who sought to cross the color line by "passing" as a member of another racial group disrupted the systems on which American society had been ordered and contributed to the considerable anxiety about shifting racial boundaries that developed in the 1920s as a consequence of increased immigration from areas outside northern Europe and the Great Migration of African Americans from the rural South to the urban North. Nella Larsen's *Passing* not only captured that anxiety but also evoked the race and class issues that fueled it and thus reveals the contradictions of the era.

"The problem of the Twentieth Century," asserted the African American scholar and activist W. E. B. Du Bois in *The Souls of Black Folk* (1903), "is the problem of the color line." The historical and cultural contexts of Nella Larsen's *Passing* affirm this assertion. The late nineteenth and early twentieth centuries, for instance, gave rise to a popular and an influential eugenics movement in the United States. A social philosophy supported by now largely discredited scientific studies and research into genetic

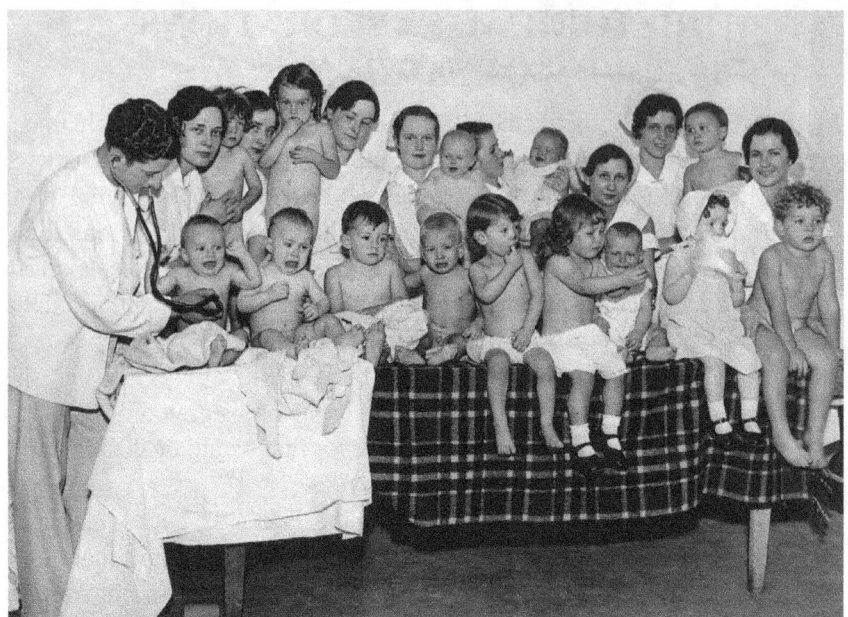

One of a staff of forty physicians and nurses begins the task of examining some of the 983 children between the ages of two months and five years who have been entered in a "Better Babies" Contest. Like the "Fitter Families" contests, the "Better Babies" contests, based on the "science" of eugenics popular in the Jazz Age, were intended to identify the finest specimens of children based on an "objective" set of standards. (Underwood & Underwood/Corbis)

disorders, especially mental conditions such as schizophrenia, bipolar disorder, and depression, eugenics is the application of selective breeding for the improvement of human hereditary qualities. Through selective breeding, in other words, humans, eugenicists believed, could direct their own evolution. Because the practice of eugenics promised to eliminate inferior genes, the philosophy was embraced by many leaders of the Progressive Era, including the birth control activist Margaret Sanger. In addition, various corporate foundations, including the Carnegie Institution, the Rockefeller Foundation, the Harriman railroad fortune, and the Kellogg fortune, funded the eugenics movement's activities and initiatives. In 1906, the American Breeder's Association, the first eugenics body in the United States, was established under the direction of the biologist Charles B. Davenport to "investigate and report on heredity in the human race, and emphasize the value of superior blood and the menace to society of inferior blood" (Chase 114). Among its members were the inventor Alexander Graham Bell and the botanist Luther Burbank. In 1911, Davenport founded the Eugenics Record Office, which collected family pedigrees and supported genetic research. By the late 1920s, eugenics was included in the curriculum of many high schools and leading universities, including Harvard, Colombia, Cornell, and Brown, effectively legitimizing the movement and the science on which it was based.

Unifying the eugenics philosophy was the view that some people were more "fit" than others and that the fittest should be encouraged to procreate while the "unfit" should be discouraged and even prevented from bearing children. Throughout the late nineteenth and early twentieth centuries, this view also gained acceptance among the general public at least in part because it came to be linked to progressive belief in the improvement of society, especially through science. In 1908, for instance, the Louisiana State Fair launched the first "Scientific Baby Contest," a competition to find the ideal child based on health and intelligence standards. By 1913, when the *Women's Home Companion* magazine began to cosponsor these "Better Babies Contests," they rivaled in popularity the produce and livestock competitions at as many as forty state fairs. Proud mothers submitted their children for inspection by doctors and nurses in hopes that their child would be determined to possess "a sound mind in a sound body," as the winners' certificate proclaimed. In 1920, at the Kansas State Free Fair, "Better Babies Contests" expanded to include "Fitter Families Contests." Competitors submitted an "Abridged Record of Family Traits" and then underwent physical and psychological testing by medical doctors. Each family received a letter grade of eugenic health. The "Grade A Individuals" received a silver trophy. All contestants with a grade of B+ or higher took home a coveted bronze medal bearing the inscription "Yea, I have a goodly heritage" (eugenicsarchive.org). By linking health to scientific measurement, these competitions thus helped popularize eugenics philosophy and paved the way for legislative reforms aimed at the problem of the "unfit."

Racial passing, the subject of Nella Larsen's novel, contributed to this anxiety because the practice of crossing the color line to live as a member of another race disrupted the stereotypes of "fit" and "unfit" and undermined the social structures built on them. While nobody could know for certain the prevalence of the practice, headlines like that published in 1928 by the *New York World*, "Crossing the Color Line: Social and Economic Ambitions Lead Negroes to 'Pass' at Rate of 5,000 a Year to White Fold," would have alarmed a white majority whose superiority was based on a biological construction of race. That majority would also have been both appalled and fascinated by a sensational trial, known as the Rhinelander

Case, that highlighted and confirmed some of their worst fears about the practice. The case, to which Larsen refers late in her novel, when Irene speculates about Clare's fate should her racist white husband discover her mixed-race status, "What if Bellew should divorce Clare? Could he?" There was the Rhinelander case" (228), clearly provides a context for her Jazz Age tale.

On October 14, 1924, after a difficult three-year courtship, Alice Beatrice Jones and Leonard "Kip" Rhinelander married despite his family's disapproval. He, after all, was the son of a prominent New York family whose name appeared on the *Social Register* alongside the Vanderbilts and the Astors and heir to a $100 million fortune. She, in contrast, was the daughter of working-class English immigrants and employed as a domestic. Scandal about the marriage arose a month later when the New Rochelle *Standard Star* published a story under the headline "Rhinelanders' Son Marries Daughter of a Colored Man." What had formerly been a marriage of disparate class had suddenly become a case of miscegenation, and all the nation was interested. While New York law did not ban interracial marriage, as twenty-eight states did in the 1920s, it was socially prohibited throughout the nation. Alice's name, for instance, had been included in the *Social Register* after her elopement with Leonard, but it was quickly deleted after the allegations of her mixed-race heritage surfaced. Moreover, Leonard's father understood what his son, who clearly loved Alice, apparently did, or perhaps cared, not to acknowledge, that no respectable white woman of the Rhinelanders' class would marry Leonard unless he secured an annulment, which would have rendered the marriage null and void, as if it had never happened. Two weeks after the revelations that Alice's father descended from a West Indian, Leonard, capitulating to family pressure, filed for an annulment of the marriage, alleging, among other charges, that Alice had deceived him about her race. One year later, in November 1925, the case of *Rhinelander vs. Rhinelander* produced headlines that testified to the nation's racial anxieties.

In prosecuting Leonard's case, his lawyer argued that Alice, who was four years older than her husband, had deliberately deceived a shy, awkward young man who at the time of their meeting was being treated at the Orchard School, an inpatient clinic, for various nervous conditions, including stammering. Alice, moreover, had used sex, he argued, reading from their love letters, which provided irrefutable evidence of sexual intimacy, to coerce Leonard, "slave" to his affection for her, into marriage. Alice, at the urging of her husband, had initially denied her mixed-race heritage, the only hope that she and Leonard might socially preserve their marriage, but at trial, she surprised both her husband and his lawyers by abandoning her claim of whiteness to maintain that Leonard had known and accepted the truth of her racial identity. The letters that were intended to portray her as a predatory and licentious black woman suddenly provided evidence to support Alice's honesty. Given their premarital intimacy, Leonard, after all, who had seen her naked body, would have had to know that at least one drop of non-white blood flowed through her veins, and that drop, so far as society was concerned, determined her racial identity.

As the trial progressed, both sides introduced a variety of sensational evidence to support their claims. In addition to the love letters, which women were excluded from hearing to protect their sensibilities, the entertainer Al Jolson, famous as a blackface performer of jazz and blues songs, was called to corroborate Alice's claim that she had once met him, which he denied. Most sensational of all, however, Alice's lawyer asked his client to disrobe to allow an all-white, all-male, all-married jury as well as her husband to inspect her skin color. The truth written on her body, Alice's attorney, who had also called into question Leonard's honesty and criticized his exploitation as a privileged white gentleman of a working-class black woman, rested his case, and the jury began its deliberations. On December 5, 1925, it returned a verdict in favor of Alice. In 1929, Leonard and Alice Rhinelander divorced. Neither married again, and their sensational case slipped into obscurity. In the mid-1920s, however, the scandal as well as the jury's verdict had challenged the nation to consider race and racial identity and to formulate an answer to a question that Leonard's attorney had put to the jury in his summation: "Can the Ethiopian change his skin?"

Larsen's novel issues that same challenge to both its black and white readers in its treatment of what is known as "the talented tenth." A term that originated among Northern white liberals in 1896, the "talented tenth" refers to the African American leadership class in the early twentieth century and is today associated chiefly with an influential essay of the same phrase by W. E. B. Du Bois in which he challenged the views of another African American leader, Booker T. Washington, in his Atlanta Exposition Speech of 1895. In that speech, Washington advocated mutual cooperation between the races and a technical education for blacks that would prepare them for useful contributions to the nation's, and their own, prosperity. In "The Talented Tenth," in contrast, Du Bois, who favored a classical education of the sort that he had received at Fisk and Harvard universities, argued, "The Negro race, like all races, is going to be saved by its exceptional men. The problem of education, then, among Negroes must first of all deal with the Talented Tenth; it is a problem of developing the

W. E. B. Du Bois (1868–1963), African American writer and intellectual, was considered one of the midwives of the Harlem Renaissance and the father of pan-Africanism. (Library of Congress)

Best of this race that they may guide the Mass away from the contamination and death of the Worst, in their own and other races" (33). Unabashedly elitist, the notion of the Talented Tenth might have been endorsed by proponents of the eugenics movement, implying, as it does, that some people are more fit than others, yet its assertions of African American "fitness" likely would have affronted those same proponents. Larsen's novel, with its black middle-class characters, would also have done so.

Passing's social world is distinctly upscale. Irene Redfield, the novel's protagonist, is married to a physician who practices in Manhattan and the mother of two school-age sons who, in the novel's opening scene, are away at summer camp. A fashionable woman who knows the difference between a dress designed by Worth or Lanvin (219) and has traveled in Europe, she fills her days flitting from social engagement to social engagement, from teas to bridge parties to dances, where she mingles not only with an African American elite but also with white philanthropists and liberals, such as Hugh Wentworth (as well as race tourists drawn to her Harlem home by the thrill of the exotic). A member of the Negro Welfare League, she also works tirelessly to improve the lives of the less fortunate, prompting her dissatisfied husband to taunt about her earnestness, "Uplifting the brother's no easy job" (186). The Redfields' lifestyle places them firmly within the era's thriving black middle class and thus provides evidence of the African American's ability to surmount class barriers that effectively disrupts racial stereotypes. Yet because their lifestyle is also anchored in a distinctly white bourgeois ethos, it reinforces the complexities of racial identity signified in the act of passing. In effect, the novel simultaneously undermines and reinforces the eugenicists' belief that whites are superior to people of color.

While the reasons for which every individual chooses to pass as a member of another race are always personal, Larsen suggests that they are chiefly social and economic, rooted in the desire to enjoy the privileges of superiority and to avoid the persecution and discrimination experienced by those of the lower classes. Irene, for example, is proud of her racial heritage. At one point, in fact, observing her husband dancing with her friend Clare Kendry, she is pleased "that Clare was having the opportunity to discover that some coloured men were superior to some white men" (204). Nevertheless, Irene, who could pass as white but chooses not to do so, cannot on occasion resist the temptation to pass, especially when passing secures an advantage. Had she not been passing, after all, she could not have sheltered from Chicago's summer heat in the Drayton Hotel's tearoom.

Clare's decision to pass as a white woman is also based on social and economic advantage. Aware early of her mixed-race identity, a teenage Clare had been raised to know her place as a "daughter of the indiscreet Ham" (159) by her white father's "good Christian" aunts following his death in a bar fight. Expected to earn her keep doing housework and the laundry, the sixteen-year-old was soon chafing against this "hard life." "Determined to get away, to be a person and not a charity or a problem" (159), she was also aware of advantages available to whites. Soon it was rumored about school that she had been seen dining with whites at a fashionable hotel and driving with a white man in a chauffeur-driven Packard in Lincoln Park. When John "Jack" Bellew returns to the city from South America with "untold gold" (159), Clare seizes the opportunity to abandon her "coloured" heritage and marries him on her eighteenth birthday. As she tells Irene, "Money's awfully nice to have. In fact, all things considered, . . . it's even worth the price" (160). As Irene soon discovers, that price includes marriage to an unredeemed racist who calls his wife "Nig" (171) because her skin is a tawny white. To live the life she wants, Clare is clearly willing to make any sacrifice.

Despite their differing views on passing, both women share the desire to enjoy the social and economic benefits of white society. Clare has attained them by passing. Irene, however, enjoys them as a member of a black elite modeled on a distinctly white ethos. Her world of teas and dances and charity functions is no different from the white elites' whose names and photos appeared on the society pages of newspapers and whose lives were chronicled in the gossip magazines that gained popularity in the Jazz Age.

Nor is her deep concern for respectability. She assures herself, for example, that she is not "a snob" who "cared greatly for the petty restrictions and distinctions with which what called itself Negro society chose to hedge itself about" (157), but Irene is in fact deceiving herself. Indeed, she has "a natural and deeply rooted aversion to the kind of front-page notoriety that Clare Kendry's presence in [the Michigan summer resort of] Idlewild, as her guest, would expose her to." She is a conventional woman who fears the collapse of her secure life among the black elite and thus distrusts anything that she perceives as "menaces" (190) to it, including her husband's restless longing to practice medicine in Brazil and Clare's dangerous insistence on reconnecting to her race.

Everything about Irene's world, from the "fat-bellied German coffee-pot" (184) from which she pours the morning coffee prepared by her housemaid Zulena to her plan to send her son for a European education (19), from her tasteful wardrobe to her carefully chosen circle of friends, replicates upper middle-class white society and its bourgeois ethos, which may account at least in part for her insecurities. Just as passing reinforced notions of white superiority, so, too, did the creation of a black elite that reproduced the white paradigm, so any deviation from that paradigm, any social *faux pas*, would constitute a fall from grace, not only in the black community but also in the white. For a woman like Irene, who has defined herself as a superior black woman within a community of the "talented tenth," such a fall would be intolerable.

A candid conversation between Irene and Hugh Wentworth at the Negro Welfare League dance makes clear that Larsen was acutely aware of the complex and contradictory status of the black elite during the Jazz Age. Surveying the guests circulating about the venue, Irene and Hugh remark first on its diversity, but then, having observed Clare dancing with a handsome black man, Hugh seizes on the topic of the popularity of "gentlemen of colour," complaining a bit tongue-in-cheek but not without an edge of pique that they have displaced "a mere Nordic" like him from his accustomed position. Even his wife Bianca, he notes, has spent the night "being twirled about by some Ethiopian" (205). In response, Irene quickly corrects Hugh's assumptions about the reason for black popularity, locating it not in superiority, not in "patronizing kindness" (205), not in "predatory sexuality" (206), but in the exotic. It springs, she tells him, from an "emotional excitement; . . . the sort of thing you feel in the presence of something strange and even, perhaps, a bit repugnant to you" (205). Otherness, the strange and exotic, prompts curiosity, Irene explains, but as her use of the word "repugnant" implies, it does not confer equality. She reinforces her point when the topic of conversation moves on to passing. Noting that the practice primarily involves blacks who pass as white, Irene responds to Hugh's statement that he had never considered the point with a remark that exposes the unspoken assumptions about race in the United States: "No, you wouldn't. Why should you?" (206). As a wealthy white man, the most privileged of all classes, Hugh would never have contemplated passing as a black man, for in doing so, he would have devalued himself. Although nothing about his talents and skills, his intelligence and achievements, or even his appearance would have been different, to identify himself and pass as a black man would have changed entirely the basis on which society judged him, and he would have been found inferior. The implications of Hugh's obliviousness to this truth unify the various historical and cultural contexts of Nella Larsen's Jazz Age novel. In a country based on a white paradigm and where color mattered, only a man of Hugh's race and class could so easily have assumed his superiority, but then science, after all, as well as the legal system, affirmed his status. Moreover, the African American middle class, modeled as it was on a white bourgeois ethos, conceded it.

In the midst of the Harlem Renaissance, that first full flowering of African American culture, "when hundreds of white people of Hugh Wentworth's type" (198) trekked north for an experience of otherness, Larsen exposed the reality of the color line, even for its "Talented Tenth." Indeed, when Irene's husband Brian observes, "Pretty soon the coloured people won't be allowed in [to Harlem events] at all, or will have to sit in Jim Crowed sections" (198), she captured its ironies as well.

DOCUMENTING *PASSING*

The Harlem Renaissance

The Harlem Renaissance, the first full flowering of African American culture, expanded American cultural life to make popular all things African American for the first time in the nation's history. No longer were African American writers constrained by the forms of the slave narrative or the tale of racial uplift that had historically been their primary literary genres. They could instead create tales of African American life within the nation's urban centers, novels and short stories that certainly explored issues of race but were not limited to them. African American musicians were also revolutionizing the modern sound and rhythms, inventing all that jazz that would give rise to an era. The following selections, the first two by participants in this Renaissance, the poet Langston Hughes and novelist Wallace

Thurman, bear witness to a time when Harlem was in vogue not only for the African American community but also for fashionable white liberals. All three selections make clear that despite the new inclusiveness of the era the Harlem Renaissance did not effect a sea change in race relations.

Document: From *The Big Sea*, Langston Hughes, 1940

The 1920's were the years of Manhattan's black Renaissance. It began with *Shuffle Along, Running Wild,* and the Charleston. Perhaps some people would say even with *The Emperor Jones,* Charles Gilpin, and the tom-toms at the Provincetown. But certainly it was the musical revue, *Shuffle Along,* that gave a scintillating send-off to that Negro vogue in Manhattan, which reached its peak just before the crash of 1929, the crash that sent Negroes, white folks, and all rolling down the hill toward the Works Progress Administration.

Shuffle Along was a honey of a show. Swift, bright, funny, rollicking, and gay, with a dozen danceable, signable tunes. Besides, look who were in it: The now famous choir director, Hall Johnson, and the composer, William Grant Still, were a part of the orchestra. Eubie Blake and Noble Sissle wrote the music and played and acted in the show. Miller and Lyles were the comics, Florence Mills skyrocketed to fame in the second act. Trixie Smith sang "He May Be Your Man But He Comes to See Me Sometimes." And Caterina Jarboro, now a European prima donna, and the internationally celebrated Josephine Baker were merely in the chorus. Everybody was in the

Langston Hughes (1902–1967), one of the best known leaders of the Harlem Renaissance, famously wrote about the period when "the negro was in vogue" and championed pride in African American identity and its diverse culture. (Library of Congress)

audience—including me. People came back to see it innumerable times. It was always packed. When I saw it, I was thrilled and delighted. . . . It gave just the proper push—a pre-Charleston kick—to that Negro vogue of the 20's, that spread to books, African sculpture, music, and dancing. . . .

White people began to come to Harlem in droves. For several years they packed the expensive Cotton Club on Lenox Avenue. But I was never there, because the Cotton Club was a Jim Crow club for gangsters and monied whites. They were not cordial to Negro patronage, unless you were a celebrity like Bojangles. So Harlem Negroes did not like the Cotton Club and never appreciated its Jim Crow policy in the very heart of their dark community. Nor did ordinary Negroes like the growing influx of whites toward Harlem after sundown, flooding the little cabarets and bars where formerly only colored people laughed and sang, and where now the strangers were given the best ringside tables to sit and stare at the Negro customers—like amusing animals in a zoo. . . .

It was a period when, at almost every Harlem upper-crust dance or party, one would be introduced to various distinguished white celebrities there as guests. It was a period when almost any Harlem Negro of any social importance at all would be likely to say casually: "As I was remarking the other day to Heywood—," meaning Heywood Broun. Or: "As I said to George—," referring to George Gershwin. It was a period when local and visiting royalty were not at all uncommon in Harlem. And when the parties of A'Lelia Walker, the Negro heiress, were filled with guests whose names would turn any Nordic social climber green with envy. It was a period when Harold Jackman, a handsome young Harlem school teacher of modest means, calmly announced one day that he was sailing for the Riviera for a fortnight, to attend Princess Murat's yachting party. It was a period when Charleston preachers opened up shouting churches as sideshows for white tourists. It was a period when at least one charming colored chorus girl, amber enough to pass for a Latin American, was living in a pent house, with all her bills paid by a gentleman whose name was banker's magic on Wall Street. It was a period when every season there was at least one hit play on Broadway acted by a Negro cast. And when books by Negro authors were being published with much greater frequency and much more publicity than ever before or since in history. It was a period when white writers wrote about Negroes more successfully (commercially speaking) than Negroes did about themselves. It was the period (God help us!) when Ethel Barrymore appeared in blackface in *Scarlet Sister Mary!* It was the period when the Negro was in vogue.

Source: Excerpt from "Parties" from THE BIG SEA by Langston Hughes. Copyright © 1940 by Langston Hughes. Copyright renewed 1968 by Arna Bontemps and George Houston Bass. Reprinted by permission of Hill and Wang, a division of Farrar, Straus and Giroux, LLC.

Document: From *Negro Life in New York's Harlem*, Wallace Thurman, 1928

... Harlem's famed night clubs have become merely side shows staged for sensation-seeking whites. ... [T]hey cannot approximate the infectious rhythm and joy always found in a Negro cabaret.

Take the Sugar Cane Club on Fifth Avenue near 135th Street, located on the border of the most "low-down" section of Harlem. This place is visited by few whites or few "dicty" Negroes. Its customers are the rough-and-ready, happy-go-lucky more primitive type—street walkers, petty gamblers and pimps, with an occasional adventurer from other strata of society.

The Sugar Cane Club is a narrow subterranean passageway about twenty-five feet wide and 125 feet long. Rough wooden tables, surrounded by rough wooden chairs, and the orchestra stands, jammed into the right wall center, use up about three-quarters of the space. The remaining rectangular area is bared for dancing. With a capacity for seating about one hundred people, it usually finds room on gala nights for twice that many. The orchestra weeps and moans and groans as only an unsophisticated Negro Jazz orchestra can. A blues singer croons vulgar ditties over the tables to individual parties or else wah-wahs husky syncopated blues songs from the center of the floor. Her act over, the white lights are extinguished, red and blue spot lights are centered on the diminutive dancing space, couples push back their chairs, squeeze out from behind the tables and from against the wall, then finding one another's bodies, sweat gloriously together, with shoulders hunched, limbs obscenely intertwined and hips wiggling; animal beings urged on by liquor and music and physical contact. ...

One particular place known as the Glory Hole is hidden in a musty damp basement behind an express and trucking office. It is a single room about ten feet square and remains an unembellished basement except for a planed down plank floor, a piano, three chairs and library table. The Glory Hole is typical of its class. It is a social club, commonly called dive, convenient for the high times of a certain group. The men are unskilled laborers during the day, and in the evenings they round up their girls or else meet them at the rendezvous in order to have what they consider and enjoy as a good time. The women, like the men, swear, drink and dance as much and as vulgarly as they please. Yet they do not strike the observer as being vulgar. They are merely being and doing what their environment and their desire for pleasure suggest. . . .

The other extreme of amusement places in Harlem is exemplified by the Bamboo Inn, a Chinese-American restaurant that features Oriental cuisine, a jazz band and dancing. It is the place for select Negro Harlem's night life, the place where debutantes have the coming out parties, where college lads take their co-eds and society sweethearts and dignified matrons entertain. It is a beautifully decorated establishment, glorified by a balcony with booths, and a large gyroflector, suspending from the center of the ceiling, on which colored spotlights play, flecting the room with triangular bits of varicolored light. The Bamboo Inn is *the* place to see "high Harlem" just like the Glory Hole is *the* place to see "low Harlem." Well-dressed men escorting expensively garbed women and girls; models from Vanity Fair with brown, yellow and black skins. Doctors and lawyers, Babbitts and their ladies with fine manners (not necessarily learned through Emily Post), fine clothes and fine homes to return to when the night's fun has ended. . . .

When Harlem people wish to dance, without attending a cabaret, they go to the Renaissance Casino or to the Savoy, Harlem's two most famous public dance halls. The Savoy is the pioneer in the field of giving dance-loving Harlemites some place to gather nightly. It is an elaborate ensemble with a Chinese garden (Negroes seem to have a penchant for Chinese food—there are innumerable Chinese restaurants all over Harlem), two orchestras that work in relays, and hostesses provided at twenty-five cents per dance for partnerless young men. The Savoy opens at three in the afternoon and closes at three in the morning. One can spend twelve hours in this jazz palace for sixty-five cents, and the price of a dinner or an occasional sustaining sandwich and drink. The music is good, the dancers are gay, and setting is conducive to joy.

Source: Wallace Thurman, *Negro Life in New York's Harlem*, Girard, KS: Haldeman-Julius Publications, 1928.

Document: From "'Charleston' Dance Sweeps New York City by Storm; Louis Chalif Is Forced to Instruct in Dance That Is Distasteful," Maxine Davis, 1925

From the battery to the Bronx, from the darkest dives of Harlem to the flittering splendor of Fifth av., everybody in New York is dancing the "Charleston."

With utmost reluctance, the most exclusive dancing masters of the country accepted the wiggle-wiggle that drifted into the light, from the black and tan resorts of New York into the homes of the indigo-blooded with the insidious impartiality of the cholera. They were forced to adopt the form of these aboriginal gyrations as a regular ballroom dance to teach the youngsters and their grandmothers because public sentiment of high and low forced it. The American Society of Teachers of Dancing, the dancing masters of the four hundred in all the great cities of the nation—with modifications, and their convention at the Waldorf this week.

Behold then Louis Chalif, who teaches his art to his fashionable disciples in a pink marble temple on the creme de la creme of thorough-fares, Fifty-seventh st., near Fifth Av.; he who had been teacher of royalty and is preceptor of the aristocracy of Manhattan, is preparing with utmost distaste to teach the Charleston.

Chalif numbers among his pupils whom he instructs for the trifling sum of $6 a half hour—Gloria Gould and her family (he has taught Gloria since she was nine years old), all the Vanderbilt children and some of the Vanderbilts, no longer children, Mrs. August Belmont, Mrs. Sarah Payne Whitney, her son and two daughters and, in a word, the offspring of the social register.

Chalif, who is a preacher of beauty and grace of movement, admits that the high as well as the low want the "Charleston," and that Newport and Tuxedo are swaying and wriggling and kicking in the same measures as Avenue A.

And this fall even the little children of the social powers that want to gyrate in imitation of their elders. Chalif and his conferees will have to teach them.

"I hate to make clowns of the children," he mourned, "but what would you do?"

The best dancing masters, however, led by the fashionable Russian, will teach a modified version, in which smooth gliding motions will be substituted for the free motions of the African savage and which the foot will be tilted but 45 degrees off the floor.

That no one really expects folks to dance a characterization revised to have the thrill of a Virginia reel is apparent. "We teach them the polite steps. We cannot be responsible for the way they perform them outside our halls," apologized Chalif.

This master has real hopes, however, that the innate culture of the "upper classes" will take the Charleston and make it a decent, if popular, exercise.

"Just because the Charleston has come up to us from the lowest social level, does not mean that it might not become a polished and beautiful dance," he says optimistically, pointing out the lowly origin of dances popular for generations. . . .

France, according to Chalif, has given the world most of its formal dances. Now it is America's turn. All the world is Charleston-mad and assuredly the Charleston is of American vintage.

The close dancing and the habit of dancing all evening on floor space no larger than that of a telephone booth is not altogether the product of the war or current immorality, he states. It is because of the modern practice of many people dancing in public on tiny café floors. "Picture people dancing the quadrille or a stately minuet at the Del Fey club," he smiles. . . .

Source: Maxine Davis, "'Charleston' Dance Sweeps New York City by Storm; Louis Chalif Is Forced to Instruct in Dance That Is Distasteful," *The Miami Daily News,* August 29, 1925.

THE AFRICAN AMERICAN ELITE

The world of Nella Larsen's Passing *is decidedly upscale. Clare Kendry and Irene Redfield enjoy European travel and a social life that revolves around teas and dances and charity events. Their children attend private schools and summer camp. Irene possesses a sense of* noblesse oblige *to those less fortunate than she is. Their lives make clear, in other words, that the African American community replicated the class system of the larger white culture, a hierarchal structure into which people earned their place based on marks of status such as income, profession, education, and, perhaps surprisingly, color. The ability of Irene and Clare to "pass" as white, for example, makes available to them privileges that would not have been shared by dark-toned African Americans. The following selections document the reality of this African American elite and in so doing challenge the assumptions of the eugenics movement, documents about which follow this section, that achieved both popular and scientific acceptance during the 1920s.*

Document: From "The Talented Tenth," W. E. B. Du Bois, 1903

The Negro race, like all races, is going to be saved by its exceptional men. The problem of education, then, among Negroes must first of all deal with the Talented Tenth; it is the problem of developing the Best of this race that they may guide the Mass away from the contamination and death of the Worst, in their own and other races. Now the training of men is a difficult and intricate task. Its technique is a matter for educational experts, but its object is for the vision of seers. If we make money the object of man-training, we shall develop money-makers but not necessarily men; if we make technical skill the object of education, we may possess artisans but not, in nature, men. Men we shall have only as we make manhood the object of the work of the schools—intelligence, broad sympathy, knowledge of the world that was and is, and of the relation of men to it—this is the curriculum of that Higher Education which must underlie true life. On this foundation we may build bread winning, skill of hand and quickness of brain, with never a fear lest the child and man mistake the means of living for the object of life.

If this be true—and who can deny it—three tasks lay before me; first to show from the past that the Talented Tenth as they have risen among American Negroes have been worthy of leadership; secondly, to show how these men may be educated and developed; and thirdly, to show their relation to the Negro problem.

You misjudge us because you do not know us. From the very first it has been the educated and intelligent of the Negro people that have led and elevated the mass, and the sole obstacles that nullified and retarded their efforts were slavery and race prejudice; for what is slavery but the legalized survival of the unfit and the nullification of the work of natural internal leadership? Negro leadership, therefore, sought from the first to rid the race of this awful incubus that it might make way for natural selection and the survival of the fittest. . . .

And so we come to the present—a day of cowardice and vacillation, of strident wide-voiced wrong and faint hearted compromise; of double-faced dallying with Truth and Right. Who are to-day guiding the work of the Negro people? The "exceptions" of course. And yet so sure as this Talented Tenth is pointed out, the blind worshippers of the Average cry out in alarm: "These are exceptions, look here at death, disease and crime—these are the happy rule." Of course they are the rule, because a silly nation made them the rule: Because for three long centuries this people lynched Negroes who dared to be brave, raped black women who dared to be virtuous, crushed dark-hued youth who dared to be ambitious, and encouraged and made to flourish servility and lewdness and apathy. But not even this was able to crush all manhood and chastity and aspiration from black folk. A saving remnant continually survives and persists, continually aspires, continually shows itself in thrift and ability and character. Exceptional it is to be sure, but this is its chiefest promise; it shows the capability of Negro blood, the promise of black men. Do Americans ever stop to reflect that there are in this land a million men of Negro blood, well-educated, owners of homes, against the honor of whose womanhood no breath was ever raised, whose men occupy positions of trust and usefulness, and who, judged by any standard, have reached the full measure of the best type of modern European culture: Is it fair, is it decent, is it Christian to ignore these facts of the Negro problem, to belittle such aspiration, to nullify such leadership and seek to crush these people back into the mass out of which by toil and travail, they and their fathers have raised themselves?

Can the masses of the Negro people be in any possible way more quickly raised than by the effort and example of this aristocracy of talent and character? Was there ever a nation of God's fair earth civilized from the bottom upward? Never; it is, ever was and ever will be from the top downward that culture filters. The Talented Tenth rises and pulls all that are worth the saving up to their vantage ground. This is the history of human progress; and the two historic mistakes which have hindered that progress were the thinking first that no more could ever rise save the few already risen; or second, that it would better the unrisen to pull the risen down.

Source: W. E. B. Du Bois, "The Talented Tenth," from *The Negro Problem: A Series of Articles by Representative Negroes of To-day*, New York, 1903.

Document: From "The Task of Negro Womanhood," Elise Johnson McDougald, 1925

Throughout the years of history, woman has been the weather-vane, the indicator, showing in which direction the wind of destiny blows. Her status and development have augured now calm and stability, now swift currents of progress. What then is to be said of the Negro woman of to-day, whose problems are of such import to her race?

A study of her contributions to any one community, throughout America, would illuminate the pathway being trod by her people. There is, however, an advantage in focusing upon the women of Harlem—modern city in the world's metropolis. Here, more than anywhere else, the Negro woman is free from the cruder handicaps of primitive household hardships and the grosser forms of sex and race subjugation. Here, she has considerable opportunity to measure her powers in the intellectual and industrial fields of the great city. The questions naturally arise: "What are her difficulties" and, "How is she solving them?"

To answer these questions, one must have in mind not any one Negro woman, but rather a colorful pageant of individuals, each differently endowed. Like the red and yellow of the tiger-lily, the skin of one is brilliant against the star-lit darkness of a racial sister. From grace to strength, they vary in infinite degree, with traces of the race's history left in physical and mental outline on each. With a discerning mind, one catches the multiform charm, beauty and character of Negro women, and grasps the fact that their problems cannot be thought of in mass.

Because only a few have caught this vision, even in New York, the general attitude of mind causes the Negro woman serious difficulty. She is conscious that what is left of chivalry is not directed toward her. She realizes that the ideals of beauty, built up in the fine arts, have excluded her almost entirely. Instead, the grotesque Aunt Jemimas of the streetcar advertisements, proclaim only an ability to serve, without grace or loveliness. Nor does the drama catch her finest spirit. She is most often used to provoke the mirthless laugh of ridicule; or to portray feminine viciousness or vulgarity not peculiar to Negroes. This is the shadow over her. To a race naturally sunny comes the twilight of self-doubt and a sense of personal inferiority. It cannot be denied that these are potent and detrimental influences, though not generally recognized because they are in the realm of the mental and spiritual. More apparent are the economic handicaps which follow her recent entrance into industry. It is conceded that she has special difficulties because of the poor working conditions and low wages of her men. It is not surprising that only the most determined women forge ahead to results other than mere survival. To the gifted, the zest of meeting a challenge is a compensating factor which often brings success. The few who do prove their mettle, stimulate one to a closer study of how this achievement is won under contemporary conditions.

Better to visualize the Negro woman at her job, our vision of a host of individuals must once more resolve itself into groups on the basis of activity. First, comes a very small leisure group—the wives and daughters of men who are in business, in the professions and a few well-paid personal service occupations. Second, a most active and progressive group, the women in business and the professions. Third, the many women in the trades and industry. Fourth, a group weighty in numbers struggling on in domestic service, with an even less fortunate fringe of casual workers, fluctuating with the economic temper of the times.

The first is a pleasing group to see. It is picked for outward beauty by Negro men with much the same feeling as other Americans of the same economic class. Keeping their women free to preside over the family, these women are affected by the problems of every wife and mother, but touched only faintly by their race's hardships. They do share acutely in the prevailing difficulty of finding competent household help. Negro wives find Negro maids unwilling generally to work in their own neighborhoods, for various reasons. They do not wish to work where there is a possibility of acquaintances coming into contact with them while they serve and they still harbor the misconception that Negroes of any station are unable to pay as much as persons of the other race. It is in these homes of comparative ease that we find the polite activities of social exclusiveness. The luxuries of well-appointed homes, modest motors, tennis, golf and country clubs, trips to Europe and California, make for social standing. The problem confronting the refined Negro family is to know others of the same achievement. The search for kindred spirits gradually grows less difficult; in the past it led to the custom of visiting all the large cities in order to know similar groups of cultured Negro people. In recent years, the more serious minded Negro woman's visit to Europe has been extended from months to years for the purpose of study and travel. The European success which meets this type of ambition is instanced in the conferring of the doctorate in philosophy upon a Negro woman, Dr. Anna J. Cooper, at the last commencement of the Sorbonne, Paris. Similarly, a score of Negro women are sojourning abroad in various countries for the spiritual relief and cultural stimulation afforded there.

Source: Elise Johnson McDougald, "The Task of Negro Womanhood," in Alain Locke, *The New Negro, An Interpretation*, New York: Albert and Charles Boni, 1925.

RACE AND THE EUGENICS MOVEMENT IN THE JAZZ AGE

By the 1920s, scientists and social scientists had begun to apply the theories of Charles Darwin to efforts to improve the human race. Eugenics, then considered a progressive idea, sought to engineer "better babies" and "fitter families" through mapping of the gene pool and selective breeding. While the eugenics movement that reached the height of its popularity during the Jazz Age may not have been intentionally racist, the following documents make clear that whiteness was privileged by those who supported and encouraged the adoption of its principles and methods. The first two documents thus provide appropriate context for a novel that explores issues of race and racial identity. The third document, a newspaper account of the sensational Rhinelander *trial to which Larsen refers in* Passing, *provides evidence of the conflicts associated with race in the United States.*

Document: From "Eugenics Seeks to Improve the Natural, Physical, Mental and Temperamental Qualities of the Human Family," Eugenics Record Office, 1927

This office is devoted to the study of the biological forces which determine the natural capacities and limitations of mankind. It looks forward to having ultimately a good working pedigree-index of the natural traits of a large portion of the families of America. Science can not [sic] experiment with human beings. It desires merely to learn and publish the actual results of man's experiments on himself. Every marriage is an experiment in heredity. Every person should be interested in the actual biological results of matings among his own kin, and should look forward to securing a scientific analysis of the hereditary potentialities of himself and all his descendants which may result from matings with persons with specific hereditary qualities. When this desire becomes general, the science of eugenics will become firmly established and will be able to contribute to the practical conservation of the better family traits of the American people. . . .

The principle business of eugenics is:

1. To find out what matings are fittest for society as organized. This presupposes, among other things, an understanding of the social, economic and biological factors that govern mate selection and fecundity, and also a knowledge of the method of inheritance of human traits. To these tasks scientific investigators have set themselves earnestly.
2. To disseminate a knowledge of the facts of inheritance as they are ascertained.
3. To secure such social ideals as will facilitate the mating of the fittest—i.e., a large opportunity for acquaintanceship among young persons, and a fuller knowledge, on the part of all, of the hereditary traits carried by each.
4. To educate organized society, especially as represented by the several state governments, to a point, where it will act with an eye to racial progress, encouraging the reproduction of the "best blood," and discouraging or preventing the reproduction of its worst strains. Eugenical improvement means the diversification, purification, and conservation of highly effective and talented human families.
5. To encourage every intelligent and patriotic family to establish an Eugenical Family Archive for preserving genealogical and

biographical materials, and for working out as accurately and as completely as possible a record of the family distribution of natural physical, mental, and temperamental traits. The establishment of the custom would aid greatly the practical applications of eugenics.

In a few words, then, if a race is to make progress along the lines of natural abilities, those in control must see to it that there shall be fit matings and many children among those most richly endowed by nature, and that hereditary defectives and degenerates shall not be permitted to reproduce at all. The accomplishment of these ends will require much effort and interest on the part of individual citizens. The State can be expected to take means to bring about these ends only when due pressure is brought to bear by aroused citizens. Thus law, science, social effort, individual enlightenment, and personal resolve—each has its part to play in working out the eugenical ideal, that is, in improving the inborn character and talents of succeeding generations. Eugenics, like other practical pedigree studies, is primarily a biological science. When a child is conceived, "the gates of heredity are closed;" after that, so far as control is concerned, the child's development, education, and betterment are a matter of environment. Thus it is easily seen that if the race is to be improved in its natural qualities, family records, giving a thorough account of the natural physical, mental and temperamental traits of members of many families, must be provided for the use of science in discovering the laws of heredity, and for the particular family itself in predicting profitable lines of education for its young, in guarding against inborn weakness, and in determining whether a contemplated marriage may be biologically fortunate.

Record of Family Traits. Every person interested in conserving the best racial qualities of his family should apply to this office for two copies of the schedule, "Record of Family Traits." The record is sent in duplicate to all persons who ask for it, provided they are further seriously interested in studying the origin, segregation, transmission, and recombination of the inborn traits within their family pedigrees, and will agree, in each case, after filling out these schedules and retaining one copy for his own family archives, to return the second to be added to the permanent files of the Eugenics Record Office.

Family Tree Folder. Besides the Record of Family Traits, there are numerous other genealogical and pedigree forms supplied to interested persons by this office. The Family Tree Folder is one of the most useful of these forms. It provides space and instructions for plotting the family tree and for indicating the distribution, in the family, of one or more striking hereditary traits. This folder provides also for a short biographical outline of each person charted. This is the shortest and most condensed pedigree-plotting system outlined by this office.

Short Schedules for Special Traits. In addition to the two schedules above described, the Eugenics Record Office issues a few briefer forms for recording special traits. These are: (1) Musical Talent, (2) Tuberculosis, (3) Harelip and Cleft Palate, (4) Hair Form, Hair and Eye Color, and Complexion, (5) Stature, (6) Weight, (7) Physical Measurement Record, (8) Twins, (9) Mathematical Ability, and finally a small (10) Special Trait Sheet for recording the family distribution and brief description of any striking trait that seems to "run in families." . . .

Source: "Eugenics Seeks to Improve the Natural, Physical, Mental and Temperamental Qualities of the Human Family," Eugenics Record Office, 1927.

Document: From "Fitter Families for Future Firesides," 1924

Forward [*sic*]

The Fitter Families' Project is a legitimate outgrowth of scientific agriculture. It is the application of the principles of scientific plant and animal husbandry to the next higher order of creation, the human family, and contemplates the development of a science of practical human husbandry.

The basic principle underlying modern agricultural procedure is the fact that the character and vitality of every living thing is determined by two factors, heredity and environment. After the germ cell of plant or animal is fertilized, nothing can alter the traits that plant or animal will have, but it then depends entirely upon the nurture and care as to whether that plant or animal will become the best possible individual of its kind.

It is now believed that the time has come when these two factors must be taken into consideration in human mating and in family habits, if the best elements of our civilization are to dominate or even survive. This must be done by stimulating the interest of intelligent families and arousing a family consciousness by which each family will conceive of itself as a genetic unit with a definite obligation to study its heredity and build up its health status.

The movement for the competitive health examination of pre-school children originated at the Iowa State Fair in 1911, and the winners provided the climax in the million dollar parade of prize stock and other agricultural products, as they rode in an automobile with a runner on the side proclaiming them to be "Iowa's Best Crop". The examiners of these babies followed the only criterion extant at that time and observed and used, in considerable part, the methods of the stock judges. They soon observed that the stock judges always took inheritance into consideration in judging. Charles B. Davenport said to the Iowa group in the very beginning, "You should score 50% for heredity before you begin to examine a baby", and again, a year later, "A prize winner at two may be an epileptic at ten". It remained for the Kansas Free Fair to give the Better Baby a pedigree. It is now demanded that the Better Baby be supported by a Family, fit both in their inheritance and in the development of their mental, moral, and physical traits.

It is highly appropriate that this movement should rise out of the vigorous, progressive, rural life of the present day, which is giving to the world not only material sustenance but a very important and substantial reserve vigor of brain and body.

In the Free Fair Book, announcing the newly-created Eugenics Department, appeared the following appropriate challenge:

TO THE MEN OF AMERICA
You talk of your breed of cattle,
And plan for the higher strain;
You double the food of the pasture,
And heap up the measure of grain;
You draw on the wits of the nation,
To better the barn and the pen;
But what are you doing my brothers,
To better the breed of men?

You boast of your Morgans and Herefords,
Of the worth of a calf or a colt,
And scoff at the scrub and the mongrel,
As worthy a fool or a dolt;
You mention the points of your roadster,
With man a "wherefore" and "when",
But ah, are you conning, my brothers,
The worth of the children of men?

And what of your boy—Have you measured
His needs for a growing year?
Does your mark, as his sire, in his features,
Mean less than your brand on a steer?
Thoroughbred—that is your watchword
For stable and pasture and pen—

But what is your word for the homestead?
Answer, you breeders of men!
Rose Trumall, Scottsdale, Arizona

Source: "Fitter Families for Future Firesides: A Report of the Eugenics Department of the Kansas Free Fair, 1920–1924," 1924.

Document: From "Body of Woman Shown to Jury," *The Florence* [AL] *Times*, 1925

Mrs. Rhinelander Viewed to Settle Question of Color.

White Plains, NY, Nov 23

In the jury room of the West Chester county supreme court today, Alice Jones Rhinelander undressed with her body from the waist up and her lower limbs exposed, was viewed by the jury trying her husband's suit for annulment.

Leonard Kip Rhinelander, who charges that his wife deceived him as to her color, Justice Mortschauser, stenographers and opposing counsel accompanied the girl, the daughter of a negro cab man, into the jury room.

Preceding this astounding development, two letters written by Leonard to Alice were read in court. They described minutely pre-marital intimacies and Lee Parsons Davis, the defendant's counsel, hoped to prove by the color of her body that young Rhinelander could not but suspect that she had negro blood in her veins.

Mrs. Rhinelander and her mother went behind a screen in the jury room while the former disrobed. She was seen by the jury for only a few minutes and no questions were asked her.

Former Judge Isaac N. Mills, Rhinelander's counsel, was shocked at the proceedings. Again and again the venerable attorney proclaimed his protest at the "indecent procedure."

Ten minutes after the scene had again been transferred to the court room, Mrs. Rhinelander left the court house. She was weeping hysterically. Her two sisters, Mrs. Grace Miller and Mrs. Emily Brooks, were at her arm.

Davis resumed cross-examination of Rhinelander. He asked the witness whether his wife's body was the same color as it was in 1922. Rhinelander replied that it was.

Court then recessed for luncheon.

As soon as court reconvened after the recess, Davis announced that he had completed the cross-examination of Rhinelander, which began a week ago today.

Mrs. Rhinelander, composed, but her eyes bearing traces of her weeping spell, was back in court as were many other women who had been ordered out when Davis read the "mystery" letters.

Source: "Body of Woman Shown to Jury." *The Florence* [AL] *Times*, November 23, 1925.

Suggested Readings

Blackmer, Corinne. "The Veils of the Law: Race and Sexuality in Nella Larsen's *Passing*." *College Literature* 22.3(October 1995): 50–67.

Brown-Guillory, Elizabeth. "Nella Larsen (1891–1964)." *Black Women and America: An Historical Encyclopedia*. Vol. 1. Brooklyn: Carlson Publishing, 1993.

Chase, Allan. *The Legacy of Malthus. The Social Costs of the New Scientific Racism*. New York: Knopf, 1980.

Christian, Barbara. *Black Women Novelists: The Development of a Tradition, 1892–1976*. Westport, CT: Greenwood, 1980.

Cutter, Martha J. "Sliding Significations: *Passing* as a Narrative and Textual Strategy in Nella Larsen's Fiction." In *Passing and the Fictions of Identity*. Ed. Elaine Ginsburg. Durham, NC: Duke University Press, 1996: 75–100.

Davis, Thadious M. "Nella Larsen." *Dictionary of Literary Biography: Afro American Writers from the Harlem Renaissance to 1940*. Vol. 51. Detroit: Gale Research Co., 1987: 182–192.

Davis, Thadious M. *Nella Larsen, Novelist of the Harlem Renaissance: A Woman's Life Unveiled*. Baton Rouge: Louisiana State University Press, 1994.

Douglas, Ann. *Terrible Honesty: Mongrel Manhattan in the 1920s*. New York: Farrar Straus Giroux, 1995.

Du Bois, W. E. Burghardt. *The Souls of Black Folk*. 1903. New York: The New American Library, 1969.

Du Bois, W. E. Burghardt. "The Talented Tenth." In *The Negro Problem*. New York: Arno Press and *The New York Times*, 1969: 31–75.

English, Daylanne K. *Unnatural Selections: Eugenics in American Modernism and the Harlem Renaissance*. Chapel Hill: University of North Carolina Press, 2004.

Gross, Ariela. *What Blood Won't Tell: A History of Race on Trial in America*. Cambridge, MA: Harvard University Press, 2008.

Hobbs, Allyson. *A Chosen Exile: A History of Racial Passing in American Life*. Cambridge, MA: Harvard University Press, 2014.

Huggins, Nathan I. *The Harlem Renaissance*. New York: Oxford University Press, 1971.

Hutchinson, George. *In Search of Nella Larsen: A Biography of the Color Line*. Cambridge, MA: Harvard University Press, 2006.

Kaplan, Carla. *Miss Anne in Harlem: The White Women of the Black Renaissance*. New York: Harper, 2013.

Larson, Charles R. *Invisible Darkness: Jean Toomer and Nella Larsen*. Iowa City: University of Iowa Press, 1993.

Lewis, David Levering. *When Harlem Was in Vogue*. New York and Oxford: Oxford University Press, 1981.

Lewis, Earl, and Heidi Ardizzone. *Love on Trial: An American Scandal in Black and White*. New York: Norton, 2001.

Locke, Alain, ed. *The New Negro. An Interpretation*. 1925. New York: Arno Press and *The New York Times*, 1968.

López, Ian Haney. *White by Law: The Legal Construction of Race*. New York: New York University Press, 2006.

Madigan, Mark J. "Miscegenation and 'The Dicta of Race and Class': The Rhinelander Case and Nella Larsen's *Passing*." *Modern Fiction Studies* 36.4(Winter 1990): 523–528.

McLendon, Jacquelyn Y. *The Politics of Color in the Fiction of Jessie Fauset and Nella Larsen*. Charlottesville: University Press of Virginia, 1995.

Onwuachi-Willig, Angela. "A Beautiful Lie: *Rhinelander v. Rhinelander* as a Formative Lesson on Race, Identity, Marriage, and Family." *California Law Review* 95.6(December 2007): 1–60.

Pfeiffer, Kathleen, *Race Passing and American Individualism*. Amherst: University of Massachusetts Press, 2003.

Singh, Amritjit. *The Novels of the Harlem Renaissance: Twelve Black Writers, 1923–1933*. University Park: Penn State University Press, 1976.

Smith-Pryor, Elizabeth M. *Property Rites: The Rhinelander Trial, Passing, and the Protection of Whiteness*. Chapel Hill: University of North Carolina Press, 2009.

Thaggert, Miriam. "Racial Etiquette: Nella Larsen's *Passing* and the Rhinelander Case." *Meridians* 5.2(Spring 2005): 1–29.

Wall, Cheryl. "Passing for What? Aspects of Identity in Nella Larsen's Novels." *Black American Literature Forum* 20.102(Spring/Summer 1986): 97–111.

Zackodnik, Teresa C. *The Mulatta and the Politics of Race*. Jackson: University Press of Mississippi, 2004.

Index

ABC of the Invisible Empire, 40. *See also* Ku Klux Klan; Simmons, William J.
Advertising, 6, 16–18, 23
African American, xvii, xviii, xxiv, 40, 135, 150, 151, 152, 190, 191, 192, 193, 195, 196, 197, 203, 204, 207, 213
"Ain't We Got Fun?," xviii
Alger, Horatio, 48
American Birth Control League, xxiv
American Breeder's Association, 200
American Civil Liberties Union, 41
American Dream, 46–49, 57, 58
Amos 'n Andy, xx
Anderson, Sherwood, 99, 134, 136, 139

Anti-Semitism, 40, 111, 149–50, 164–69
Arrowsmith (Sinclair Lewis), 4, 8
Art Deco, xx
Ashley, Lady Brett (*The Sun Also Rises*), 131, 133, 142, 143, 145, 146, 147–49
Atlanta Exposition Speech, 203
Automobile, xix, xx, 3, 4, 5, 11, 13, 50–54, 60–65

Babbitt (Sinclair Lewis), xxii, xxiv, 1–33; Documenting, 22–31; Historical Background to, 3–7; Historical Explorations of, 13–22; Synopsis, 1–3; Why We Read, 10–12

Babbitt, George F. (*Babbitt*), 1–3, 4–5, 6, 7, 10–12, 14, 15, 16, 18–19, 20, 21, 28
Babbitt, Myra (*Babbitt*), 1, 3
Babbitt, Ted (*Babbitt*), 1, 2, 3, 11, 12, 21
Babbitt, Tinka (*Babbitt*), 1
Babbitt, Verona (*Babbitt*), 1, 2, 11
"Babbittry," 7, 22
Bagnold, Enid, 148
Baker, Jordan (*The Great Gatsby*), 35, 36, 52, 54
Baker, Josephine, 135, 151, 158, 159
Bankhead, Tallulah, 57
Barnes, Djuna, 136
Barnes, Jake (*The Sun Also Rises*), 131, 133, 142, 143, 144, 145, 146–47, 148, 149, 150, 151, 152
Barton, Ralph, 106
Beach, Sylvia, 136
The Beautiful and Damned (F. Scott Fitzgerald), 44
Bell, Alexander Graham, 200
Bell, Alphonzo, 111
Bellew, John "Jack" (*Passing*), 189, 190, 196–97, 202, 205
Bernays, Edward, 17
"Better Babies," 200, 201, 217
"Big Two-Hearted River" (Ernest Hemingway), 139
Biograph Company, 100, 101
The Birth of a Nation, 111
"Black Sox" scandal, xx
"Black Tuesday," xx, xxvi, 159–60
Bolsheviks, 114
Bootleggers, 10, 36, 55, 56, 65, 74–76, 96, 106, 114, 149
Bow, Clara, xxi, 16, 17, 57, 109, 112, 113
Boyle, Kay, 136, 137, 156–57, 160–62

Breakaway, xviii
Brittain, Vera, 147–48
Brooke, Rupert, 144
Bryan, William Jennings, 41
Broadway, 101, 102
Bronfman, Samuel, 56
Browne, Lewis, 9
Brush, Katherine, 112
Buchanan, Daisy Fay (*The Great Gatsby*), 35, 36, 42, 48, 52, 53, 54, 58
Buchanan, Tom (*The Great Gatsby*), 35, 36, 48, 52, 53, 54, 55, 57
Bullfighting, 133, 152–54, 160–63
Burbank, Luther, 200
Burke, Billie, 101, 112
Burton, Beatrice, 108. *See also* Flapper novels
Business, xx, 3, 4, 5, 6, 8, 13–20, 22–28
Business culture, 13–14
But Gentlemen Marry Brunettes (Anita Loos), 98, 102
Butler Act, 41

Campbell, Mike (*The Sun Also Rises*), 132, 133, 142, 145, 147, 148, 150
Capone, Al, xix, 38, 57
Carnegie, Andrew, 13
Carnegie Institution, 200
Carraway, Nick (*The Great Gatsby*), 35, 36, 41, 47, 48, 49, 52, 54, 55, 57, 58, 59
A Cast of Thousands (Anita Loos), 102
Celebrity culture, xxi, 16–17, 50, 57–59, 76–90, 111–12
Cézanne, Paul, 135
Channing, Carol, 102, 103
Chaplin, Charlie, xxi, xxv, 57, 76, 77–79, 112

Charleston, xviii, xxv, 106, 114, 211–13
Chéri (Colette and Anita Loos), 102
Chocolat the clown, 151
Christie, Al, 111
Chrysler Building, xx
Class consciousness and conflict, 38, 50, 51–56, 57, 58, 59, 97, 98, 99, 149, 190, 191, 192, 195, 197, 199, 202–7, 213–17
Cobb, Ty, xxi, 57, 76
Cohn, Robert (*The Sun Also Rises*), 131, 143, 146, 147, 148, 149–50, 152, 153, 158
Colette, Sidonie-Gabrielle, 102
Conformity, 3, 5–6, 7, 8, 9, 19, 20–22, 28–31
Consumer credit, xx, 3, 19–20
Consumer culture, xix, xx, xxvi, 3, 5, 6, 8, 9, 11, 13, 16–19, 22, 37, 50, 57, 135
Coolidge, Calvin, xx, xxv, 3–4, 13
Cooper, James Fenimore, 48
Corey, Maybelle Gilman, 114
Cotton Club, xviii, 135
The Crack-Up (F. Scott Fitzgerald), 46
Crane, Hart, 137
Crash of 1929, 113
Crawford, Joan, 101, 112
Cullen, Countée, 196, 198
Cultural conflicts, 41, 106–9, 135, 142, 164

Dancing Mothers, 112. *See also* Flapper films
Darrow, Clarence, 41
Darwin, Charles, 41, 217
Davenport, Charles B., 200
Davies, Marion, 101
Death in the Afternoon (Ernest Hemingway), 152

De Mille, Cecil B., 111
Dempsey, Jack, xx, xxi, 57
"Diamonds Are a Girl's Best Friend," 103
Dodsworth (Sinclair Lewis), 8
Dolly sisters, 114
Doolittle, Hilda (H. D.), 136
Dorothy Shaw (*Gentlemen Prefer Blondes*), 94, 95, 96, 97, 98, 102, 105, 114
Dos Passos, John, 136, 137
Dreiser, Theodore, 9, 99
"Drug-stores," 55, 106
Du Bois, W. E. B., 195, 199, 203, 204, 213–15
"Dulce et Decorum Est" (Wilfred Owen), 144

Earhart, Amelia, xxi, xxvi, 57, 76
East Egg (*The Great Gatsby*), 35, 51, 52, 58, 59
Easter Parade, New York City, 17–18
Eighteenth Amendment (Prohibition), 10, 37, 65
Ellington, Duke, xviii
Elmer Gantry (Sinclair Lewis), 8
Emerson, John, 101
Eugenics movement, 199–201, 213, 217–22
Eugenics Record Office, 201
"Eulogy on the Flapper" (Zelda Fitzgerald), 108, 109
Expatriates, 132, 134, 135, 136, 139, 142, 143, 144, 146, 149, 152, 154

Fairbanks, Douglas, xxi, 57, 76, 101, 112
A Farewell to Arms (Ernest Hemingway), 139
Faulkner, William, 12, 97, 99
Fauset, Jessie Redmon, 192, 195

Festival of San Fermín, 132, 133, 139, 144, 150
Fine Arts-Triangle, 101, 110
"Fitter Families," 200, 201, 217, 220–22
Fitzgerald, Frances Scott "Scottie," 44, 45, 46
Fitzgerald, F. Scott, xvii, xxi, xxii, xxv, 3, 12, 37, 41, 42–46, 47, 49, 50, 51, 53, 54, 57, 58, 59, 99, 108, 112, 136, 137, 145, 149
Fitzgerald, Zelda Sayre, xxi, 43–44, 45, 46, 108, 109
Flaming Youth, 109, 112. *See also* Flapper films
Flanner, Janet "Genet," 159
Flapper, xviii, xxi, 6, 10, 11, 38–39, 42, 97, 99, 100, 104, 106–9, 114, 115–23, 147
The Flapper, 109. *See also* Flapper films
Flapper films, 109, 112–13. *See also* Dancing Mothers; *Flaming Youth*; *The Flapper*; *It*; *The Offshore Pirate*; *Our Dancing Daughters*; *Our Modern Maidens*; *The Perfect Flapper*
Flapper novels, 108. *See also* Burton, Beatrice; *The Flapper Wife*; *The Petter*
The Flapper Wife (Beatrice Burton), 108. *See also* Flapper novels
Flowers, Theodore "Tiger," 150, 151
Ford, Ford Madox, 137
Ford, Henry, xix, xxv, 14, 22, 50
For Whom the Bell Tolls (Ernest Hemingway), 140
Franklin, Benjamin, 48, 57

Gable, Clark, 101
Gangsters, xix, xxvi, 10, 38, 57, 58, 149
Garbo, Greta, 112
Garson, Greer, 101
Gatsby, Jay (*The Great Gatsby*), 35, 36, 42, 47, 48, 49, 51, 52, 53, 54, 55, 56, 57, 58, 59, 65. *See also* Gatz, James
Gatz, James (*The Great Gatsby*), 47, 48, 57. *See also* Gatsby, Jay
Gehrig, Lou, xxi, 57
Gellhorn, Martha, 139–40
Gender in the Jazz Age, xviii, xxi, 17–18, 38–39, 50, 56, 59, 96–97, 98, 99, 103–5, 106–9, 112–13, 143, 146, 147–49, 153, 160, 191, 215–17
Gentlemen Prefer Blondes (Anita Loos), xxi xxv, 93–130; Documenting, 114–28; Historical Background to, 96–99; Historical Explorations of, 106–14; Synopsis, 93–96; Why We Read, 103–5
Gibson, Charles Dana, 107
Gibson girl, 107
Gigi (Colette and Anita Loos), 102
"The Gilded Six-Bits" (Zora Neale Hurston), 192
A Girl Like I (Anita Loos), 102
Gish, Lillian, 102
Glyn, Elinor, 113
The Gold Rush, xxv
Gordon, Ruth, 102
Gorton, Bill (*The Sun Also Rises*), 132, 133, 150, 151, 152
Gottlieb, Morton, 102, 103
Grand Old Opry, xx, xxv
Grand Tour of Europe, 104, 105
Great Depression, 46, 113
The Great Gatsby (F. Scott Fitzgerald), xix, xxii, xxv, 35–92, 108, 149; Documenting, 60–90;

Historical Background to, 37–42; Historical Explorations of, 50–59; Synopsis, 35–36; Why We Read, 46–49
Great Migration, xviii, 40, 191, 199
The Great Train Robbery, 110
Great War, 134. *See also* World War I
Griffith, David Wark, 40, 101, 110, 111, 123–24
Guggenheim Fellowship, 195

Harding, Warren G., xxiii, xxiv, 3, 13, 44
Harlem, 190, 192, 195
Harlem Renaissance, xviii, 191–93, 194, 196, 198, 204, 207–13. *See also* Negro Awakening; New Negro Movement
Harlow, Jean, 101
Harmon Foundation Award, 194
Harris, Paul P., 15, 16, 23–24
Harvard Business School, 13
Hayes, Helen, 102
Hegger, Grace Livingstone, 9
Held, John, Jr., 108
Helicon Home Colony, 8
Hemingway, Ernest, xxi, xxv, 9, 12, 99, 134, 135, 136, 137–41, 142, 143, 144, 145, 146, 148, 151, 152, 153, 154, 160
Hemingway, Hadley Richardson, 134, 139
Henderson, Fletcher, xviii
"Heritage" (Countée Cullen), 196
Hitler, Adolf, 152
Hollywood, xx, 46, 93, 96, 101, 102, 110, 111, 113, 123–28
Hoover, Herbert, xxvi, 13
Hoover, J. Edgar, xxv
Hopalong Cassidy, 48, 57
Houdini, Harry, 57

"How to Live on $36,000 a Year" (F. Scott Fitzgerald), 44
Hughes, Langston, 191, 207, 208–9
"Hugh Selwyn Mauberley" (Ezra Pound), 144, 149
Humor in *Gentlemen Prefer Blondes*, 99, 105
Hurston, Zora Neale, 191–92

Imagism, 136. *See also* Modernism
Imes, Elmer, 194–95, 196
Immigration, xxiv, xxvi, 28, 38, 39, 40, 55, 111
Industrialization, xix, xx, 3, 13, 40, 50, 135
In Our Time (Ernest Hemingway), 139
International Imitation Hemingway Competition, 141
Intolerance, 101, 110
It, 109, 112, 113. *See also* Flapper films
It Can't Happen Here (Sinclair Lewis), 8–9
"It" girl, xxi, 17, 113

Jazz, xvii, xviii, 6, 37, 50, 106, 114, 190, 203, 207
Jazz Age, xvii, xviii, xxi, xxii, 7, 10, 11, 12, 22, 23, 28, 29, 39, 42, 46, 49, 50, 54, 58, 59, 65, 76, 77, 97, 98, 99, 100, 102, 104, 105, 106, 109, 113, 114, 115, 123, 134, 135, 137, 142, 147, 148, 151, 159, 164, 190, 193, 196, 199, 200, 202, 205, 207, 217
The Jazz Singer, xxvi
Jim Crow, 191, 194, 207
Johnson, James Weldon, 195
Jolson, Al, 203
Joyce, James, 97, 136, 137, 139
Joyce, Peggy Hopkins, 114

232 Index

Kansas City Star, 138
Kaye-Smith, Sheila, 195
Keaton, Buster, 57
Keller, Helen, 15
Kendry, Clare (*Passing*), 189, 190, 191, 196, 197, 198, 202, 204, 205, 206, 213
Kiss Hollywood Good-Bye (Anita Loos), 102
Kiwanis Club, 15, 16
"Knowledge in Contempt in America, Believe Europeans" (H.L. Mencken), 29–31
Ku Klux Klan, xxi, xxv, 40–41, 143, 152, 164, 169–84. *See also ABC of the Invisible Empire*; Simmons, William J
Kurowsky, Agnes, 138

Lansky, Meyer, xix
Larsen, Nella, xxi, xxvi, 190, 191, 192, 193–96, 197, 201, 202, 203, 204, 204, 207, 213, 217
The Last Tycoon (F. Scott Fitzgerald), 46
League of Nations, xxiii
Leatherstocking novels (James Fenimore Cooper), 48
Lee, Lorelei (*Gentlemen Prefer Blondes*), 93, 94, 95, 96, 97, 98, 99, 102, 103, 104, 105, 106, 108, 109, 110, 112, 114
Leisure activities, xx, 20, 51, 110, 113
Lerman, Leo, 102
Les Années Folles, 135, 142. *See also* Roaring Twenties
Lewis, Sinclair, xxii, xxiv, 1, 3, 5, 7–10, 13, 18, 19, 20, 21, 22, 28
Life, 108
Lindbergh, Charles, xx, xxi, xxv, 57, 76, 80–83, 158–59

Lindsay, Vachel, 11
Lindy Hop, xviii
Lions Club, 15, 22
Littlefield, Eunice (*Babbitt*), 3, 11, 12
Locke, Alain, 191
Logan, Josh, 102
London, Jack, 7, 8
Loos, Corinne Anita, xxi, xxv, 96, 97, 98, 99–103, 104, 105, 106, 110, 111, 112
Lost Generation, xxi, 45, 105, 132, 134, 137, 141, 142–43, 144–45, 146, 153, 154–60
Loy, Myrna, 101
Luciano, Lucky, xix, 38
Lucky Strikes, 17
Lumìere brothers, 110

Madonna (Ciccone), 103
Main Street (Sinclair Lewis), 7, 8
"Make It New," 136. *See also* Modernism
The Man Nobody Knows (Bruce Barton), 14–15, 23, 24–28
Mason, Charlotte Osgood, 192
Matisse, Henri, 135–36
May Day Riots, 40
McKay, Claude, 192
McPherson, Aimee Semple, 142
Mellon, Andrew, 13
Mencken, H. L., 10, 11, 20, 22, 28, 29–31, 41, 96, 97
The Merchant of Venice, 149
Metro-Goldwyn-Mayer (MGM), 101
Mickey Mouse, xxvi
Mills, Florence, 114
Minogue, Kylie, 103
Mippipopolous, Count (*The Sun Also Rises*), 132, 145–46
Miró, Joan, 139

Miss America, xxiv
"Miss Annes," 192
Mitchison, Naomi, 148
Model T, xx, xxv, 50. *See also* Automobile
Modernism, xvii, 12, 105, 134, 135, 136, 139. *See also* Imagism; "Make It New"
Monroe, Marilyn, 103
Moore, Colleen, 112, 123, 124–25
Moran, George "Bugs," xix
Morgan, J. P., 13
Motion pictures, xx, xxiv, xxvi, 11, 37, 57, 76, 95, 100, 101, 102, 106, 109, 110–14, 123–28
A Mouse Is Born (Anita Loos), 102
A Moveable Feast (Ernest Hemingway), 136, 139, 140

National Association for the Advancement of Colored People (NAACP), 191, 195
National Socialist German Workers' Party (Nazis), 152
National Urban League, xxiv, 191
Negro Awakening, 195. *See also* Harlem Renaissance
Negro Welfare League (NWL), 190, 197, 204
Nestor Studios, 111
New Adam, 47–48
New Eden, 47
New Negro Movement, 190, 192, 195. *See also* Harlem Renaissance
New Woman, xviii, 38, 107, 147
New World, 46, 47, 48, 105
"The New York Hat" (Anita Loos), 101
New York Yankees, xx, xxiv

Nineteenth Amendment (women's suffrage), xviii, xxiii, 37, 38
Nobel Prize in Literature, 7, 9–10, 137, 140

The Odyssey (Homer), 148
The Offshore Pirate, 112. *See also* Flapper films
The Old Man and the Sea (Ernest Hemingway), 140
Old World, 47, 105
Origin of Species (Charles Darwin), 41
Our Dancing Daughters, 109, 112. *See also* Flapper films
Our Modern Maidens, 112. *See also* Flapper films
Our Mr. Wrenn (Sinclair Lewis), 8
Owen, Wilfred, 144

Palloma, Frank, 101, 110
Palmer, William, 40
Paris, France, 131, 132, 133, 134, 135, 136, 137, 138, 139, 140, 141, 142–43, 146, 151, 154–160, 196
Passing (Nella Larsen), xxi, xxvi, 189–225; Documenting, 207–223; Historical Background to, 190–193; Historical Explorations of, 199–207; Synopsis, 189–90; Why We Read, 196–98
"Passing Our Tenth Milestone" (Paul P. Harris), 23–24
Pat Hobby stories (F. Scott Fitzgerald), 46
The Perfect Flapper, 109. *See also* Flapper films
The Perils of Pauline, 114
The Petter (Beatrice Burton), 108. *See also* Flapper novels

Index

Pfeiffer, Pauline, 139, 140
Picasso, Pablo, 135, 137, 139
Pickford, Mary, xxi, 57, 76, 112
Plum-Bun (Jessie Redmon Fauset), 192
Porter, Edwin, 110
"Potter palm" concerts, xviii
Pound, Ezra, 12, 136, 137, 139, 144, 145, 149
Progressive Era, 200
Prohibition, xviii, xix, xxiii, 2, 6, 10, 37–38, 50, 54, 55–57, 65–76, 98, 106, 114, 135, 142
Prosperity, xix, xxi, xxvi, 3, 4, 5, 6, 7, 13, 16, 19, 20, 22, 37, 42, 51, 59, 135
Pulitzer Prize, 8

Quicksand (Nella Larsen), 193, 194, 195, 196

Race relations, xviii, xxi, xxiv, 40, 50, 59, 98, 147, 149, 150–52, 164–84, 191, 192–93, 197, 199–207
Racial identity, xxi, 189, 190, 192, 193–94, 195, 196–98, 199–207, 217–23
Radio, xix, xx, xxiv, xxv, 3, 13, 37, 41, 50, 76, 106, 142
Ragged Dick, 48
Reader's Digest, xxi, xxiv
Redfield, Brian (*Passing*), 190, 192, 196, 205, 206, 207
Redfield, Irene (*Passing*), 189, 190, 191, 196, 197, 198, 199, 202, 204, 205, 206, 213
Red-Headed Woman, 112
Red Scare, xxi, xxiii, 28, 40, 110
Religion of business, 9, 14–15, 16, 22–28

Remus, George, 56
Republican Party, xx, 3, 6, 13, 14, 22
Rhinelander, Alice Jones, 202, 203
Rhinelander, Leonard "Kip," 202, 203
Rhinelander Case, 201–3, 217, 222–23
Roaring Twenties, xvii, 13, 106, 135. See also Jazz Age; *Les Années Folles*
Rockefeller, John D., 13
Rockefeller Foundation, 200
Rockne, Knute, xx
Rolls Royce, 51, 53
Roman Catholicism, 38, 40, 139, 145, 152
Romero, Pedro (*The Sun Also Rises*), 133, 143, 146, 147, 148, 149, 153
Rotary Club, 15, 22, 23–24
Russian Revolution, 39
Russell, Rosalind, 101
Ruth, George "Babe," xx, xxi, xxvi, 16, 57, 76, 83–90

Sacco (Nicola) and Vanzetti (Bartolomeo) Case, xxvi, 40
"Sanctuary" (Nella Larsen), 195
Sanger, Margaret, xxiv, 200
Sassoon, Siegfried, 144
Saturday Evening Post, 8, 108
Save Me the Waltz (Zelda Fitzgerald), 45
Schultz, Dutch, xix
Scopes, John T., 20–21, 41
Scopes "Monkey" Trial, xxi, xxv, 20–21, 41, 142
Self-Made Man, 48
Shakespeare and Company, 136
Sherwood, Robert, 123
Shimmy, 106, 114
Shylock (*The Merchant of Venice*), 149

Simmons, William J., 40. *See also ABC of the Invisible Empire*; Ku Klux Klan
Sinclair, Upton, 8
"The Snows of Kilimanjaro" (Ernest Hemingway), 136, 140–41
The Social Register (Anita Loos), 102
The Souls of Black Folk (W. E. B. Du Bois), 199
Spanish Civil War, 140
Speakeasies, xix, 6, 10, 38, 50, 55, 56, 106
Spofford, Henry (*Gentlemen Prefer Blondes*), 95, 96, 114
Sports, xx, xxiv, 17, 140
Stein, Gertrude, xxi, 135, 136, 137, 139, 142, 145, 154, 159
St. Valentine's Day Massacre, xix, xxvi
The Sun Also Rises (Ernest Hemingway), xxi, xxv, 131–87; Documenting, 154–84; Historical Background to, 133–36; Historical Explorations of, 144–54; Synopsis, 131–33; Why We Read, 141–43
Sunday, Billy, 15, 142
Symington Side Lacer, 39

"The Talented Tenth" (W. E. B. Du Bois), 203–4, 206, 207, 213–15
Tales of the Jazz Age (F. Scott Fitzgerald), 37
Talmadge, Constance, 101, 112
Talmadge, Norma, 112
Taylor, Ruth, 103
Teapot Dome scandal, xxiv, xxvi, 4
Tender Is the Night (F. Scott Fitzgerald), 45
Testament of Youth (Vera Brittain), 148

This Side of Paradise (F. Scott Fitzgerald), 37, 43, 44, 46, 108, 114, 145
Thompson, Dorothy, 9
Three Comrades, 46
Three Lives (Gertrude Stein), 135
Thurman, Wallace, 207–8, 210–11
Time, xxi, xxiv
"Tin Lizzie," 50
To Have and Have Not (Ernest Hemingway), 140
Toomer, Jean, 192
"Torches of Freedom," 17
Toronto Star, 134, 139
The Torrents of Spring (Ernest Hemingway), 139
Town Topics, 57, 58
Tracy, Spencer, 101
Treaty of Versailles, xxiii
Twentieth-Century Fox, 101

Ulysses (James Joyce), 136
United Artists, 101
University of Notre Dame, xx

Valentino, Rudolph, xxi, 57, 76, 112
Van Vechten, Carl, 192
The Vegetable (F. Scott Fitzgerald), 44
The Virtuous Vamp, 112. *See also* Flapper films
Volstead Act, 37, 65, 72, 109. *See also* Eighteenth Amendment
Voluntary Aid Detachment (VAD), 145, 147

Walgreen's, 55
Washington, Booker T., 194, 203
Wells, H. G., 9
Welsh, Mary, 140
Wentworth, Hugh (*Passing*), 197, 204, 206, 207

West Egg (*The Great Gatsby*), 35, 51, 58, 59
Wharton, Edith, 9, 97
The Wharton School, 13
"What Became of the Flappers?" (Zelda Fitzgerald), 109
White, Pearl, 114
White middle-class values, xviii, 5, 6–7, 10, 11, 16, 18, 19, 20–22, 38, 40, 55, 206
Wilson, George (*The Great Gatsby*), 36, 51–53
Wilson, Myrtle (*The Great Gatsby*), 35, 36, 52, 53, 54, 57, 59, 76
Wilson, Woodrow, 38, 144–45
Wolfsheim, Meyer (*The Great Gatsby*), 36, 55, 57, 149
Women's Home Companion, 201
World War I, xviii, xix, xxi, xxiii, 3, 13, 35, 37, 39, 41, 42, 43, 107, 131, 132, 134–35, 137, 138, 140, 141, 142, 143, 144–45, 146, 147–48, 149, 151, 153, 154. *See also* Great War
World War II, 140, 141, 150–51

Yale Club, 56
Youth culture, xviii, 11–12, 37, 142–43

Zenith (*Babbitt*), 1, 2, 4, 5, 6, 10, 14, 15, 21, 28

About the Author

Linda De Roche, PhD, is professor of English and American Studies at Wesley College, Dover, Delaware. Her published works include ABC-CLIO's *Mary Higgins Clark: Life and Letters* and Greenwood's *Student Companion to Willa Cather* and *Student Companion to F. Scott Fitzgerald*. She holds a doctorate in English from the University of Notre Dame.